THE CAMBRIDGE BIBLE COMMENTARY

NEW ENGLISH BIBLE

GENERAL EDITORS

P. R. ACKROYD, A. R. C. LEANEY,
J. W. PACKER

DEUTERONOMY

To Vicky

with gratitude and in the hope that
when Christopher and James ask 'What
is the meaning of the precepts, statutes,
and laws?', this book will be of help.

DEUTERONOMY

COMMENTARY BY

ANTHONY PHILLIPS

*Fellow, Dean and Chaplain of
Trinity Hall, Cambridge*

CAMBRIDGE

AT THE UNIVERSITY PRESS

1973

Published by the Syndics of the Cambridge University Press
Bentley House, 200 Euston Road, London NW1 2DB
American Branch: 32 East 57th Street, New York, N.Y.10022

© Cambridge University Press 1973

Library of Congress Catalogue Card Number: 73-77172

ISBNS:
0 521 08636 1 hard covers
0 521 09772 x paperback

Printed in Great Britain
at the University Printing House, Cambridge
(Brooke Crutchley, University Printer)

GENERAL EDITORS' PREFACE

The aim of this series is to provide the text of the New English Bible closely linked to a commentary in which the results of modern scholarship are made available to the general reader. Teachers and young people have been especially kept in mind. The commentators have been asked to assume no specialized theological knowledge, and no knowledge of Greek and Hebrew. Bare references to other literature and multiple references to other parts of the Bible have been avoided. Actual quotations have been given as often as possible.

The completion of the New Testament part of the series in 1967 provides a basis upon which the production of the much larger Old Testament and Apocrypha series can be undertaken. The welcome accorded to the series has been an encouragement to the editors to follow the same general pattern, and an attempt has been made to take account of criticisms which have been offered. One necessary change is the inclusion of the translators' footnotes since in the Old Testament these are more extensive, and essential for the understanding of the text.

Within the severe limits imposed by the size and scope of the series, each commentator will attempt to set out the main findings of recent biblical scholarship and to describe the historical background to the text. The main theological issues will also be critically discussed.

Much attention has been given to the form of the volumes. The aim is to produce books each of which will be read consecutively from first to last page. The introductory material leads naturally into the text, which itself leads into the alternating sections of the commentary.

The series is accompanied by three volumes of a more general character. *Understanding the Old Testament* sets out to provide the larger historical and archaeological background, to say something about the life and thought of the people of the Old Testament, and to answer the question 'Why should we study the Old Testament?'. *The Making of the Old Testament* is concerned with the formation of the books of the Old Testament and Apocrypha in the context of the ancient near eastern world, and with the ways in which these books have come down to us in the life of the Jewish and Christian communities. *Old Testament Illustrations* contains maps, diagrams and photographs with an explanatory text. These three volumes are designed to provide material helpful to the understanding of the individual books and their commentaries, but they are also prepared so as to be of use quite independently.

P. R. A.

A. R. C. L.

J. W. P.

CONTENTS

LIST OF MAPS

THE FOOTNOTES TO THE
N.E.B. TEXT

The footnotes to the N.E.B. text are designed to help the reader either to understand particular points of detail – the meaning of a name, the presence of a play upon words – or to give information about the actual text. Where the Hebrew text appears to be erroneous, or there is doubt about its precise meaning, it may be necessary to turn to manuscripts which offer a different wording, or to ancient translations of the text which may suggest a better reading, or to offer a new explanation based upon conjecture. In such cases, the footnotes supply very briefly an indication of the evidence, and whether the solution proposed is one that is regarded as possible or as probable. Various abbreviations are used in the footnotes.

(1) Some abbreviations are simply of terms used in explaining a point: *ch(s).*, chapter(s); *cp.*, compare; *lit.*, literally; *mng.*, meaning; *MS(S).*, manuscript(s), i.e. Hebrew manuscript(s), unless otherwise stated; *om.*, omit(s); *or*, indicating an alternative interpretation; *poss.*, possible; *prob.*, probable; *rdg.*, reading; *Vs(s).*, Version(s).

(2) Other abbreviations indicate sources of information from which better interpretations or readings may be obtained.

Aq.   Aquila, a Greek translator of the Old Testament (perhaps about A.D. 130) characterized by great literalness.

Aram.   Aramaic – may refer to the text in this language (used in parts of Ezra and Daniel), or to the meaning of an Aramaic word. Aramaic belongs to the same language family as Hebrew, and is known from about 1000 B.C. over a wide area of the Middle East, including Palestine.

Heb.   Hebrew – may refer to the Hebrew text or may indicate the literal meaning of the Hebrew word.

Josephus   Flavius Josephus (A.D. 37/8–about 100), author of the *Jewish Antiquities*, a survey of the whole history of his people, directed partly at least to a non-Jewish audience, and of various other works, notably one on the *Jewish War* (that of A.D. 66–73) and a defence of Judaism (*Against Apion*).

Luc. Sept.   Lucian's recension of the Septuagint, an important edition made in Antioch in Syria about the end of the third century A.D.

Pesh.   Peshitta or Peshitto, the Syriac version of the Old Testament. Syriac is the name given chiefly to a form of Eastern Aramaic used by the Christian community. The translation varies in quality, and is at many points influenced by the Septuagint or the Targums.

Sam. Samaritan Pentateuch – the form of the first five books of the Old Testament as used by the Samaritan community. It is written in Hebrew in a special form of the Old Hebrew script, and preserves an important form of the text, somewhat influenced by Samaritan ideas.

Scroll(s) Scroll(s), commonly called the Dead Sea Scrolls, found at or near Qumran from 1947 onwards. These important manuscripts shed light on the state of the Hebrew text as it was developing in the last centuries B.C. and the first century A.D.

Sept. Septuagint (meaning 'seventy'; often abbreviated as the Roman numeral LXX), the name given to the main Greek version of the Old Testament. According to tradition, the Pentateuch was translated in Egypt in the third century B.C. by 70 (or 72) translators, six from each tribe, but the precise nature of its origin and development is not fully known. It was intended to provide Greek-speaking Jews with a convenient translation. Subsequently it came to be much revered by the Christian community.

Symm. Symmachus, another Greek translator of the Old Testament (beginning of the third century A.D.), who tried to combine literalness with good style. Both Lucian and Jerome viewed his version with favour.

Targ. Targum, a name given to various Aramaic versions of the Old Testament, produced over a long period and eventually standardized, for the use of Aramaic-speaking Jews.

Theod. Theodotion, the author of a revision of the Septuagint (probably second century A.D.), very dependent on the Hebrew text.

Vulg. Vulgate, the most important Latin version of the Old Testament, produced by Jerome about A.D. 400, and the text most used throughout the Middle Ages in western Christianity.

[...] In the text itself square brackets are used to indicate probably late additions to the Hebrew text.

(Fuller discussion of a number of these points may be found in *The Making of the Old Testament* in this series.)

THE HISTORICAL BACKGROUND
TO DEUTERONOMY

Date B.C.

601   Judah rebels.

598   Jerusalem falls to the Babylonians under Nebuchadnezzar (605–562) who take King Jehoiachin (598–597) into exile. Zedekiah (597–587) put on the throne in his place.

589   Judah again rebels.

587   Jerusalem sacked, temple destroyed, Zedekiah taken prisoner, and Judah absorbed into the Babylonian empire.

561   Although Jehoiachin is released from prison in Babylon (2 Kings 25: 28), he is not restored to his throne.

560–540   In this period the Deuteronomic Work (Deuteronomy to 2 Kings) is completed (cp. p. 3).

539   Cyrus of Persia takes Babylon.

538   Edict of Cyrus allowing Jews to return to Palestine and re-establish the temple and its worship.

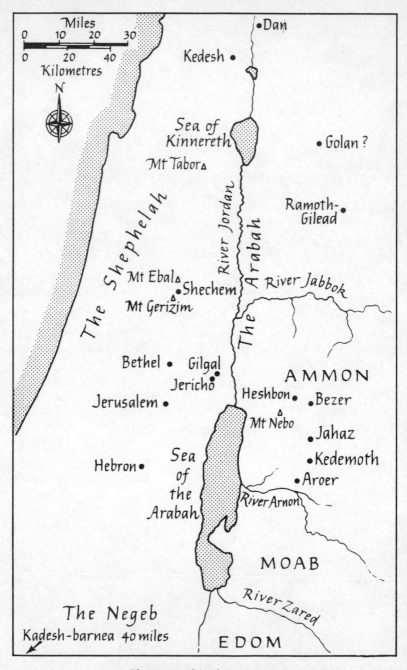

1. Places named in the commentary.

DEUTERONOMY

✳   ✳   ✳   ✳   ✳   ✳   ✳   ✳   ✳   ✳   ✳   ✳   ✳

WHAT IS DEUTERONOMY?

The title 'Deuteronomy' derives from the Greek translation
of the Old Testament, the Septuagint, where the Hebrew
phrase 'a copy of this law' in Deut. 17: 18 was mistranslated
as 'this second law' (*deuteronomion*). The Jews have followed
their normal custom in calling the book after its opening
phrase, in this case 'These are the words', or more simply
'Words'. The 'words' are those of Moses speaking in Moab
on the eve of Israel's crossing of the Jordan into the promised
land of Canaan. They are presented as his last will and testament, and the work concludes with his death and burial.

Deuteronomy takes the form of three separate addresses
followed by a series of appendices. The first address (1: 1 –
4: 43) outlines the main events in Israel's journey from Mount
Horeb (the deuteronomic name for Sinai) to the plains of
Moab, and concludes with the exhortation to observe the
law. The second address (4: 44 – 29: 1) begins by reminding
the Israelites of the terms of the Mosaic covenant set out in the
Ten Commandments which demanded above all else Israel's
exclusive allegiance to her God. It is on obedience to this
law that possession of the land depends. The major portion of
this address consists of supplementary laws to the Ten
Commandments, which although very varied in scope have
the overall purpose of helping Israel to maintain the covenant
relationship through which she receives divine blessing.
Hence the law is not considered a burden, but a benefit. But
as the concluding passage of this address makes clear with its
lists of blessings and curses, failure to observe the divine law
can only result in disaster. The third address (29: 2 – 30: 20)
outlines the choice that faces Israel – obedience or disobedi-

ence. But Moses reminds Israel that even if she is punished for failure to observe the law, on repentance she can still have her fortunes restored, including possession of the land. The appendices deal with the writing down of the law, its deposit in the Ark, and the appointment of Joshua as Moses' successor (31); the recitation of the Song of Moses (32); his Blessing (33); death and burial (34).

As with the first four books of the Old Testament, the Jews have traditionally regarded Moses as the author of Deuteronomy. But in fact Judaism was not so much concerned with maintaining a particular view about authorship, but rather with giving Mosaic authority to the deuteronomic law, and so seeing it as an integral part of the Torah (the Law), the Jewish name for the first five books of the Old Testament, which together are commonly called the Pentateuch.

However, close examination of the text of Deuteronomy shows that it has a completely different character from the other books of the Pentateuch. Indeed its style is so distinctive that it can be more readily identified than any other of the literary sources of these five books. It is therefore clear that originally Deuteronomy did not belong with the rest of the Pentateuch. Further, this distinctive style is not confined to Deuteronomy, but continues in the historical books Joshua to 2 Kings. Scholars have therefore been able to put forward the view that originally there were two quite separate literary works, the Tetrateuch (the four books Genesis to Numbers) and the Deuteronomic Work (Deuteronomy to 2 Kings). Only in the period after the exile was Deuteronomy detached and added to the Tetrateuch. In their subsequent handing-down, the two works have to some extent influenced one another, which explains why a few deuteronomic notes appear in Genesis to Numbers. Further deuteronomic literary activity is also found in the prose sermons inserted into the prophecies of Jeremiah.

Deuteronomy has long been connected with the finding of

the law book in the temple in Josiah's reign in 621 B.C. (2 Kings 22f.). On hearing of the contents of this book, the king was so shocked that he forthwith embarked on a radical religious reform which resulted in the centralization of all worship in Jerusalem, and the consequent destruction of every other shrine. Since such centralization of worship is the main innovation of the deuteronomic law, the majority of scholars hold that the book discovered in the temple must at least have contained the major legal material (12–26, 28) around which the original book of Deuteronomy comprising the second and third addresses (4: 44 – 30: 20) was formed.

That the present book of Deuteronomy is not the original book can readily be recognized from the fact that Deuteronomy now has two introductions, 1 – 4: 43 and 4: 44–11: 32. This is due to the deuteronomic historian who in the period of the exile used the original book of Deuteronomy for the introduction to his Work (Deuteronomy to 2 Kings), and wrote Israel's history from the conquest to the exile in the light of the deuteronomic law. Thus 1 – 4: 43 acts as the introduction to the whole Deuteronomic Work, while 4: 44 – 11: 32 is the introduction to the original book. Further, it has long been noted that while normally the author of the original book uses the singular form of address, there are a number of passages in which the plural form is adopted. These have also been identified as interpolations of the deuteronomic historian.

Since the last event recorded in the Deuteronomic Work is the release of the exiled King Jehoiachin from prison in Babylon in 561 B.C. (2 Kings 25: 28), but there is no mention of the advent of the Persian king, Cyrus, and the return from exile in 538 B.C., the deuteronomic historian must have completed his Work soon after Jehoiachin's release. Thus when Deuteronomy in its final form appeared, Israel had in fact already experienced the punishment which it constantly threatens. Whether the deuteronomic historian wrote in Babylon or Palestine remains a matter of dispute.

WHAT IS DEUTERONOMY'S LITERARY FORM?

2 Kings 23 : 2 describes the book discovered in the temple as a 'covenant document' (better than the N.E.B's 'book of the covenant'). A considerable number of secular covenant documents have been discovered dating from the middle of the second millennium to the seventh century B.C. They take the form of political suzerainty treaties whereby one party, the suzerain, agrees to protect the other, his vassal, provided that the latter fulfils certain conditions specified in the treaty. While the treaties do not follow a strict stereotyped form, they generally include (i) preamble, (ii) historical prologue, (iii) statement of general principles, (iv) detailed obligations imposed on the vassal, (v) direction as to deposit of the treaty and future public reading, (vi) list of gods who witness the treaty, (vii) curses and blessings. Some scholars have argued that from the first Israel interpreted her relationship with her God inaugurated in the Mosaic covenant at Sinai in terms of these treaties. But because not all of the usual suzerainty treaty components can be found in the story of Sinai in Exod. 20, in particular the curses and blessings formula, other scholars have held that it was only later that Israel came to understand her relationship with her God in this way. Whether or not this is so, it is quite clear that in its present form Deuteronomy interprets the covenant relationship in terms of the political suzerainty treaties, whose literary form it follows closely. While the first commandment (Exod. 20: 3; Deut. 5: 7) prohibiting Israel from dealing with any other god prevented the inclusion of a list of gods as witnesses, all the other usual treaty provisions are present. So chs. 1–4 contain the preamble and historical prologue, 5–11 a statement of general principles, 12–26 the detailed obligations, 27–30 the curses and blessings, and 31–4 provisions as to the future including the deposit and public reading of the covenant document. Judah, as a vassal state of Assyria, was familiar enough with this kind of treaty: indeed just such a political

treaty may have acted as the actual model for Deuteronomy in its present form.

Thus Deuteronomy holds that obedience to the law determines Israel's very existence. While she formed the elect community chosen by God from all the nations of the world, her election contained within it a threat, the threat of rejection if she failed to carry out the obligations imposed on her, the chief of which was a total prohibition of any relationship with any god other than Yahweh, Israel's suzerain.

WHERE, WHEN AND BY WHOM WAS THE ORIGINAL BOOK WRITTEN?

The fact that part of Deuteronomy can be associated with the book found in the temple in Josiah's reign does not, of course, indicate that the deuteronomic law is necessarily to be dated to his time. Indeed examination of the book shows that some of the laws are in origin much older. It has in fact long been argued that the traditions behind Deuteronomy originated in the northern kingdom and were brought south following the fall of Samaria to the Assyrians in 721 B.C. Recent scholarship has, however, shown the essentially southern interest of deuteronomic theology, and there can be no doubt that the original book reached its present form in Judah.

None the less, the loss of the northern kingdom and its incorporation into the Assyrian empire had a decisive effect on neighbouring Judah, who interpreted the disaster as the direct consequence of failure to keep the covenant law imposed by God at Sinai. The prophets had in fact proclaimed total judgement on the northern kingdom, and their message had now been dramatically confirmed. In order to avoid a similar fate, Hezekiah of Judah forthwith instituted a religious reform under which he purified the cult (2 Kings 18: 1–6). This resulted in some attempt to centralize worship in Jerusalem, though it seems that the ancient sanctuaries were still allowed to exist alongside the temple in Jerusalem.

Naturally at this time the literary traditions of the north were brought to Judah by those anxious to preserve them. It seems that either in Hezekiah's reign, or shortly afterwards, these traditions were combined with those of the south into a new work called by scholars the JE redaction (or revision). The letters J and E stand for two of the literary sources found in the Tetrateuch. J is so called because it was written in Judah probably in the time of Solomon and uses the divine name Yahweh (Jehovah), while E is associated with the northern kingdom, often called Ephraim, and uses the general term Elohim for God. While a definite connected literary strand can be found for J, this is now seen to be much less certain for E. But it can still be recognized that blocks of material which may be termed collectively E, and which came from the north, were incorporated into J, and a combined work using the traditions of the two kingdoms came into being. This included that part of the Sinai narrative contained in Exod. 18–24, 32–4. Indeed Exod. 32–4, with its polemical treatment of the story of the golden calf, readily identifiable with the bulls of Jeroboam I (1 Kings 12: 28f.; cp. Hos. 8: 5f.; 10: 5; 13: 2), and its fierce anti-Canaanite legislation, seems to reflect Hezekiah's reform. Further, the provision that at the three main feasts all males are to appear at the central shrine (Exod. 34: 22–4) must result from Hezekiah's centralization policy, for earlier they would undoubtedly have attended their local sanctuaries (cp. Exod. 23: 17). It was this JE narrative of the Sinai events which served as a historical model for the deuteronomic historian, as the frequent parallels and some significant differences make plain.

Hezekiah's reform was short-lived, for Assyria quickly reasserted her political control over Judah, and Manasseh, Hezekiah's successor, remained her vassal throughout his long reign. It would seem most likely that it was at this time that the deuteronomic law was developed by building on ideas contained in Hezekiah's reform, but which were now suppressed. A casual glance through Deuteronomy reveals at once that it is no straightforward law code, for legal enactments are continually punctuated by material in sermon form. Deuteronomy has in fact been described as 'preached law'. Clearly those who were responsible for its authorship must have fulfilled a preaching or teaching office in their daily lives.

In fact all three professional offices in ancient Israel were associated with teaching and preaching: the priests, the prophets and the wise (Jer. 18: 18). It is therefore not surprising that different scholars have attributed the authorship of the deuteronomic literature to each of these circles. Thus some scholars see the deuteronomic style as a continuation of the work of the prophetic movement. But while Deuteronomy certainly betrays prophetic influence, it none the less treats prophecy with a certain reserve (cp. 13: 1–5; 18: 20–2). Other scholars find the authors of Deuteronomy among the Levites, there regarded as Israel's only legitimate priests. But in addition to their priestly functions, the Levites were also responsible for the teaching of the law (33: 8–10), which Deuteronomy assigns to their keeping (17: 18; 31: 9, 24–6). Thus, many years later, when Ezra read the law to the people, it was the Levites who were entrusted with the task of expounding it (Neh. 8). Yet other scholars feel that since through the centralization of worship, the chief innovation of the deuteronomic reform, the majority of the Levites lost their livelihood and became like the widow, orphan and resident alien dependent on charity, the Levites could not possibly have instituted the reform. Instead these scholars find the deuteronomists among the wise prominent in court circles dealing with political affairs of state, and who would certainly have been familiar with the suzerainty treaty form. In addition the widely acknowledged humanism of Deuteronomy, its stress on the doctrine of reward as the reason for the observance of the law, and its didactic approach are all typical of wisdom thought (cp. Proverbs, Ecclesiastes and Job).

The identity of the authors of Deuteronomy and the deuteronomic literature is then still an open question. But what can be maintained with reasonable certainty is that the original book of Deuteronomy (4: 44 – 30: 20) or its proto-type (12–26, 28) came into existence some time between the reforms of Hezekiah and Josiah. It was this book which was discovered in the temple, and after receiving prophetic approval (2 Kings 22: 14–20), led to Josiah's reform.

WHAT IS THE PURPOSE OF THE COMPLETED WORK?

It may at first appear ironical that Deuteronomy in its completed form appeared at a time when the covenant relationship was thought to have come to an end through the Babylonian conquest. But in publishing his Work, the deuteronomic historian had a double purpose. First he sought to identify the point at which the chosen people had gone wrong, and so forfeited their election, and second he wanted to point out the course Israel should take if she were ever given another chance.

For the deuteronomists, Israel's primary sin was her apostasy. Contrary to the first and fundamental commandment she had sought to enter into relations with other gods. Although God had continued to exercise patience, even giving Judah the fate of the northern kingdom as a warning (2 Kings 17), in the end he could do no other than bring a similar judgement upon her too. But it is the deuteronomists' view that Israel would never have been tempted into apostasy in the first place had she on entry into the promised land utterly destroyed the Canaanite population. It was through this fundamental failure on her part that Canaanite religious practices and institutions had been allowed to continue alongside her own religion, and had led Israel to reject her special covenant relationship. As a result her God had in his turn rejected her. This explains the enormous stress throughout Deuteronomy on the danger of fraternizing with the

Canaanites. They are to be utterly exterminated, thereby guaranteeing Israel's freedom from their polluting influence.

Undoubtedly on entry into Canaan, Israel did take over much of the indigenous religion and absorb it into her own. This was inevitable when a simpler culture encountered a much wealthier and more sophisticated environment. Indeed throughout the period before the exile the Old Testament witnesses to the tension between what was considered genuinely Israelite and what could be traced to Canaanite influence. This is clearly seen in the prophetic books. In the deuteronomists' eyes the affluence of life in Canaan led Israel to minimize the power of her God who had freed her from slavery in Egypt, and through whom alone she had gained possession of the promised land. For their part they maintain that Israel had no need to resort to Canaanite practices. Her religion brought with her from Horeb (Sinai) was quite sufficient to meet the new situation of life in Canaan.

But this overall deuteronomic assessment is decidedly one-sided, for the influence of Canaanite religion on Israel was by no means entirely negative. As the Psalter clearly indicates, Israel's religion was a synthesis between the pre-conquest exodus traditions associated with a God who acts in history, and Canaanite ideas related to a God who governs nature and fertility. It was with the help of these Canaanite ideas that Israel was led to recognize that her God was not merely a tribal deity who aided her in her military encounters, but was also lord of the universe, which he himself both created and controlled (cp. comment on 11: 1–32). Although there were minority puritan sects like the Rechabites (Jer. 35) who totally renounced everything to do with life in Canaan, they were not representative of the mainstream of Israel's religious thought. Thus while Hosea attacks the excesses of Canaanite religion and the fact that Israel's God was being treated as if he were Baal, he none the less draws on Canaanite theological ideas concerning nature and fertility to reinterpret Israel's religion for his contemporaries.

9

But the Deuteronomic Work is not only concerned with the past but also with the future. While eager to point out Israel's past mistakes, the deuteronomic historian also aims to give her encouragement for the future. While he recognizes that the exilic generation are experiencing judgement under the Mosaic covenant, he still envisages the possibility that their merciful God might one day again lead his people across the Jordan into the promised land: there might yet be a second exodus. But this could only happen if despite her present misfortune Israel remained loyal to her God. So the deuteronomic historian sets out the deuteronomic law as an introduction to his Work. Israel knows what is required of her: she cannot blame God if through her disobedience he should ultimately reject her.

It is probable that the Deuteronomic Work was in fact inspired by the release of Jehoiachin. This must have caused considerable excitement throughout Judaism both in Babylon and Palestine. Was this the prelude to another mighty act of Israel's God, leading to the resumption of her special relationship with him summed up in the Mosaic covenant?

But as it turned out, Israel's theology did not develop along these lines. So fundamental was the judgement brought about by the Babylonian conquest that a totally new way of understanding Israel's covenant relationship with her God arose. This was achieved through the work of Ezekiel and the Priestly theologians who, adding their own literary strand known as P to the JE redaction, produced the other post-exilic literary work, the Tetrateuch. They saw the elect community of Israel reborn entirely due to God's grace (Ezek. 37). Her continued existence was no longer to depend on obedience to the covenant law, but was to exist irrespective of the law. The cult, with its Day of Atonement (Lev. 16), was to provide the means whereby Israel might ever renew and reform herself, and thus be in continual relationship with her God. Thus for post-exilic Israel the covenant relationship no longer contained both threat and promise.

What is the purpose of the completed work?

Israel was the elect community whose election could never again be thrown in doubt. And so when she did reappear after the exile, she came back not as a political entity, but as a worshipping community centred on the temple and its cult presided over by the high priest.

But this new understanding of the covenant relationship as based solely on God's grace, that is, his freely expressed and utterly undeserved love for Israel, did not mean that the law was therefore of no importance. For the law alone determined who could come within the cult and so be a member of the elect community. While this community itself was protected by the covenant of grace, only those who accepted the law could be brought within it. All others had to be rigorously excluded, which explains the reforming work of Nehemiah and Ezra (cp. Neh. 13: 23–7; Ezra 9–10). Only in this way could the purity of the cult be maintained. In other words, responsibility under the law was now transferred from the community to the individual (cp. Jer. 31: 29–34; Ezek. 18).

And the law in question was not merely the Priestly law of the Tetrateuch, but also Deuteronomy, whose authority had been recognized by Josiah and whose enactment concerning the centralization of the cult at Jerusalem was fundamental for post-exilic Judaism. So Deuteronomy was severed from the Deuteronomic Work and joined to the Tetrateuch to become the Law (Torah), the criterion of Jewish orthodoxy. And when the cult itself disappeared in A.D. 70 after the destruction of Jerusalem by the Romans, it was the Law alone which survived as the visible guarantee of Israel's divine election.

✳   ✳   ✳   ✳   ✳   ✳   ✳   ✳   ✳   ✳   ✳   ✳   ✳

Primary charge of Moses to the people

✻ The first eleven chapters of Deuteronomy are not a unity but form two separate introductions. 1 – 4: 43 describes in very abbreviated form Israel's journey through the wilderness from Horeb to Beth-peor in the Jordan valley, and concludes with a sermon on the necessity of avoiding idolatry. Most of the material in 1–3 can be found in the JE narrative (mainly in Numbers). This has been consciously rewritten for preaching purposes by the deuteronomic historian and together with 4: 1–43 now forms the introduction to the whole deuteronomic history (Deuteronomy to 2 Kings). 4: 44 – 11: 32 consists of a series of sermons reminding the Israelites of the importance of keeping the covenant law once they enter Canaan. While these chapters contain the original introduction to the book of Deuteronomy, they have been considerably supplemented by the deuteronomic historian as his use of the plural form of address makes clear. Once more he has reworked the JE narrative (9: 7*b* – 10: 11), and it is probable that the insertion of the Ten Commandments as well as their setting (5: 1 – 6: 1) is also due to the same hand in spite of the retention of the singular form of address. ✻

THE SUMMONS TO ENTER CANAAN

1 THESE ARE THE WORDS that Moses spoke to all Israel in Transjordan, in the wilderness, that is to say in the Arabah opposite Suph, between Paran on the one side and Tophel, Laban, Hazeroth, and Dizahab on 2 the other. (The journey from Horeb through the hill-country of Seir to Kadesh-barnea takes eleven days.)

On the first day of the eleventh month of the fortieth 3–4
year, after the defeat of Sihon king of the Amorites who
ruled in Heshbon, and the defeat at Edrei of Og king of
Bashan who ruled in Ashtaroth, Moses repeated to the
Israelites all the commands that the LORD had given
him for them. It was in Transjordan, in Moab, that Moses 5
resolved to promulgate this law. These were his words:
The LORD our God spoke to us at Horeb and said, 'You 6
have stayed on this mountain long enough; go now, 7
make for the hill-country of the Amorites, and pass on
to all their neighbours in the Arabah, in the hill-country,
in the Shephelah, in the Negeb, and on the coast, in
short, all Canaan and the Lebanon as far as the great
river, the Euphrates. I have laid the land open before 8
you; go in and occupy it, the land which the LORD swore
to give to your forefathers Abraham, Isaac and Jacob,
and to their descendants after them.'

* The first five verses have suffered considerable editorial
additions. They seek to identify the time and place where
Moses gave his new law to Israel on the eve of their entry into
Canaan. The position is very confused since most of the
places named cannot be identified. There then follows the
summons to enter the promised land, whose boundaries
reflect those of the once powerful Davidic empire.

1. *all Israel*: Moses' words are intended for every individual
within the community, which is regarded by Deuteronomy
as a unity in spite of the history of the divided kingdoms.
in the Arabah: the Jordan valley and adjacent land. These
words may be an addition to conform with 3: 29; 34: 6,
where it is recorded that Moses made his speech at Beth-peor.
The other place names probably refer to an area of Moab some
distance to the east of the Jordan. Verse 2 is out of context.

13

3. *On the first day of the eleventh month of the fortieth year*: this is an addition perhaps by the editor of the Pentateuch who having combined Deuteronomy with the Tetrateuch was anxious to tie it in with the system of dating adopted there by the Priestly theologians. For the defeat of the Canaanite kings, Sihon and Og, cp. on 2: 26 – 3: 11.

7. *the Amorites*: general term for the inhabitants of the land east and west of Jordan. *the Shephelah*: the land between the Judaean hills and the coastal plain. *the Negeb*: the south of Palestine.

8. *your forefathers Abraham, Isaac and Jacob*: the covenant with Abraham (here regarded as made with all three patriarchs) that his descendants would become a nation and possess the land of Canaan (Gen. 15) is understood by Deuteronomy to be fulfilled through the Horeb covenant. This scheme of promise and fulfilment thus points to the centrality of the latter covenant in deuteronomic theology. The covenant with Abraham was one of promise only: Deuteronomy is anxious to remind Israel that the promise was in fact conditional. It rested on obedience to the covenant law. ✳

THE REORGANIZATION OF ISRAEL'S JUDICIARY

9 At that time I said to you, 'You are a burden too heavy
10 for me to carry unaided. The LORD your God has increased you so that today you are as numerous as the
11 stars in the sky. May the LORD the God of your fathers increase your number a thousand times and may he
12 bless you as he promised. How can I bear unaided the heavy burden you are to me, and put up with your
13 complaints? Choose men of wisdom, understanding, and repute for each of your tribes, and I will set them in
14 authority over you.' Your answer was, 'What you have

14

told us to do is right.' So I took[a] men of wisdom and 15
repute and set them in authority over you, some as
commanders over units of a thousand, of a hundred, of
fifty or of ten, and others as officers, for each of your
tribes. And at that time I gave your judges this command: 16
'You are to hear the cases that arise among your kinsmen
and judge fairly between man and man, whether fellow-
countryman or resident alien. You must be impartial 17
and listen to high and low alike: have no fear of man, for
judgement belongs to God. If any case is too difficult for
you, bring it before me and I will hear it.' At the same 18
time I instructed you in all these duties.

* Drawing on the JE narrative (Exod. 18: 13ff.), the deuteronomic historian prefaces his account of the giving of the law
with the reorganization of the judiciary (cp. Num. 11: 14ff.).
Initially legal cases were heard locally by the elders of each
town, that is the male heads of each family. But under
Jehoshaphat (873–849 B.C.) professional judges were appointed
to all the fortified cities (2 Chron. 19: 5–11). Exod. 18: 13–26,
most probably written to justify this innovation, indicates
that these possessed both military and judicial authority.
In contrast, Deut. 1: 9–18 appears at first sight to
differentiate the military and executive officers from the
judiciary. While this might reflect the contemporary political
situation, such differentiation is unlikely since the 'commanders' of verse 15, like the professional judges in 16: 18,
continue to have the support of the 'officers' and appear to
have been appointed specifically to deal with 'complaints'
(verse 12). Verses 16ff. are perhaps then best understood as a
hortatory addition.

15. *some as commanders*: the Hebrew *sarim* (translated by
'officers' in Exod. 18: 21, 25) indicates those in a position

[a] *So Sept.; Heb. adds* the heads of your tribes.

to command, and is particularly applied to royal officials. Isa. 1: 21ff. describes Jerusalem as being governed by corrupt *sarim* (translated 'rulers') and looks forward to a return to an earlier system of justice. *others as officers*: the Hebrew *shoterim* refers to court officials who would have been in charge of all aspects of its administration including the enforcement of judgement.

16. *resident alien*: the Hebrew *ger* indicates a foreigner who has taken up permanent residence in Israel. Initially, and indeed under the deuteronomic laws themselves (12-26), the *ger* had no right to legal protection. Like the widow and the orphan, he had to rely on charity (Exod. 22: 21f.; 23: 9). It was only following Josiah's reform that his legal position was equated with that of a full Israelite, and in consequence he became entitled to the protection of the courts, and also liable as a full Israelite for breach of Israel's law (Lev. 20: 2; 24: 10-23). Cp. on 14: 21.

17. *If any case is too difficult for you*: this probably alludes to the right of appeal to the central appeal court at Jerusalem (cp. on 17: 8-13) which replaced appeal to the monarch (2 Sam. 15: 1-6). *

THE STORY OF THE SPIES

19 Then we set out from Horeb, in obedience to the orders of the LORD our God, and marched through that vast and terrible wilderness, as you found it to be, on the way to the hill-country of the Amorites; and so we came 20 to Kadesh-barnea. Then I said to you, 'You have reached the hill-country of the Amorites which the LORD our 21 God is giving us. The LORD your God has indeed now laid the land open before you. Go forward and occupy it in fulfilment of the promise which the LORD the God of your fathers made you; do not be discouraged or

afraid.' But you all came to me and said, 'Let us send 22
men ahead to spy out the country and report back to
us about the route we should take and the cities we shall
find.' I approved this plan and picked twelve of you, one 23
from each tribe. They set out and made their way up 24
into the hill-country as far as the gorge of Eshcol, which
they explored. They took samples of the fruit of the 25
country and brought them back to us, and made their
report: 'It is a rich land that the LORD our God is giving
us.'

But you refused to go up and rebelled against the 26
command of the LORD your God. You muttered treason 27
in your tents and said, 'It was because the LORD hated
us that he brought us out of Egypt to hand us over to
the Amorites to be wiped out. What shall we find up 28
there? Our kinsmen have discouraged us by their report
of a people bigger and taller than we are, and of great
cities with fortifications towering to the sky. And
they told us they saw there the descendants of the
Anakim.'[a]

Then I said to you, 'You must not dread them nor be 29
afraid of them. The LORD your God who goes at your 30
head will fight for you and he will do again what you
saw him do for you in Egypt and in the wilderness. You 31
saw there how the LORD your God carried you all the
way to this place, as a father carries his son.' In spite of 32
this you did not trust the LORD your God, who went 33
ahead on the journey to find a place for your camp. He
went in fire by night to show you the way you should
take, and in a cloud by day.

[a] the descendants...Anakim: *or* the tall men.

34 When the LORD heard your complaints, he was indig-
35 nant and solemnly swore: 'Not one of these men, this
wicked generation, shall see the rich land which I swore
36 to give your forefathers, except Caleb son of Jephunneh.
He shall see it, and to him and his descendants I will
give the land on which he has set foot, because he fol-
37 lowed the LORD with his whole heart.' On your account
the LORD was angry with me also and said, 'You yourself
38 shall never enter it, but Joshua son of Nun, who is in
attendance on you, shall enter it. Encourage him, for he
39 shall put Israel in possession of that land. Your dependants
who, you thought, would become spoils of war, and
your children who do not yet know good and evil, they
shall enter; I will give it to them, and they shall occupy it.
40 You must turn back and set out for the wilderness by
way of the Red Sea.'ᵃ

41 You answered me, 'We have sinned against the LORD;
we will now go up and attack just as the LORD our God
commanded us.' And each of you fastened on his weapons,
42 thinking it an easy thing to invade the hill-country. But
the LORD said to me, 'Tell them not to go up and not
to fight; for I will not be with them, and their enemies
43 will defeat them.' And I told you this, but you did not
listen; you rebelled against the LORD's command and
44 defiantly went up to the hill-country. The Amorites
living in the hills came out against you and like bees they
45 chased you; they crushed you at Hormah in Seir. Then
you came back and wept before the LORD, but he would
46 not hear you or listen to you. That is why you remained
in Kadesh as long as you did.

[a] Or the Sea of Reeds.

✻ Israel refuses to invade Canaan after her spies have reported on the strength of the inhabitants around Hebron (cp. Num. 13–14). For this lack of faith in taking what God was so richly providing, only Caleb and Joshua of the adult population are to be allowed to enter the promised land. Having doubted God's ability to carry out his promise, the exodus generation is considered no longer fit to enjoy its fulfilment. When the people do try and invade, they are heavily defeated for this further act of disobedience, and return to Kadesh.

24. *Eshcol*: near Hebron. The name means 'cluster' and refers to the clusters of fruit which would be found in this rich valley.

28. *Anakim*: a tribal name known from Egyptian execration texts of the nineteenth century B.C. comprising curses on the enemies of the Pharaoh. The *Anakim* are usually connected with the area round Hebron, and were regarded as exceptionally tall (cp. N.E.B. footnote). A thirteenth-century B.C. Egyptian letter describes certain Bedouin as between 4 or 5 cubits high (7 to 9 feet, or about 2 to 2·7 metres).

36. *Caleb*: originally this story was probably concerned to explain how the Calebites came to be found in the region of Hebron. No such considerations apply here.

37. *You yourself shall never enter it*: although innocent, Moses suffers with the guilty (cp. 3: 26–8; 4: 21). In the JE narrative in Exod. 32: 32 Moses offers personally to atone for the sins of his people after the incident of the golden calf. This tradition that Moses suffered innocently may well have been used by Deutero-Isaiah (Isa. 40–55) as the model for his picture of the suffering servant (Isa. 53). The Priestly theologians reinterpreted God's refusal to allow Moses to cross the Jordan by explaining this refusal as due to sin on Moses' part (Num. 20: 12; Deut. 32: 51).

46. *as long as you did*: this verse is probably a later addition reflecting the JE tradition that the thirty-eight years in the wilderness were spent at Kadesh and not, as the deuteronomic historian records, in journeying through Edom (2: 14). ✻

2   19   PDY

THE JOURNEY TO THE PROMISED LAND

2 So we turned and set out for the wilderness by way of
the Red Sea as the LORD had told me we must do, and
we spent many days marching round the hill-country of
2, 3 Seir. Then the LORD said to me, 'You have been long
enough marching round these hills; turn towards the
4 north. And give the people this charge: "You are about
to go through the territory of your kinsmen the descendants of Esau who live in Seir. Although they are afraid
5 of you, be on your guard and do not provoke them; for
I shall not give you any of their land, not so much as a
foot's-breadth: I have given the hill-country of Seir to
6 Esau as a possession. You may purchase food from them
for silver, and eat it, and you may buy*a* water to drink."'
7 The LORD your God has blessed you in everything you
have undertaken; he has watched your journey through
this great wilderness; these forty years the LORD your
God has been with you and you have gone short of
8 nothing. So we went on past our kinsmen, the descendants
of Esau who live in Seir, and along*b* the road of the
Arabah which comes from Elath and Ezion-geber, and
we turned and followed the road to the wilderness of
9 Moab. There the LORD said to me, 'Do not harass the
Moabites nor provoke them to battle, for I will not give
you any of their land as a possession. I have given Ar to
10 the descendants of Lot as a possession.' (The Emim once
lived there – a great and numerous people, as tall as the
11 Anakim. The Rephaim also were reckoned as Anakim;
12 but the Moabites called them Emim. The Horites lived

[a] *Or* dig for.   [b] *So Sept.; Heb.* past.

in Seir at one time, but the descendants of Esau occupied their territory: they destroyed them as they advanced and then settled in the land instead of them, just as Israel did in their own territory which the LORD gave them.) 'Come now, cross the gorge of the Zared.' So we 13 went across. The journey from Kadesh-barnea to the 14 crossing of the Zared took us thirty-eight years, until the whole generation of fighting men had passed away as the LORD had sworn that they would. The LORD's 15 hand was raised against them, and he rooted them out of the camp to the last man.

When the last of the fighting men among the people 16 had died, the LORD spoke to me, 'Today', he said, 'you 17, 18 are to cross by Ar*a* which lies on the frontier of Moab, and when you reach the territory of the Ammonites, 19 you must not harass them or provoke them to battle, for I will not give you any Ammonite land as a possession; I have assigned it to the descendants of Lot.' (This also 20 is reckoned as the territory of the Rephaim, who lived there at one time; but the Ammonites called them Zam-zummim. They were a great and numerous people, as 21 tall as the Anakim, but the LORD destroyed them as the Ammonites advanced and occupied their territory instead of them, just as he had done for the descendants 22 of Esau who lived in Seir. As they advanced, he destoyed the Horites so that they occupied their territory and took possession instead of them: so it is to this day. It was 23 Caphtorites from Caphtor who destroyed the Avvim who lived in the hamlets near Gaza, and settled in the land instead of them.) 'Come, set out on your journey 24

[a] by Ar: *or* the gully.

and cross the gorge of the Arnon, for I have put Sihon
the Amorite, king of Heshbon, and his territory into
your hands. Begin to occupy it and provoke him to
25 battle. Today I will begin to put the fear and dread of
you upon all the peoples under heaven; if they so much
as hear a rumour of you, they will quake and tremble
before you.'

* Israel after her failure to enter Canaan direct from the
south via Hebron is ordered to journey east of Jordan through
Edom, Moab and Ammon. But God commands her that she
should not provoke the indigenous peoples as he himself
has allocated their land to them. In the same way, he is now
about to give Canaan to Israel. He is the universal God to
whom the whole world belongs to do with as he likes
(cp. Amos 9: 7). While Num. 20: 14-21 provides a parallel
account to the journey through Edom, there is no other
mention of similar journeys through Moab and Ammon. The
passage contains in parenthesis (verses 10-12, 20-3) a number
of precedents for the displacement of peoples by invading
nations drawn from local folklore, and indicates Israel's
considerable interest in the origins of her neighbours.

4. *descendants of Esau who live in Seir*: the Edomites. The
story here differs markedly from that in Num. 20: 14-21
where Israel twice petitions the king for permission to pass
through his territory and is refused.

5. *for I shall not give you any of their land*: in 32: 8 the
allocation of territories to the nations is attributed to the pre-
Davidic Canaanite God of Jerusalem, Elyon (translated
'Most High' in the N.E.B.), and now identified with Israel's
God. This may indicate that the idea of God parcelling out to
the nations their land has been inherited from Canaanite
theology. But it is also possible that this idea derives from the
ancient suzerainty treaties under which the suzerain granted

land to his vassals. For in addition to the gift of the land and the command to possess it (cp. 1: 8), the treaty warned the vassal not to trespass beyond its boundaries which the suzerain had determined.

6. *purchase food . . . buy water*: Israel is not to plunder the land nor raid local wells.

7. *these forty years*: the traditional time of Israel's journeying in the wilderness (Amos 2: 10; Ps. 95: 10). It exactly spans the lifetime of one generation.

9. *Ar*: unknown, perhaps a geographical term.

10. *Emim*: giants like the Anakim (cp. Gen. 14: 5).

11. *Rephaim*: mentioned in Gen. 15: 20; Josh. 17: 15 as part of the pre-Israelite population of Canaan. But here they are probably to be understood as a collective term for various tall peoples.

12. *The Horites*: these are the Hurrians whose language indicates that originally they came from the region of Armenia. By the middle of the second millennium they filled northern Mesopotamia and Syria.

13. *Zared*: an eastern tributary to the south of the Dead Sea.

14. *took us thirty-eight years*: cp. 1: 46. No information is given as to what Israel did in this time. But it was of sufficient duration for the exodus generation of adult males to die out in accordance with God's decree (1: 34–40).

20. *Zamzummim*: another race of giants.

23. *Caphtorites*: the Philistines who settled on the south-western coastal plain (cp. Amos 9: 7). Caphtor is usually identified with Crete. *Avvim*: the original inhabitants of the south-western coastal plain displaced by the Philistines (cp. Josh. 13: 3f.). *

THE DEFEAT OF THE CANAANITE KINGS,
SIHON AND OG

26 Then I sent messengers from the wilderness of Kedemoth to Sihon king of Heshbon with these peaceful
27 overtures: 'Grant us passage through your country by
the highway: we will keep to the highway, trespassing
28 neither to right nor to left, and we will pay you the full
29 price for the food we eat and the water we drink. The
descendants of Esau who live in Seir granted us passage,
and so did the Moabites who live in Ar. We will simply
pass through your land on foot, until we cross the
Jordan to the land which the LORD our God is giving us.'
30 But Sihon king of Heshbon refused to grant us passage;
for the LORD your God had made him stubborn and
obstinate, in order that he and his land might become
31 subject to you, as it still is. So the LORD said to me,
'Come, I have begun to deliver Sihon and his territory
32 into your hands. Begin now to occupy his land.' Then
Sihon with all his people came out to meet us in battle
33 at Jahaz, and the LORD our God delivered him into our
hands; we killed him with his sons and all his people.
34 We captured all his cities at that time and put to death
everyone in the cities, men, women, and dependants;
35 we left no survivor. We took the cattle as booty and
36 plundered the cities we captured. From Aroer on the
edge of the gorge of the Arnon and the level land of
the gorge, as far as Gilead, no city walls were too lofty
37 for us; the LORD our God laid them all open to us. But
you avoided the territory of the Ammonites, both the
parts along the gorge of the Jabbok and their cities in

the hills, thus fulfilling all[a] that the LORD our God had commanded.

Next we turned and advanced along the road to Bashan. **3** Og king of Bashan, with all his people, came out against us at Edrei. The LORD said to me, 'Do not be afraid of him, 2 for I have delivered him into your hands, with all his people and his land. Deal with him as you dealt with Sihon the king of the Amorites who lived in Heshbon.' So the 3 LORD our God also delivered Og king of Bashan into our hands, with all his people. We slaughtered them and left no survivor, and at the same time we captured all his 4 cities; there was not a single town that we did not take from them. In all we took sixty cities, the whole region of Argob, the kingdom of Og in Bashan; all these were 5 fortified cities with high walls, gates, and bars, apart from a great many open settlements. Thus we put to death all 6 the men, women, and dependants in every city, as we did to Sihon king of Heshbon. All the cattle and the spoil 7 from the cities we took as booty for ourselves.

At that time we took from these two Amorite kings 8 in Transjordan the territory that runs from the gorge of the Arnon to Mount Hermon (the mountain that the 9 Sidonians call Sirion and the Amorites Senir), all the 10 cities of the tableland, and the whole of Gilead and Bashan as far as Salcah and Edrei, cities in the kingdom of Og in Bashan. (Only Og king of Bashan remained as the 11 sole survivor of the Rephaim. His sarcophagus of basalt[b] was nearly fourteen feet long and six feet wide,[c] and it may still be seen in the Ammonite city of Rabbah.)

[a] *So Sept.; Heb.* and all.   [b] *Or* iron.
[c] *Lit.* nine cubits long and four cubits wide by the common standard.

✻ Israel first asks Sihon for free passage through his territory. But this is not in accord with God's will for Israel has now reached the land which he has decreed shall be hers. Sihon takes up arms against Israel, is defeated and killed, his land taken, and its inhabitants exterminated. Og suffers a similar fate. Israel now holds all the land from Mount Hermon to the Arnon.

26. *Kedemoth*: a city near the Arnon. *Heshbon*: Sihon's capital 16 miles (about 25 kilometres) east of Jordan. The Canaanite kingdoms of Heshbon and Bashan were probably formed in the thirteenth century following the break-up of the Canaanite city-state pattern. Cp. Num. 21: 21–31.

30. *the LORD your God had made him stubborn and obstinate*: Sihon is a mere pawn in God's hands.

32. *Jahaz*: a city north of the Arnon and mentioned on the ninth-century stele of Mesha, king of Moab, known as the Moabite Stone. This stele, now in the Louvre, commemorates Mesha's victories over Israel whereby Moab gained her independence (cp. 2 Kings 3: 5ff.).

34. *put to death everyone in the cities*: this refers to the ḥerem ('ban') which was a feature of the holy war, and could be of varying severity: (1) total destruction of all persons and property (20: 16–18; 1 Sam. 15: 3); (2) total destruction of all persons, but not property (2: 34f.; 3: 6f.); (3) destruction of all males only (20: 10–15). It was interpreted as a sacrifice to God to whom the enemy had been dedicated, and therefore failure to carry it out resulted in severe penalties. So following the siege of Jericho, Achan and his family were themselves executed for trying to appropriate certain objects which fell under the ban, and therefore belonged to God (Josh. 7). The ban is to be inflicted on the Canaanites in order to ensure that there should be no survivors who might lead Israel into apostasy. The utter annihilation of the Canaanites would lead to the complete extermination of their alien religious life and worship for ever. The mention of the ban here is, of course, theoretical and reflects the deuteronomic view as to what

ought to have happened at the original entry into the land. How often in ancient times the ban was inflicted remains uncertain, but evidence for it is found on the Moabite Stone. This records that Mesha exterminated the inhabitants of the Israelite city of Nebo whom he had dedicated to his god, Ashtar-Chemosh.

36. *Aroer*: also mentioned on the Moabite Stone.

3: 1. *Og*: there is no earlier report of this second conquest, for Num. 21: 33–5 is itself late. But Sihon and Og may have long been connected in the liturgy. Thus they are found together in Ps. 135: 11; 136: 19f. in the liturgical creeds celebrating the history of Israel's election and deliverance. And these psalms are not necessarily to be thought of as late and therefore dependent on traditions in Deuteronomy and elsewhere, for they may well have a pre-exilic background associated with the festival of the renewal of the covenant. *Bashan*: meaning 'fertile' was well known for its pastures and flocks, and also for its oak trees from which oars were made (Ezek. 27: 6).

3. *and left no survivor*: cp. 2: 34.

11. *His sarcophagus of basalt*: the size of this stone coffin of Og confirms that he was the last of the giants. Perhaps this legend came to be attached to a particular prominent rock. *Rabbah*: modern Amman. ✳

THE ASSIGNMENT OF TRANSJORDAN

At that time, when we occupied this territory, I 12 assigned to the Reubenites and Gadites the land beyond Aroer on the gorge of the Arnon and half the hill-country of Gilead with its towns. The rest of Gilead and the 13 whole of Bashan the kingdom of Og, all the region of Argob, I assigned to half the tribe of Manasseh. (All Bashan used to be called the land of the Rephaim. Jair 14 son of Manasseh took all the region of Argob as far as

the Geshurite and Maacathite border. There are tent-
15, 16 villages in Bashan still called by his name, Havvoth-jair.[a])
To Machir I assigned Gilead, and to the Reubenites and
the Gadites I assigned land from Gilead to the gorge of
the Arnon, that is to the middle of the gorge; and its
territory ran[b][c] to the gorge of the Jabbok, the Ammonite
17 frontier, and included the Arabah, with the Jordan and
adjacent land, from Kinnereth to the Sea of the Arabah,
that is the Dead Sea, below the watershed of Pisgah on the
18 east. At that time I gave you this command: 'The LORD
your God has given you this land to occupy; let all your
fighting men be drafted and cross at the head of their
19 fellow-Israelites. Only your wives and dependants and
your livestock – I know you have much livestock – shall
20 stay in the towns I have given you. This you shall do
until the LORD gives your kinsmen security as he has
given it to you, and until they too occupy the land which
the LORD your God is giving them on the other side of
the Jordan; then you may return to the possession which
I have given you, every man to his own.'

21   At that time also I gave Joshua this charge: 'You have
seen with your own eyes all that the LORD your God has
done to these two kings; he will do the same to all the king-
22 doms into which you will cross over. Do not be afraid of
them, for the LORD your God himself will fight for you.'

✱ Transjordan is now divided up between the tribes of
Reuben and Gad who take the southern portion, and the half

[a] *That is* Tent-villages of Jair.
[b] that is...ran: *or* including the bed of the gorge and the adjacent
strip of land...
[c] and its territory ran: *prob. rdg.; Heb.* and territory and...

tribe of Manasseh which is assigned the north. But before those of military age can settle in their new lands, Moses orders them to help in the conquest of the rest of Canaan west of Jordan. Joshua is to lead the campaign.

14. *Jair son of Manasseh*: cp. Num. 32: 41 where Jair is reported as being active in Gilead and not as here in Bashan. He was one of the so-called minor judges (Judg. 10: 1–5; 12: 7–15) responsible for the overall administration of the covenant law in the pre-monarchical period of Israel's settlement in Canaan. *the Geshurite and Maacathite border*: two Aramaean tribes on the western border of Bashan.

15. *Machir*: understood as part of Manasseh.

17. *from Kinnereth to the Sea of the Arabah*: this describes the length of the Jordan from the Sea of Galilee to its entrance into the north of the Dead Sea. *

MOSES' LAST REQUEST

At that same time I pleaded with the LORD, 'O Lord 23, 24 GOD, thou hast begun to show to thy servant thy greatness and thy strong hand: what god is there in heaven or on earth who can match thy works and mighty deeds? Let me cross over and see that rich land which 25 lies beyond the Jordan, and the fine hill-country and the Lebanon.' But because of you the LORD brushed me 26 aside and would not listen. 'Enough!' he answered. 'Say no more about this. Go to the top of Pisgah and look 27 west and north, south and east; look well at what you see, for you shall not cross this river Jordan. Give Joshua 28 his commission, encourage him and strengthen him; for he will lead this people across, and he will put them in possession of the land you see before you.'

So we remained in the valley opposite Beth-peor.   29

✻ Moses pleads to be allowed to cross the Jordan, but because of Israel's sin, God turns down his request. Instead he must be content to view the promised land from afar before his death.

26. *because of you*: cp. Deut. 1: 37; 4: 21.

27. *look well at what you see*: Moses is here being invited to take actual possession of the promised land on Israel's behalf, for the legal transfer of property took place when the purchaser looked it over (cp. Gen. 13: 14–17). Thus the similar passage in Deut. 34 records the actual conveyance to Israel of the land of Canaan, which is then immediately confirmed by the account of the conquest. The same method of transferring land is found in the New Testament both in the story of Jesus' temptation by the devil (Matt. 4: 8f.), and in the parable of the guests who refused to come to the dinner party (Luke 14: 18), where the man who goes to inspect his land is not to be understood as engaged in some idle activity, but as actually taking legal possession. This method of transfer of land is also found in Roman law. ✻

AN INJUNCTION TO OBSERVE THE COVENANT LAW

4 Now, Israel, listen to the statutes and laws which I am teaching you, and obey them; then you will live, and go in and occupy the land which the LORD the God of
2 your fathers is giving you. You must not add anything to my charge, nor take anything away from it. You must carry out all the commandments of the LORD your God which I lay upon you.

3 You saw with your own eyes what the LORD did at Baal-peor; the LORD your God destroyed among you
4 every man who went over to the Baal of Peor, but you who held fast to the LORD your God are all alive today.
5 I have taught you statutes and laws, as the LORD my God

commanded me; these you must duly keep when you
enter the land and occupy it. You must observe them 6
carefully, and thereby you will display your wisdom and
understanding to other peoples. When they hear about
these statutes, they will say, 'What a wise and understanding people this great nation is!' What great nation 7
has a god*a* close at hand as the LORD our God is close to
us whenever we call to him? What great nation is there 8
whose statutes and laws are just, as is all this law which
I am setting before you today? But take good care: be 9
on the watch not to forget the things that you have seen
with your own eyes, and do not let them pass from your
minds as long as you live, but teach them to your sons
and to your sons' sons. You must never forget that day 10
when you stood before the LORD your God at Horeb,
and the LORD said to me, 'Assemble the people before
me; I will make them hear my words and they shall learn
to fear me all their lives on earth, and they shall teach
their sons to do so.' Then you came near and stood at the 11
foot of the mountain. The mountain was ablaze with fire
to the very skies: there was darkness, cloud, and thick mist.
When the LORD spoke to you from the fire you heard a 12
voice speaking, but you saw no figure; there was only a
voice. He announced the terms of his covenant to you, 13
bidding you observe the Ten Words,*b* and he wrote
them on two tablets of stone. At that time the LORD 14
charged me to teach you statutes and laws which you
should observe in the land into which you are passing
to occupy it.

[a] *Or* gods.
[b] *Or* Ten Commandments.

31

* Having dealt with the history of the wilderness period, Moses returns to the situation now facing Israel. She must keep his law which on no account is to be varied. Failure to do so can only result in direct divine punishment as on the apostates at Baal-peor. Indeed, Israel's veneration of her law is to lead other nations to a recognition of the uniqueness of her covenant relationship so graciously inaugurated by her God on Mount Horeb, where she received the Ten Commandments.

2. *must not add. . .nor take anything away*: the idea of the immutability of legal obligations is found throughout the ancient Near East (cp. 12: 32 and the conclusion to the nineteenth-century B.C. Babylonian Code of Lipit-Ishtar). The deuteronomists thought of their law as complete in spite of the fact that it contained none of the civil law provisions found in the Book of the Covenant (Exod. 20: 22 – 23: 33) which involved an action for damages by the injured party. The explanation for this can only be that the deuteronomists did not understand such issues as threatening the covenant relationship, but as domestic matters which merely involved the parties directly concerned. Instead their primary concern was with those legal provisions by which Israel's exclusive allegiance to her God could be maintained, and on observance of which the existence of the nation depended.

3. *Baal-peor*: cp. Num. 25 where the story of Israel's unfaithfulness is related.

6. *your wisdom and understanding*: for the Hebrews the wise man was the person who could discern or bring about order (1 Kings 3: 16–28). The establishment of order was also the function of the law. It was the unique ability of Israelite law in achieving this which was to win the admiration of the heathen nations.

7. *a god close at hand*: as long as Israel kept the covenant law there was no need to fear that God would not answer her prayers. The Hebrew here could be translated 'gods' (cp. N.E.B. footnote), which is, of course, entirely appropriate

for the other nations who knew nothing of the commandment to worship one god alone.

9. *teach them to your sons*: everyone must know the law
since it was obedience to the law alone which ensured the
life of the nation. It was the duty of the father to instruct
his children both in law and religion and to explain Israel's
unique position. The practice of his own religion provided
occasions when questions could be asked and answers given.
So even today at the celebration of Passover the youngest
child present asks certain set questions of the celebrant who
in reply tells the story of Israel's miraculous deliverance from
Egypt and explains the symbolism of the meal (cp. Exod.
12: 26f.).

13. *the Ten Words*: the use of the term *Words* to describe
the covenant stipulations reflects the ancient suzerainty treaties,
where the obligations imposed on the vassal were similarly
described (cp. Exod. 20: 1; 34: 27f.; Deut. 10: 4). *two tablets
of stone*: the Commandments are not to be thought of as
written partly on one tablet and partly on the other. Each
tablet would have contained all Ten Commandments. This
again reflects the normal practice of the suzerainty treaties
under which one copy was retained by the suzerain and the
other given to the vassal for deposit in the temple of his god.
In Israel's case both copies were placed in the Ark (Deut.
10: 1–5; 31: 9, 26), the throne of her invisible God, thereby
symbolizing his permanent presence with his vassal, Israel. *

A WARNING AGAINST IDOLATRY

On the day when the LORD spoke to you out of the 15
fire on Horeb, you saw no figure of any kind; so take
good care not to fall into the degrading practice of 16
making figures carved in relief, in the form of a man or a
woman, or of any animal on earth or bird that flies in the 17
air, or of any reptile on the ground or fish in the waters 18

33

19 under the earth. Nor must you raise your eyes to the heavens and look up to the sun, the moon, and the stars, all the host of heaven, and be led on to bow down to them and worship them; the LORD your God assigned these for the worship of[a] the various peoples under

20 heaven. But you are the people whom the LORD brought out of Egypt, from the smelting-furnace, and took for

21 his own possession, as you are to this day. The LORD was angry with me on your account and swore that I should not cross the Jordan nor enter the rich land which the

22 LORD your God is giving you for your possession. I shall die in this country; I shall not cross the Jordan, but you

23 are about to cross and occupy that rich land. Be careful not to forget the covenant which the LORD your God made with you, and do not make yourselves a carved figure of anything which the LORD your God has for-

24 bidden. For the LORD your God is a devouring fire, a jealous god.

* The tradition that at Horeb Israel saw no figure of her God, but merely heard his voice, is interpreted theologically as an indication that Israel was from the first to abstain from making images. These verses are in effect a sermon on the second commandment (cp. on 5: 8ff.), and take it one stage further to include not merely the prohibition of all images, but also of the worship of any heavenly body. While originally the second commandment specifically sought to prevent the making of an actual image of Israel's God, later it was reinterpreted to cover images of all other deities whom she might be tempted to worship. It is this fear of apostasy which lies behind this passage.

[a] assigned...worship of: *or* created these for.

16. *in the form of a man or a woman*: this reflects the intention of the original commandment (Exod. 20: 4*a*; Deut. 5: 8*a*) in prohibiting any image of Israel's God in human form, for from the first she visualized him in this way. Her relationship with him was of such an intimate nature that he could only be thought of in personal terms.

17f. *or of any animal...bird...reptile...or fish*: this reflects the expansion of the original commandment to include images from nature now thought of as images of other deities (Exod. 20: 4*b*; Deut. 5: 8*b*).

19. *raise your eyes to the heavens*: here the commandment is further extended to include the worship of astral powers, a practice which seems to have arisen late in Israel. But in fact the belief that the heavenly bodies control human destiny (astrology) is one which appears particularly in periods of political uncertainty, such as the last years of the Judaean monarchy (e.g. 2 Kings 21: 3–6). *for the worship of the various peoples*: surprise has sometimes been expressed at such an apparently tolerant attitude to the idolatrous practices of the heathen nations. But it is more probable that their religion is being deliberately ridiculed.

20. *from the smelting-furnace*: a metaphor for the ordeal which Israel went through in Egypt (cp. 1 Kings 8: 51).

21f. *The LORD was angry with me*: cp. 1: 37; 3: 26.

24. *a jealous god*: Israel's God demands her exclusive allegiance. This phrase is only used of Israel's God when his claims over Israel are being threatened by other deities (cp. Exod. 20: 5; Deut. 5: 9; 6: 15). *

THE CONSEQUENCES OF DISOBEDIENCE

When you have children and grandchildren and grow 25 old in the land, if you then fall into the degrading practice of making any kind of carved figure, doing what is wrong in the eyes of the LORD your God and provoking

26 him to anger, I summon heaven and earth to witness against you this day: you will soon vanish from the land which you are to occupy after crossing the Jordan. You 27 will not live long in it; you will be swept away. The LORD will disperse you among the peoples, and you will be left few in number among the nations to which the 28 LORD will lead you. There you will worship gods made by human hands out of wood and stone, gods that can 29 neither see nor hear, neither eat nor smell. But if from there you seek the LORD your God, you will find him, 30 if indeed you search with all your heart and soul. When you are in distress and all these things come upon you, you will in days to come turn back to the LORD your 31 God and obey him. The LORD your God is a merciful god; he will never fail you nor destroy you, nor will he forget the covenant guaranteed by oath with your fore-fathers.

* If in the future Israel falls victim to idolatry, then she will lose possession of the land which she is about to occupy, and being scattered among the foreign nations, will worship their gods. Yet even then, if Israel turns to her God she will find him. Being by nature merciful, he cannot ultimately forget his promise to the forefathers. This passage clearly betrays knowledge of the exile in Babylon, which led to widespread apostasy. Yet the deuteronomic historian can still hope that in spite of the terrible judgement wrought by God, the covenant relationship might even now be restored. It is this hope which forms the motive for his Work.

26. *heaven and earth to witness*: this reflects the suzerainty treaty form in which both divine and natural phenomena are cited as witnesses to the treaty. While the first commandment ruled out any recourse to divine witnesses on Israel's part,

the use of natural witnesses is found both in the prophets and the psalms (cp. Mic. 6: 2). Here *heaven and earth* represent the full created universe (cp. Deut. 30: 19; 31: 28).

27. *few in number*: this should not be interpreted as a reference to the remnant doctrine particularly associated with Isaiah, for such a doctrine is quite foreign to Deuteronomy. Rather it stresses the very severe nature of God's punishment.

29. *you seek the LORD your God*: cp. Jer. 29: 12-14.

31. *guaranteed by oath with your forefathers*: for the deuteronomic historian, even the Babylonian conquest had not ultimately invalidated the earlier promise to the patriarchs. Here lies the hope for the future, though that future will still be governed by whether or not Israel will obey the covenant law. *

THE UNIQUENESS OF ISRAEL'S GOD

Search into days gone by, long before your time, 32 beginning at the day when God created man on earth; search from one end of heaven to the other, and ask if any deed as mighty as this has been seen or heard. Did 33 any people ever hear the voice of God speaking out of the fire, as you heard it, and remain alive? Or did ever a god 34 attempt to come and take a nation for himself away from another nation, with a challenge, and with signs, portents, and wars, with a strong hand and an outstretched arm, and with great deeds of terror, as the LORD your God did for you in Egypt in the sight of you all? You 35 have had sure proof that the LORD is God; there is no other. From heaven he let you hear his voice for your 36 instruction, and on earth he let you see his great fire, and out of the fire you heard his words. Because he loved 37 your fathers and chose their children after them,[a] he in

[a] *So Sept.; Heb.* his children after him.

his own person brought you out of Egypt by his great
38 strength, so that he might drive out before you nations
greater and more powerful than you and bring you in
39 to give you their land in possession as it is today. This
day, then, be sure and take to heart that the LORD is
God in heaven above and on earth below; there is no
40 other. You shall keep his statutes and his commandments
which I give you today; then all will be well with you
and with your children after you, and you will live long
in the land which the LORD your God is giving you for
all time.

☆ Moses appeals to the two great saving acts in Israel's
history, the exodus from Egypt and the revelation at Horeb,
as proof of the unique nature of her God. He is utterly
incomparable with the gods of the other nations.

32. *when God created man on earth*: all human history is to
be examined. *from one end of heaven to the other*: every part
of the universe is to be searched out.

35. *there is no other*: this is best interpreted as 'there is no
other *like him*', rather than as an explicit statement of monotheism, that is the doctrine that there is only one God.
Whether this passage influenced Deutero-Isaiah, the first
Old Testament theologian specifically to enunciate this
doctrine, remains uncertain. Cp. on Deut. 32: 39.

37. *Because he loved your fathers*: both the exodus and Horeb
are interpreted as further acts of divine graciousness first seen
in the promise to the patriarchs.

38. *as it is today*: the author has forgotten that this is
supposed to be part of a speech by Moses before entry into
the promised land. ☆

THE ESTABLISHMENT OF THE TRANSJORDANIAN CITIES OF REFUGE

Then Moses set apart three cities in the east, in Trans- 41
jordan, to be places of refuge for the homicide who 42
kills a man without intent, with no previous enmity
between them. If he takes sanctuary in one of these
cities his life shall be safe. The cities were: Bezer-in-the- 43
Wilderness on the tableland for the Reubenites, Ramoth
in Gilead for the Gadites, and Golan in Bashan for the
Manassites.

∗ These verses are a late interpolation of someone already
familiar with Num. 35: 9–15 and Josh. 20, from which
the names of the Transjordanian cities of refuge are taken.
The interpolator was evidently perplexed that there was no
mention of the establishment of these cities before the invasion
west of the Jordan. It has generally been argued that the cities
of refuge owe their origin to the centralization of the cult
at Jerusalem with the consequent destruction of the local
sanctuaries at which the murderer who maintained that he
had acted without intent could hitherto have sought asylum
(Exod. 21: 13). The list of cities in Josh. 20: 7f. (Kedesh in
Galilee, Shechem, Hebron, Bezer, Ramoth in Gilead, and
Golan) would then be understood as a late imaginative
reconstruction (cp. map, p. xiv). But this assertion cannot be
maintained since in Hos. 6: 8f. direct allusion is made to two
of these cities as 'cities of refuge', namely Ramoth in Gilead
(there called Gilead) and Shechem. The first is pictured as
full of murderers who ought to have been executed, while
those who should have been given access to the second are
themselves murdered *en route* by the priests. The establishment of the cities of refuge is therefore older than Hosea
(*c.* 750–724 B.C.) and must in fact be traced back to the period

of the united monarchy of David and Solomon, since only then would all six cities have been in Israelite hands. Cp. on 19: 1–13.

43. *Bezer-in-the-Wilderness*: also mentioned on the Moabite Stone. *Ramoth in Gilead*: Jeroboam II (786–746 B.C.) restored to the northern kingdom the territory lost since the reign of Solomon (2 Kings 14: 25), which would have included Ramoth in Gilead. Hence in Hosea's time it was again able to act as a city of refuge for the surrounding territory. ✶

THE PREFACE

44 This is the law which Moses laid down for the Israelites.
45 These are the precepts, the statutes, and the laws which Moses proclaimed to the Israelites, when they came out of
46 Egypt and were in Transjordan in the valley opposite Beth-peor in the land of Sihon king of the Amorites who lived in Heshbon. Moses and the Israelites had
47 defeated him when they came out of Egypt and had occupied his territory and the territory of Og king of Bashan, the two Amorite kings in the east, in Trans-
48 jordan. The territory ran from Aroer on the gorge of
49 the Arnon to Mount Sirion,[a] that is Hermon; and all the Arabah on the east, in Transjordan, as far as the Sea of the Arabah below the watershed of Pisgah.

✶ These verses, with some later additions, begin the introduction to the original book of Deuteronomy.

48. *Mount Sirion*: the Hebrew reads 'Sion'. This cannot refer to the mountain on which Jerusalem was built, but must be an error for Sirion. Cp. 3: 9. ✶

[a] *So Pesh., cp. 3: 9; Heb.* Sion.

THE COVENANT AT HOREB

Moses summoned all Israel and said to them: Listen, O **5**
Israel, to the statutes and the laws which I proclaim in
your hearing today. Learn them and be careful to observe
them. The LORD our God made a covenant with us at 2
Horeb. It was not with our forefathers that the LORD 3
made this covenant, but with us, all of us who are alive
and are here this day. The LORD spoke with you face to 4
face on the mountain out of the fire. I stood between the 5
LORD and you at that time to report the words*a* of the
LORD; for you were afraid of the fire and did not go up
the mountain. And the LORD said:

I am the LORD your God who brought you out of 6
Egypt, out of the land of slavery.

You shall have no other god*b* to set against me.   7

You shall not make a carved image for yourself nor*c* 8
the likeness of anything in the heavens above, or on the
earth below, or in the waters under the earth.

You shall not bow down to them or worship*d* them; 9
for I, the LORD your God, am a jealous god. I punish the
children for the sins of the fathers to the third and fourth
generations of those who hate me. But I keep faith with 10
thousands, with*e* those who love me and keep my
commandments.

You shall not make wrong use of the name of the 11
LORD your God; the LORD will not leave unpunished the
man who misuses his name.

[a] *So Sam.; Heb.* word.   [b] *Or* gods.
[c] nor: *so many MSS.; others om.*   [d] *Or* or be led to worship...
[e] with...with: *or* for a thousand generations with...

12 Keep the sabbath day holy as the LORD your God
13 commanded you. You have six days to labour and do all
14 your work. But the seventh day is a sabbath of the LORD
   your God; that day you shall not do any work, neither
   you, your son or your daughter, your slave or your
   slave-girl, your ox, your ass, or any of your cattle, nor
   the alien within your gates, so that your slaves and slave-
15 girls may rest as you do. Remember that you were
   slaves in Egypt and the LORD your God brought you out
   with a strong hand and an outstretched arm, and for
   that reason the LORD your God commanded you to keep
   the sabbath day.

16 Honour your father and your mother, as the LORD
   your God commanded you, so that you may live long,
   and that it may be well with you in the land which the
   LORD your God is giving you.

17 You shall not commit murder.

18 You shall not commit adultery.

19 You shall not steal.

20 You shall not give false evidence against your neighbour.

21 You shall not covet your neighbour's wife; you shall
   not set your heart on your neighbour's house, his land,
   his slave, his slave-girl, his ox, his ass, or on anything that
   belongs to him.

✻ The use of the plural form of address indicates that the
passages surrounding the Ten Commandments are the work
of the deuteronomic historian. And although the singular
form of address is retained in the Commandments, their total
lack of connection with other passages in the singular form
shows that they too have been inserted here. Following the

literary pattern of the JE narrative (Exod. 18–24), the deuteronomic historian has used the Commandments as a prologue
to the deuteronomic law, just as earlier they had come to be
used in the same way to introduce the Book of the Covenant
(Exod. 20: 22 – 23: 33). In both instances the ensuing later
law is intended to be interpreted as deduced from the Commandments upon which it is dependent.

Although in the JE narrative the Ten Commandments are
contained in an E block of material, their authorship is not
to be attributed to E, for they undoubtedly existed as a self-
contained unit before being written into the Sinai narrative.
But their actual date continues to be a matter of dispute.
While it seems almost certain that the Commandments
antedate the monarchy, those scholars who accept that Israel's
covenant relationship with her God was from the first
interpreted in terms of the ancient suzerainty treaties argue
that they can in fact be traced back to Moses himself. They
find confirmation for their view not only in the I–Thou form
of address, but also in the demand for exclusive allegiance,
both typical of the suzerainty treaties. While the Commandments have suffered considerable later revision and expansion,
there is nothing in the content of the original short direct
commands which on first sight is inapplicable to a desert
setting. For while in any event the Hebrew word for 'house'
found in the tenth commandment could refer to a tent, the
tradition that the clans made bricks in Egypt (Exod. 5: 6–19)
perhaps indicates that they would have made permanent
buildings for their stay at the oasis of Kadesh (cp. Deut.
1: 46). Further, detailed examination of the Book of the
Covenant, usually dated to the period of the settlement,
indicates that there two types of law are consciously being
differentiated: crimes which require the death penalty, and
civil actions for which damages are paid (Exod. 21: 12ff.).
In all cases the crimes are to be traced back to the Ten Commandments, breach of which alone appears to have carried
the death penalty in pre-exilic Israel. This could reflect the

process of integrating the Ten Commandments with the indigenous Canaanite law following entry into the land.

Be this as it may, the deuteronomists certainly understood Israel's relationship with her God in terms of the suzerainty treaties. For them therefore obedience to the Ten Commandments determined Israel's entire fate. Hence their prominent position in the finished Work. While the deuteronomic version contains a number of minor variations from that in Exod. 20: 2–17, there are significant differences in the treatment of both the fourth and tenth commandments.

3. *all of us who are alive and are here this day*: this appears to contradict the earlier statement that the Horeb generation had died out (2: 14). But the covenant is made with *Israel*, and is therefore considered to be binding on every Israelite in every age. It is as if those now gathered east of Jordan, and for that matter the deuteronomic historian's generation too, had in fact been present at Horeb.

5. *I stood between the LORD and you*: Moses is to act as the covenant mediator. Yet verses 4 and 22ff. imply that God spoke direct to Israel. It is probably best to interpret this apparent inconsistency by holding that while Israel heard the thunder of God's voice, only Moses understood his precise words.

6. *I am the LORD your God*: dramatically Israel's God, Yahweh, identifies himself in the first person. This indicates the intimate nature of the covenant relationship now being inaugurated. His claim on Israel's allegiance is based on the historical deliverance from Egypt. Covenant and exodus are thus inseparable from one another, both constituting events in Israel's salvation history. Consequently the commandments which follow are to be interpreted as part of Yahweh's blessing. The pronunciation of the divine name remains uncertain since the original vowels between the consonants YHWH are no longer known. The hybrid form Jehovah used in the N.E.B. (e.g. Exod. 3: 15) results from the combination of these four consonants with the vowels of

Adonai meaning Lord. This combination reflects the piety of later Old Testament Judaism, which regarded the divine name as too sacred to pronounce. Instead, the word for 'Lord' was read out, the vowels of this word being inserted between the consonants YHWH in the scriptural text as a reminder to do so.

7. *You shall have no other god to set against me*: this fundamental commandment established the exclusive covenant relationship between Israel and her God. But there is here no thought of monotheism. The commandment does not seek to repudiate the *existence* of other gods, but to prevent Israel from having anything to do with them. Two important practical results follow from this prohibition. First, it ruled out any idea of Israel's God having a female consort. This was in stark contrast to Canaanite religion with its strong sexual element designed to ensure the fertility of crops and herds. And second, it effectively imposed on Israel a policy of political neutrality, for to enter into an alliance with one of the great empires meant acknowledging their gods. Israel was to rely on her God alone who had triumphed over Pharaoh and his men, and would triumph over all enemies provided she remained faithful to him. The Hebrew word for *god* can and probably should be translated here by the plural form 'gods' (cp. verse 9).

8. *You shall not make a carved image for yourself*: since relations with any other god had already been forbidden, the image would have been of Yahweh himself whom the Israelites always pictured as a human male figure. But one must not imagine that primitive peoples thought that their god could be confined to his image. They knew that a god could not be imprisoned in a piece of wood or stone carved by man, but they did think that the god concerned could be made to enter the image, and thereby become available for man to use to his own advantage. But it was a fundamental principle of Israel's religion that on no account was she to be allowed to exercise control over her God. He was to be

entirely free of man's manipulations, and could never be restricted to any place where it could be asserted that he *must* be present. So, uniquely among her neighbours, Israel was forbidden images of her God. That the Israelites took this commandment very seriously is confirmed by the fact that all her *official* shrines, including the temple at Jerusalem, remained imageless. Further, it can hardly be coincidence that in archaeological excavations to date no images of human male figures have been found at any Israelite shrine. *nor the likeness of anything in the heavens...on the earth...or in the waters*: this represents a later expansion of the original commandment, which also includes the following two verses. Images from nature are now also prohibited (cp. on 4: 15-24).

9. *You shall not bow down to them or worship them*: *them* does not refer to the singular *image* of verse 8, but to 'the gods' of the first commandment, and shows that whoever expanded the commandment took these two commandments together, thereby reinterpreting the prohibited images as those of heathen deities who might be worshipped, rather than of Israel's God. This new approach is probably best understood as part of the general reaction against animal images following the fall of the northern kingdom associated with the bull images of Jeroboam I (cp. on 9: 6ff.), and seen also in Hezekiah's destruction of the bronze serpent, Nehushtan (2 Kings 18: 4). *a jealous God*: cp. on 4: 24. *to the third and fourth generations*: that is all living members of each family, namely all Israel. The occurrence of a fifth generation is not envisaged as a physical possibility.

11. *You shall not make wrong use of the name of the LORD your God*: in order that the covenant relationship could be inaugurated, Yahweh had been forced to disclose his name to Israel. But the Israelites believed that to know the name of someone meant that one could exercise power over him: and this applied even to a god. So by disclosing his name, God had given Israel considerable power over him. Indeed, knowledge of his name was almost like having an image, so

concretely did the Israelites think of it. Its use therefore had to be protected. The particular abuse envisaged was not blasphemy, for the Israelites believed that if a man cursed God, then God would automatically strike him dead: it was the quickest way to commit suicide (Job 2: 9). Nor had the commandment anything to do with false oaths, for again the Israelites believed that God would take direct action against anyone who swore falsely. Rather it sought to prevent God's name being used for magical purposes. All magicians hope that by the use of special words or actions they can persuade supernatural powers to carry out their will. But the Israelites were never to be allowed to exercise power over their God. And since the first commandment prohibited recourse to any other god, the third commandment therefore effectively denied the Israelites the power to effect curses, spells, bewitchings and other magical practices. Consequently each individual Israelite was thereby guaranteed complete freedom from the world of magical influence, the importance of which can hardly be exaggerated.

12. *Keep the sabbath day holy*: a stronger version of the command in Exod. 20: 8 to 'Remember' the sabbath. The etymological explanation of *sabbath* is not absolutely certain, but it is probably best understood as 'the day which stops', that is, divides off one block of days from another. Although scholars have tried to find evidence for this stopping day elsewhere in the ancient Near East, they have found no exact equivalent. It therefore seems that the introduction of the seven-day week with a regular stopping day every seventh day must be traced back to the ancient Israelites who understood its observance as part of their special relationship with their God.

13f. *You have six days to labour and do all your work. But the seventh day is a sabbath*: it is probable that it is here, and not in the previous verse which presupposes the existence of the sabbath, that the original commandment is to be found (cp. Exod. 23: 12; 34: 21). It is of necessity formulated positively because the period for which work was to be forbidden had first to be defined. But the sabbath was not intended as a day of total inactivity (2 Kings 4: 22ff.) but rather as freeing men from the monotony of their daily routine labour.

15. *Remember that you were slaves in Egypt*: the fact that Israel had once been slaves not only justifies the demand that her own slaves should be released from routine work on the sabbath, but according to Deuteronomy explains why the sabbath was instituted in the first place. In contrast to Exod. 20: 11, which connects the sabbath with the Priestly account of creation (Gen. 1 – 2: 4), Deuteronomy enunciates what had always been understood, namely that the institution of the sabbath was directly related to Israel's slavery in Egypt where there would have been no regular break in daily routine work. Its creation in fact constituted an assertion of political independence. Israel no longer belonged to Pharaoh to do with as he liked, but to Yahweh upon whom she was totally dependent. But while the latter had every right to regulate Israel's working life, he did so in such a way that the sabbath became yet a further instance of his grace.

16. *Honour your father and your mother*: by *honour* is meant submission to another's authority (1 Sam. 15: 30; Ps. 86: 9). This explains why the commandment is framed positively, since it is seeking to create an unbreakable relationship. It is often argued that its purpose was to ensure that children (here understood as mature adults capable of breaking any of the Ten Commandments) would always look after their parents, even in old age, and bury them after death. But it is perhaps more probable that as with the other first four commandments, the fifth too had a religious explanation, namely that it prevented an Israelite ever rejecting his parents' faith. He was to have no freedom of religious choice. He had been born into Israel, and he was to remain within Israel for life. Thus parents were able to ensure the continuance of the ancestral religion from one generation to another. Later the emphasis of the commandment was extended to secure absolute obedience over the widest possible field from

assault (Exod. 21: 15) to simply being 'disobedient and out of control' (Deut. 21: 18–21).

17. *You shall not commit murder*: the word rendered *murder* specifically denotes a killing within the covenant community. The covenant had been made not simply with Israel, but with each individual Israelite who was therefore precious in God's sight, and entitled to protection. But there is no thought here of pacifism, the abolition of capital punishment or even vegetarianism. Israel was constantly at war, punished by execution and ate meat.

18. *You shall not commit adultery*: by *adultery* is meant sexual intercourse with a married or betrothed woman. It carried the death penalty which was inflicted by the state through the local community, and not by the husband. The probable original purpose for this prohibition was not simply to protect part of the husband's property, but to ensure that he might be certain that his wife's children were his own. This was of vital importance in a society which did not believe in life after death but rather that a man's personality went on in his children. The ancient rite in Num. 5: 11–31 may in fact be a method of assessing paternity.

19. *You shall not steal*: almost certainly refers to man-theft which was a crime carrying the death penalty (Exod. 21: 16; Deut. 24: 7), rather than theft of property which resulted in a civil action for damages (Exod. 22: 1–15). The commandment sought to prevent the sale of an Israelite outside the covenant community, which for all practical purposes was as effective as murder. As in the case of Joseph (Gen. 37), once a man had passed into the hands of foreigners, the chances of him ever being found again were very remote indeed. So it is no surprise that in Deut. 24: 7 the man-thief is described in the Hebrew as 'the stealer of life'. Naturally this commandment would have been of considerable importance to the Israelites in the desert constantly in touch with passing Bedouin caravans. But it also retained its importance long after the settlement in Canaan in preventing the Israelites

from selling off their fellow-countrymen as slaves to invading powers. Thus even a century after the return from exile, Nehemiah had to take action on this very issue (Neh. 5: 8).

20. *You shall not give false evidence*: as the translation makes plain, this commandment is not a warning against lying in general, but is solely concerned with the giving of false evidence in court. However, the situation envisaged does not involve any kind of legal action, but specifically the possible miscarriage of justice in a criminal case resulting in wrongful conviction and execution (cp. on 19: 16–21). The classic example of this crime is the case of Naboth (1 Kings 21). It should be noted that evidence in court was not given under oath, and that the accused was presumed guilty until he could prove his innocence.

21. *You shall not covet your neighbour's wife*: in Exod. 20: 17 it is the 'house' rather than the 'wife' which appears in the first clause. The change in order is due to the deuteronomic law, which apparently for the first time brought women within the scope of the covenant community (cp. 12: 12, 18; 16: 11, 14; 29: 11, 18), and so radically altered their status. They thereby became equally liable with men under the law (cp. 7: 3; 13: 6; 15: 12–17; 17: 2–5; 22: 22), and could therefore no longer be treated as simply another item of personal property. It can then be assumed that the original commandment merely concerned the house, the other forms of property being added later. As it stands, the tenth commandment does not involve any physical action, but merely refers to a mental attitude which could certainly not be enforced by the courts. This is in stark contrast to the other commandments for breach of any of which the offender would have been prosecuted. It therefore raises the possibility that the original commandment prevented actual seizure of the house (cp. Mic. 2: 2). But if this is so, then since the other commandments are nowhere interested in property, it would seem that the tenth commandment would not have been concerned with the house as such, but rather with the effect which dispossession

would have had on the owner. Now originally the administration of justice was in the hands of the elders, the heads of each household (cp. on 1: 9–18). Dispossession would therefore have involved loss of status as an elder, with the right to play one's part in the local community's affairs. This would explain the necessity for a commandment preventing the seizure of a house as opposed to other property, whether land or chattels, for it would guarantee the basic democratic nature of Israelite life. But once the elders were replaced by professional judges under Jehoshaphat's reform (2 Chron. 19: 5–11), the commandment would have lost its original purpose and so become redundant (cp. 1: 9–18). Hence in contrast to the other commandments, it could now become spiritualized, *covet* being substituted for an original word for seizing, and have added to it all other property which an Israelite might have obtained by agreement, purchase or gain. Naturally children form no part in such a list. *

THE APPOINTMENT OF MOSES AS
COVENANT MEDIATOR

These Commandments the LORD spoke in a great voice 22 to your whole assembly on the mountain out of the fire, the cloud, and the thick mist; then he said no more. He wrote them on two tablets of stone and gave them to me. When you heard the voice out of the darkness, 23 while the mountain was ablaze with fire, all the heads of your tribes and the elders came to me and said, 'The 24 LORD our God has shown us his glory and his greatness, and we have heard his voice out of the fire: today we have seen that God may speak with men and they may still live. Why should we now risk death? for this great 25 fire will devour us. If we hear the voice of the LORD our God again, we shall die. Is there any mortal man who 26

has heard the voice of the living God speaking out of the
27 fire, as we have, and has lived? You shall go near and
listen to all that the LORD our God says, and report to us
all that the LORD our God has said to you; we will listen
and obey.'

28 When the LORD heard these words which you spoke
to me, he said, 'I have heard what this people has said
29 to you; every word they have spoken is right. Would
that they always had such a heart to fear me and to
observe all my commandments, so that all might be well
30 with them and their children for ever! Go, and tell them
31 to return to their tents, but you yourself stand here
beside me, and I will set forth to you all the commandments, the statutes and laws which you shall teach them
to observe in the land which I am giving them to occupy.'

32 You shall be careful to do as the LORD your God has
commanded you; do not turn from it to right or to left.
33 You must conform to all the LORD your God commands
you, if you would live and prosper and remain long in
the land you are to occupy.

6 These are the commandments, statutes, and laws which
the LORD your God commanded me to teach you to
observe in the land into which you are passing to occupy
2 it, a land flowing with milk and honey,[a] so that you may
fear the LORD your God and keep all his statutes and
commandments which I am giving you, both you, your
sons, and your descendants all your lives, and so that you
3 may live long. If you listen, O Israel, and are careful to
observe them, you will prosper and increase greatly as
the LORD the God of your fathers promised you.

[a] a land...honey: *transposed from verse 3.*

✶ This passage again follows the JE narrative, being an expansion of Exod. 20: 18–21. After the giving of the Ten Commandments, the people refuse to draw near again to God to hear anything further which he might say. Instead they authorize Moses to act on their behalf, whose appointment God ratifies. Moses thus becomes the mediator of the covenant between God and the people. Exod. 20: 18–21 may have been created to explain the origin of this office of mediator exercised during the settlement period by the so-called minor judges (Judg. 10: 1–4; 12: 7–15) and understood by the deuteronomists to have been inherited by the prophets (cp. on 18: 15).

22. *two tablets of stone*: cp. on 4: 13.

32. *You shall be careful to do as the LORD your God has commanded you*: this refers not to the Ten Commandments but to the laws which had secondarily been revealed to Moses on Mount Horeb (verse 31), and which he had kept secret until he declared them in Moab on the eve of the conquest. ✶

THE FUNDAMENTAL COMMANDMENT

Hear, O Israel, the LORD[a] is our God, one LORD, and you must love the LORD your God with all your heart and soul and strength. These commandments which I give you this day are to be kept in your heart; you shall repeat them to your sons, and speak of them indoors and out of doors, when you lie down and when you rise. Bind them as a sign on the hand and wear them as a phylactery on the forehead; write them up on the doorposts of your houses and on your gates. 4, 5 6 7 8 9

The LORD your God will bring you into the land which he swore to your forefathers Abraham, Isaac and Jacob that he would give you, a land of great and fine cities 10

[a] *See note on Exod. 3: 15.*

11 which you did not build, houses full of good things which you did not provide, rock-hewn cisterns which you did not hew, and vineyards and olive-groves which

12 you did not plant. When you eat your fill there, be careful not to forget the LORD who brought you out

13 of Egypt, out of the land of slavery. You shall fear the LORD your God, serve him alone and take your oaths in

14 his name. You must not follow other gods, gods of the

15 nations that are around you; if you do, the LORD your God who is in your midst will be angry with you, and he will sweep you away off the face of the earth, for the LORD your God is a jealous god.

16 You must not challenge the LORD your God as you

17 challenged him at Massah.[a] You must diligently keep the commandments of the LORD your God as well as

18 the precepts and statutes which he gave you. You must do what is right and good in the LORD's eyes so that all may go well with you, and you may enter and occupy the rich land which the LORD promised by oath to your

19 forefathers; then you shall drive out all your enemies before you, as the LORD promised.

20 When your son asks you in time to come, 'What is the meaning of the precepts, statutes, and laws which the

21 LORD our God gave you?', you shall say to him, 'We were Pharaoh's slaves in Egypt, and the LORD brought

22 us out of Egypt with his strong hand, sending great disasters, signs, and portents against the Egyptians and against Pharaoh and all his family, as we saw for ourselves.

23 But he led us out from there to bring us into the land and give it to us as he had promised to our forefathers.

[a] *That is* Challenge.

The LORD commanded us to observe all these statutes and 24
to fear the LORD our God; it will be for our own good at all
times, and he will continue to preserve our lives. It will 25
be counted to our credit if we keep all these commandments in the sight of the LORD our God, as he has bidden us.'

✳ For the deuteronomists, Israel's covenant law could almost
be reduced to the first commandment, so fundamental was its
observance for her future existence. Hence the Israelites were
encouraged to use every opportunity to remind themselves of
it, lest the affluence of the rich land of Canaan might lead them
to forget their ultimate dependence on their God. Similarly
children were to be taught Israel's salvation history on which
her covenant relationship was founded.

4. *Hear, O Israel*: probably a traditional summons to
worship (cp. 5: 1; 9: 1; 20: 3; 27: 9). *the LORD is our God,
one LORD*: the Hebrew here is ambiguous. It either stresses
the uniqueness of Israel's God, or his oneness, that is that in
contrast to the multitude of Baals, it is the same Yahweh who
is worshipped at Jerusalem and Hebron (cp. 2 Sam. 15: 8).
But whichever interpretation is correct, Israel's God is to be
the exclusive object of her worship as laid down in the first
commandment.

5. *and you must love the LORD your God*: for the Israelite
the only appropriate attitude to his God is that of love.
While this does not rule out either awe or reverence, it does
indicate the true nature of the God–man relationship as one
of mutual love. God had already shown his for Israel in her
election and salvation history (7: 8).

6. *These commandments which I give you this day*: this refers
to the new deuteronomic law which will make it easier to
fulfil the fundamental law of the first commandment restated
in verses 4f.

8f. *Bind them as a sign on the hand*: originally this order was
understood metaphorically, but later it was interpreted

literally and led to the wearing of phylacteries (Exod. 13: 9, 16), and the placing of the *mezuzah* over the doorpost. Both these objects were cases for small scrolls of parchment on which the scripture passages Deut. 6: 4-9; 11: 13-21 and Exod. 13: 1-16 were inscribed.

10. *your forefathers Abraham, Isaac and Jacob*: cp. on 1: 8.

13. *You shall fear the LORD your God*: this does not indicate dread but rather reverence, and so is not incompatible with the command to love (cp. Lev. 19: 3). 'Fear of the Lord' is almost the Hebrew equivalent for religion. *and take your oaths in his name*: swearing was a part of routine worship, the oath being in effect a confession of faith (Isa. 48: 1). So to swear by another deity amounted to a direct act of apostasy and breach of the first commandment (Amos 8: 14).

15. *for the LORD your God is a jealous God*: cp. on 4: 24.

16. *as you challenged him at Massah*: the Israelites were encamped at a place where there was no water and, exhausted with thirst, accused Moses of bringing them out of Egypt to let them die in the desert (Exod. 17: 1-7). They thus questioned whether God was still active on Israel's behalf, or whether he had utterly abandoned her. This was also the basic doubt of the deuteronomic generation, and led many to commit apostasy.

20. *When your son asks you in time to come*: the deuteronomist is thinking of his own generation. Cp. on 4: 9.

21. *We were Pharaoh's slaves in Egypt*: Israel, once Pharaoh's vassal, is now the vassal of her God who delivered her from slavery in Egypt. Her salvation history and her law are thus intimately connected. The latter is the response to the former, for its observance ensures that God's grace shown in the deliverance from Egypt will continue to be exercised in Israel's favour. The absence of any mention of the revelation of the law at Sinai both in this passage and 26: 5-9 has led some scholars to argue that originally the exodus–conquest traditions were separate from those connected with Sinai, being experienced by different clans, and were only later

combined after the settlement in Canaan. But this thoroughly deuteronomic passage is not to be understood as a formal creed, but rather as a simple explanation as to how Israel acquired possession of the land of Canaan, the continuance of which depended on her obedience to the covenant law. ✶

ISRAEL'S NECESSARY EXCLUSIVISM

When the LORD your God brings you into the land 7 which you are entering to occupy and drives out many nations before you – Hittites, Girgashites, Amorites, Canaanites, Perizzites, Hivites, and Jebusites, seven nations more numerous and powerful than you – when 2 the LORD your God delivers them into your power and you defeat them, you must put them to death. You must not make a treaty with them or spare them. You must 3 not intermarry with them, neither giving your daughters to their sons nor taking their daughters for your sons; if you do, they will draw your sons away from the LORD[a] 4 and make them worship other gods. Then the LORD will be angry with you and will quickly destroy you. But this is what you must do to them: pull down their 5 altars, break their sacred pillars, hack down their sacred poles[b] and destroy their idols by fire, for you are a people 6 holy to the LORD your God; the LORD your God chose you out of all nations on earth to be his special possession.

It was not because you were more numerous than 7 any other nation that the LORD cared for you and chose you, for you were the smallest of all nations; it was 8 because the LORD loved you and stood by his oath to your forefathers, that he brought you out with his strong

[a] *Prob. rdg.; Heb.* me.   [b] sacred poles: *Heb.* asherim.

hand and redeemed you from the land of slavery, from
9 the power of Pharaoh king of Egypt. Know then that
the LORD your God is God, the faithful God; with those
who love him and keep his commandments he keeps
10 covenant and faith for a thousand generations, but those
who defy him and show their hatred for him he repays
with destruction: he will not be slow to requite any who
so hate him.

11 You are to observe these commandments, statutes, and
laws which I give you this day, and keep them.

12 If you listen to these laws and are careful to observe
them, then the LORD your God will observe the sworn
covenant he made with your forefathers and will keep
13 faith with you. He will love you, bless you and cause
you to increase. He will bless the fruit of your body and
the fruit of your land, your corn and new wine and oil,
the offspring of your herds, and of your lambing flocks,
in the land which he swore to your forefathers to give
14 you. You shall be blessed above every other nation;
neither among your people nor among your cattle shall
15 there be impotent male or barren female. The LORD
will take away all sickness from you; he will not bring
upon you any of the foul diseases of Egypt which you
know so well, but will bring them upon all your enemies.
16 You shall devour all the nations which the LORD your
God is giving over to you. Spare none of them, and do
not worship their gods; that is the snare which awaits
you.

17 You may say to yourselves, 'These nations outnumber
18 us, how can we drive them out?' But you need have no
fear of them; only remember what the LORD your

God did to Pharaoh and to the whole of Egypt, the great 19
challenge which you yourselves witnessed, the signs and
portents, the strong hand and the outstretched arm by
which the LORD your God brought you out. He will
deal thus with all the nations of whom you are afraid.
He will also spread panic among them until all who are 20
left or have gone into hiding perish before you. Be in no 21
dread of them, for the LORD your God is in your midst,
a great and terrible god. He will drive out these nations 22
before you little by little. You will not be able to exterminate them quickly, for fear the wild beasts become too
numerous for you. The LORD your God will deliver 23
these nations over to you and will throw them into great
panic in the hour of their destruction. He will put their 24
kings into your hands, and you shall wipe out their name
from under heaven. When you destroy them, no man
will be able to withstand you. Their idols you shall destroy 25
by fire; you must not covet the silver and gold on them
and take it for yourselves, or you will be ensnared by it;
for these things are abominable to the LORD your God.
You must not introduce any abominable idol into your 26
houses and thus bring yourselves under solemn ban
along with it. You shall hold it loathsome and abominable,
for it is forbidden under the ban.

* When Israel enters Canaan she must put to death its
inhabitants, and so prevent all possibility of her corruption
through their religious practices. In the opening passage
(verses 1–6), which is clearly dependent on the JE narrative
in Exod. 23: 20–33; 34: 11–16, the making of treaties, intermarriage, and the use of Canaanite shrines and their apparatus
are all specifically prohibited, though in fact historically all

had occurred. The deuteronomist sees Israel's present misfortune as the direct consequence of her failure to avoid everything Canaanite. Israel is not to make the same mistake again but to rely solely on her God who had already demonstrated his power over other nations, and, it is implied, could do so again. It was through such exclusivism, rigidly enforced by the law, that post-exilic Israel managed to survive as a definite entity, though it should be noted that anyone could have become an Israelite irrespective of earlier race or creed simply by undertaking to obey that law.

1. *drives out many nations before you*: the traditional list of peoples making up the population of Canaan appears frequently in the Old Testament with as few as three and as many as ten separate names. The exact identification of these groups remains uncertain. The *Hittites* were an offshoot of that great kingdom which flourished in Asia Minor and northern Syria in the latter half of the second millennium B.C. The *Girgashites* are rarely mentioned and nothing is known of them. The *Amorites*, originally from Mesopotamia, represent the population of the hill country, while the *Canaanites* indicate those settled along the coastal plain who had resisted earlier invasions. *Perizzites* describes those living in the open country as opposed to the towns. The *Hivites* are associated with Gibeon (Josh. 9: 7), and the *Jebusites* were the pre-Israelite occupants of Jerusalem (2 Sam. 5: 6–8).

2. *you must put them to death*: the Canaanites are to be put to the ban, that is annihilated (cp. on 2: 34). *You must not make a treaty with them*: cp. Exod. 23: 32; 34: 12, 15. Undoubtedly, as with the Gibeonites (Josh. 9; 2 Sam. 21: 1-9), treaties were made with the inhabitants of the land who were thereby brought within the covenant community.

3. *You must not intermarry with them*: in contrast to Exod. 34: 16, the prohibition of intermarriage with the indigenous Canaanites is extended from men to include women also. This reflects the deuteronomic reassessment of women,

whereby they were treated as equal partners with men within the covenant community (cp. on 5: 21).

5. *break their sacred pillars*: the sacred pillar (*massebah*) originally represented a male deity, but was reinterpreted by Israel as indicating the place where a theophany of Yahweh had occurred. It was thus considered an entirely legitimate part of cult apparatus (Hos. 3: 4). It was not until Hezekiah's reform that such apparatus was condemned (2 Kings 18: 4). Cp. Exod. 23: 24; 34: 13 which reflects this reform. *hack down their sacred poles*: in contrast the sacred pole (*asherah*) represented a female deity and was probably from the first treated as an improper cult object (cp. Exod. 34: 13; 2 Kings 18: 4), for the presence of such a symbol introduced the possibility of bisexuality into the concept of God. Cp. on 5: 7.

6. *for you are a people holy to the LORD your God*: anything *holy* is that which has been separated off for God's exclusive use. Such was Israel, for it was through her that God had chosen to manifest himself to the world (cp. Exod. 19: 5f.).

8. *and stood by his oath to your forefathers*: cp. 1: 8.

12. *If you listen to these laws*: cp. the list of blessings in Deut. 28.

15. *the foul diseases of Egypt*: cp. Exod. 15: 26; 23: 25. While God would not allow his people to contract the vile diseases of Egypt, their immunity remained conditional on their giving him their life allegiance.

20. *He will also spread panic among them*: the *panic*, translated 'hornet(s)' in earlier English versions, is to be understood as a mysterious divine force. Cp. Exod. 23: 28. It is thus being stated that it is really God who defeats his enemies.

22. *He will drive out these nations before you little by little*: a concession to the historical facts that the Canaanites were neither exterminated nor expelled.

25. *you must not covet the silver and gold on them and take it for yourselves*: cp. the case of Achan (Josh. 7), and comment on 2: 34. *

DISCIPLINE BEFORE AFFLUENCE

8 You must carefully observe everything that I command you this day so that you may live and increase and may enter and occupy the land which the LORD promised to
2 your forefathers upon oath. You must remember all that road by which the LORD your God has led you these forty years in the wilderness to humble you, to test you and to discover whether or no it was in your heart to
3 keep his commandments. He humbled you and made you hungry; then he fed you on manna which neither you nor your fathers had known before, to teach you that man cannot live on bread alone but lives by every word
4 that comes from the mouth of the LORD. The clothes on your backs did not wear out nor did your feet swell
5 all these forty years. Take this lesson to heart: that the LORD your God was disciplining you as a father disci-
6 plines his son; and keep the commandments of the LORD
7 your God, conforming to his ways and fearing him. For the LORD your God is bringing you to a rich land, a land of streams, of springs and underground waters
8 gushing out in hill and valley, a land of wheat and barley, of vines, fig-trees, and pomegranates, a land of olives,
9 oil, and honey. It is a land where you will never live in poverty nor want for anything, a land whose stones are
10 iron-ore and from whose hills you will dig copper. You will have plenty to eat and will bless the LORD your God for the rich land that he has given you.

11   Take care not to forget the LORD your God and do not fail to keep his commandments, laws, and statutes which
12 I give you this day. When you have plenty to eat and live

in fine houses of your own building, when your herds 13
and flocks increase, and your silver and gold and all
your possessions increase too, do not become proud 14
and forget the LORD your God who brought you out
of Egypt, out of the land of slavery; he led you through 15
the vast and terrible wilderness infested with poisonous
snakes and scorpions, a thirsty, waterless land, where
he caused water to flow from the hard rock; he fed you 16
in the wilderness on manna which your fathers did not
know, to humble you and test you, and in the end to
make you prosper. Nor must you say to yourselves, 17
'My own strength and energy have gained me this
wealth', but remember the LORD your God; it is he that 18
gives you strength to become prosperous, so fulfilling the
covenant guaranteed by oath with your forefathers, as
he is doing now.

If you forget the LORD your God and adhere to other 19
gods, worshipping them and bowing down to them,
I give you a solemn warning this day that you will
certainly be destroyed. You will be destroyed because 20
of your disobedience to the LORD your God, as surely
as were the nations whom the LORD destroyed at your
coming.

Listen, O Israel; this day you will cross the Jordan to **9**
occupy the territory of nations greater and more powerful than you, and great cities with walls towering to the
sky. They are great and tall people, the descendants of the 2
Anakim, of whom you know, for you have heard it
said, 'Who can withstand the sons of Anak?' Know then 3
this day that it is the LORD your God himself who goes
at your head as a devouring fire; he will subdue them and

destroy them at your approach; you shall drive them out and overwhelm them, as he promised you.

4   When the LORD your God drives them out before you, do not say to yourselves, 'It is because of my own merit that the LORD has brought me in to occupy this land.'[a]

5   It is not because of your merit or your integrity that you are entering their land to occupy it; it is because of the wickedness of these nations that the LORD your God is driving them out before you, and to fulfil the promise which the LORD made to your forefathers, Abraham, Isaac and Jacob.

* Through the forty-year journey in the wilderness, God deliberately tested Israel's loyalty, and showed her the full extent of her physical dependence on him. This experience was a necessary discipline before entry into the affluent land of Canaan where Israel might be tempted to forsake her God as no longer necessary to her, and rely solely on her new-found wealth for protection. To do so would be an act of sheer suicide. Further, possession of the land was not due to any special moral righteousness on Israel's part, but to God's grace alone. It was only through the continued exercise of that grace that the deuteronomic generation could have any hope that they would escape the fate of the previous inhabitants of the land whom God had expelled for their unrighteousness.

1. *which the LORD promised to your forefathers upon oath*: cp. on 1: 8.

3. *then he fed you on manna*: cp. Exod. 16. Manna can still be found in the Sinai area. It is formed by insects which suck the sap of certain trees and then excrete what is superfluous to their needs. This substance falls to the ground, where

[a] *So Sept.; Heb. adds* and because of the wickedness of these nations the LORD is driving them out before you.

it hardens over night. *man cannot live on bread alone*: the gift of manna is here given a new interpretation. It is the covenant relationship with God which sustains Israel and gives her life, and not the material wealth of Canaan.

4. *The clothes on your backs did not wear out nor did your feet swell*: this particular tradition of divine care does not appear in any of the stories told about the wilderness period, but it is used again in Neh. 9 in the prayer which reviews Israel's history (verse 21).

9. *a land whose stones are iron-ore*: Canaan is pictured as not only agriculturally rich but also abundant in mineral wealth. Yet in Palestine neither iron nor copper is found west of the Jordan. This indicates the idyllic nature of the description. Yahweh's gift of the land to Israel is considered such a rich blessing that in consequence the land is described in paradisial terms.

15. *with poisonous snakes and scorpions*: cp. Num. 21: 6.

17. '*My own strength and energy have gained me this wealth*': possession of Canaan is not to lead Israel to proclaim her independence of God. It was he who had won her battles, and had secured the land for her.

9: 2. *the descendants of the Anakim*: cp. 1: 28.

5. *it is because of the wickedness of these nations*: Canaanite depravity (cp. Gen. 15: 16), and the promise to the patriarchs, caused God to give the land to Israel, and not any special merit on her part. Israel's conquest of the land is therefore interpreted both as divine judgement on the previous inhabitants, and an act of grace towards Israel. ✳

THE INCIDENT OF THE GOLDEN CALF

Know then that it is not because of any merit of yours 6 that the LORD your God is giving you this rich land to occupy; indeed, you are a stubborn people. Remember 7 and never forget, how you angered the LORD your God in the wilderness: from the day when you left Egypt until you came to this place you have defied the LORD.

8 In Horeb you roused the LORD's anger, and the LORD in 9 his wrath was on the point of destroying you. When I went up the mountain to receive the tablets of stone, the tablets of the covenant which the LORD made with you, I remained on the mountain forty days and forty nights 10 without food or drink. Then the LORD gave me the two tablets of stone written with the finger of God, and upon them were all the words the LORD spoke to you out of the fire, upon the mountain on the day of the 11 assembly. At the end of forty days and forty nights the LORD gave me the two tablets of stone, the tablets of the 12 covenant, and said to me, 'Make haste down from the mountain because your people whom you brought out of Egypt have done a disgraceful thing. They have already turned aside from the way which I told them to follow and have cast for themselves an image of metal.'

13 Then the LORD said to me, 'I have considered this 14 people and I find them a stubborn people. Let me be, and I will destroy them and blot out their name from under heaven; and of you alone I will make a nation more 15 powerful and numerous than they.' So I turned and went down the mountain, and it was ablaze; and I had the 16 two tablets of the covenant in my hands. When I saw that you had sinned against the LORD your God and had cast for yourselves an image of a bull-calf, and had already turned aside from the way the LORD had told 17 you to follow, I took the two tablets and flung them down 18 and shattered them in the sight of you all. Then once again I lay prostrate before the LORD, forty days and

forty nights without food or drink, on account of all the
sins that you had committed, and because you had done
what was wrong in the eyes of the LORD and provoked
him to anger. I dreaded the LORD's anger and his wrath 19
which threatened to destroy you; and once again the
LORD listened to me. The LORD was greatly incensed 20
with Aaron also and would have killed him; so I prayed
for him as well at that same time. I took the calf, that 21
sinful thing that you had made, and burnt it and pounded
it, grinding it until it was as fine as dust; then I flung its
dust into the torrent that flowed down the mountain.
You also roused the LORD's anger at Taberah, and at 22
Massah, and at Kibroth-hattaavah. Again, when the 23
LORD sent you from Kadesh-barnea with orders to
advance and occupy the land which he was giving you,
you defied the LORD your God and did not trust him or
obey him. You were defiant from the day that the LORD[a] 24
first knew you. Forty days and forty nights I lay prostrate 25
before the LORD because he had threatened to destroy
you, and I prayed to the LORD and said, 'O Lord GOD, 26
do not destroy thy people, thy own possession, whom
thou didst redeem by thy great power and bring out of
Egypt by thy strong hand. Remember thy servants, 27
Abraham, Isaac and Jacob, and overlook the stubborn-
ness of this people, their wickedness and their sin;
otherwise the people in[b] the land out of which thou 28
didst lead us will say, "It is because the LORD was not
able to bring them into the land which he promised them
and because he hated them, that he has led them out to
kill them in the wilderness." But they are thy people, 29

[a] *So Sam.; Heb.* I.   [b] the people in: *so Sam.; Heb. om.*

thy own possession, whom thou didst bring out by thy great strength and by thy outstretched arm.'

10 At that time the LORD said to me, 'Cut two tablets of stone like the first, and make also a wooden chest, an Ark.
2 Come to me on the mountain, and I will write on the tablets the words that were on the first tablets which you broke in pieces, and you shall put them into the Ark.'
3 So I made the Ark of acacia-wood and cut two tablets of stone like the first, and went up the mountain taking the
4 tablets with me. Then in the same writing as before, the LORD wrote down the Ten Words*a* which he had spoken to you out of the fire, upon the mountain on the day of
5 the assembly, and the LORD gave them to me. I turned and came down the mountain, and I put the tablets in the Ark that I had made, as the LORD had commanded me, and there they have remained ever since.

6*b* (The Israelites journeyed by stages from Beeroth-bene-jaakan to Moserah. There Aaron died and was buried; and his son Eleazar succeeded him in the priesthood.
7 From there they came to Gudgodah and from Gudgodah
8 to Jotbathah, a land of many ravines. At that time the LORD set apart the tribe of Levi to carry the Ark of the Covenant of the LORD, to attend on the LORD and minister to him, and to give the blessing in his name, as
9 they have done to this day. That is why the Levites have no holding or patrimony with their kinsmen; the LORD is their patrimony, as he promised them.)

10 I stayed on the mountain forty days and forty nights, as I did before, and once again the LORD listened to me;

[a] Or Ten Commandments.
[b] *Verses 6, 7: cp. Num. 33: 31, 32.*

he consented not to destroy you. The LORD said to me, 11
'Set out now at the head of the people so that they may
enter and occupy the land which I swore to give to their
forefathers.'

☆ As the use of the plural form of address indicates, 9: 7 b –
10: 11 contains the second large insertion of the deuteronomic
historian into the original introduction to Deuteronomy
(4: 44 – 11: 32). This in effect amounts to a rewriting of the
main incidents in the JE narrative of Exod. 32–4, which
describes the worship of the golden calf, followed by the
breaking of the tablets of the law and their replacement.
There are, however, some significant differences in the
deuteronomic historian's version, the chief of which is that
it is expressly stated that the second set of tablets were inscribed
not with the regulations of Exod. 34: 12–26, but with a
rewriting of the Ten Commandments themselves (Deut.
10: 2–5). By this alteration the deuteronomic historian deliberately set out to indicate that Hezekiah's reform reflected
in Exod. 34: 12–26 was insufficient (cp. pp. 5f.). For while
Hezekiah did destroy the 'hill-shrines' (2 Kings 18: 4), and
laid down that the three main festivals had to be celebrated
centrally at Jerusalem (Exod. 34: 22–4), he did not bring
about a complete centralization of worship by destroying all
the ancient sanctuaries. But even these were anathema to the
deuteronomic historian writing after Josiah's reform whereby
the cult was entirely centralized at Jerusalem. Consequently
it was better that no allusion should be made to Hezekiah's
reform in his revised introduction to the deuteronomic law.

The deuteronomic historian's purpose in introducing
the narrative of the golden calf at this point was to show that
from the very first moment of the covenant relationship
Israel had rebelled against her God, who had yet been merciful
to her. The exilic generation were in effect in the same position as those who had worshipped the golden calf at Horeb,

and seen the covenant bond literally smashed before their eyes. But God of his grace had reconstituted that relationship by immediately rewriting the Ten Commandments on the new tablets of the law. He could do the same for defeated and exiled Israel.

12. *and have cast for themselves an image of metal*: while Moses is in the very act of receiving the deeds of the covenant, God warns him that the Israelites were already breaking the covenant law.

14. *Let me be, and I will destroy them*: unlike Exod. 32: 10, here God anticipates that Moses will intercede on Israel's behalf rather than accept his judgement to destroy unfaithful Israel and make a new nation from Moses himself.

16. *and had cast for yourselves an image of a bull-calf*: knowledge of Exod. 32 is presupposed. There, as the plural reference to a single object makes plain (verse 4), a later writer had deliberately associated the single Sinai bull-calf with the calves which Jeroboam I placed in the sanctuaries at Bethel and Dan following the break-up of the united monarchy (1 Kings 12: 28f.). The bull was a popular symbol in Canaanite religion indicating strength and fertility. But whereas in Canaan the image of the god was placed upon the bull, Jeroboam I left his bulls riderless. They were to act as pedestals for Israel's invisible God who under covenant law could not be physically represented. This explains why Elijah had no need to condemn the bulls, nor Jehu to destroy them (2 Kings 10: 29). Jeroboam's purpose was to provide for his new nation a suitable cult object to rival the Ark, itself the throne of the imageless Yahweh (cp. on 10: 1), which remained in the temple at Jerusalem. In doing so he daringly demythologized the chief Canaanite religious symbol. But later generations mistook Jeroboam's action and the bull images themselves came to be improperly venerated with the result that the worship of Israel's God was confused with that of Baal (Hos. 8: 5f.; 10: 5; 13: 2). To Judah such cult images were regarded as the prime cause of God's judgement on the

northern kingdom seen in the conquest by Assyria in 721 B.C.
(2 Kings 17), and therefore were rigorously rooted out in
Hezekiah's reform (2 Kings 18: 4). It is in the light of this
reform that Exod. 32 was taken over and in the JE narrative
adapted as a direct condemnation of Jeroboam I, and it was
this judgement which the deuteronomic historian inherited.
This explains his constant reference to the sin of Jeroboam.
For the deuteronomic historian, the northern kingdom was
from the first apostate because of the golden calves.

17. *I took the two tablets and flung them down*: because of
Israel's blatant breach of the covenant law, Moses recognizes
that the covenant relationship is meaningless. He therefore
breaks the two tablets and thereby brings the covenant to an
end, for, following the practice of the ancient suzerainty
treaties, the covenant only remained in force while the document recording it was in existence. Once this was destroyed,
it had to be replaced if the treaty was to continue. This is
now the issue which faces Moses on Horeb and for which he
must intercede. It was also the issue which faced the exilic
generation for whom the deuteronomic historian inserted this
passage.

18. *Then once again I lay prostrate before the LORD*: as
covenant mediator, Moses intercedes for Israel. In Exod.
32: 32 Moses offers his own life as atonement for Israel's
apostasy. While this idea is not repeated here, it is taken over
by the deuteronomic historian in his introduction to Deuteronomy where Moses is forbidden entry into the promised
land (cp. on 1: 37).

20. *The LORD was greatly incensed with Aaron*: in Exod. 32
Aaron initiates the making of the golden calf. But it is
noticeable that in contrast to this passage, there he is not
explicitly condemned. This is probably due to the fact that
the original story behind Exod. 32 was intended to justify
Jeroboam's action in making the calves by connecting them
with Aaron. Just as the serpent, Nehushtan, destroyed by
Hezekiah (2 Kings 18: 4), had been given a proper pedigree

by being directly associated with Moses (Num. 21: 8f.), though in fact it was taken over as part of the Canaanite cult apparatus at Jerusalem, so the calves were legitimized by being traced back to Aaron.

21. *and burnt it and pounded it*: in Exod. 32: 20 the people are subjected to an ordeal procedure to establish who is guilty of apostasy. They are forced to drink water into which the ground dust of the image has been mixed and which carries a curse for the guilty (cp. Num. 5: 16–28). This results in the outbreak of illness among the people (Exod. 32: 35). In contrast, here the remains of the calf are thrown into the torrent which flows down the mountain side, thereby ensuring that this abominable object should be carried away from the holy mountain, and disappear without trace (cp. on 21: 3ff.).

22f. *Taberah* (cp. Num. 11: 1–3), *Massah* (cp. on 6: 16), *Kibroth-hattaavah* (cp. Num. 11: 4–34), and *Kadesh-barnea* (cp. on 1: 19–46): all places associated with Israel's disobedience in the wilderness period.

27. *Remember thy servants, Abraham, Isaac and Jacob*: cp. on 1: 8.

28. *It is because the LORD was not able to bring them into the land*: cp. Exod. 32: 12. Israel's salvation history was meant to be interpreted by the foreign nations as evidence of the power of her God. The Babylonian conquest had now thrown all this in question, and many understood Israel's defeat as a victory for the mightier Babylonian gods. God's judgement on Israel, unless seen as punishment for her apostasy, could be entirely misinterpreted not only by other nations, but also by Israel herself. The problem of reconciling this judgement with the fact that Israel's God was still active and powerful is central to the exilic literature (cp. Deut. 32: 37; Isa. 48: 9ff.; Ezek. 20: 8ff.; 36: 22ff.).

10: 1. *and make also a wooden chest, an Ark*: the account of the making of the Ark is missing from the JE narrative in Exod. 32–4, though it must once have appeared there. While the earlier material understands the Ark as the throne of Israel's invisible God on which he manifested himself (Num. 10: 35f.), and on which he went into battle at the head of his troops (cp. 1 Sam. 4), the deuteronomic and Priestly writers interpret it as a simple container for the tablets of the law. This avoidance of any reference to the Ark as Yahweh's throne reflects the deuteronomic emphasis on the transcendence of God. Israel was to have no material means through which it might be assumed that his presence was assured. In the same way the temple became the dwelling-place not for Yahweh, but for his Name (cp. 12: 5). But since the Hebrew word translated *Ark* means 'box', it must from the first have acted as a container. Further, the practice of placing legal documents at the feet of a deity is known elsewhere in the ancient Near East. The Ark then acted as a pedestal for Israel's God who guarded the covenant law resting at his feet.

2. *I will write on the tablets the words that were on the first tablets*: God promises to restore the covenant relationship on exactly the same terms as before. See further, p. 69 and cp. Exod. 34: 12–26.

4. *the LORD wrote down the Ten Words*: in contrast to Exod. 34: 28 God, not Moses, writes down the contents of the new tablets. This alteration, like his insistence that the second set of tablets is an exact replica of the first, is due to the deuteronomic historian's desire to eradicate all reference to Hezekiah's reform. For clearly in the figure of Moses in Exod. 34: 28 the reader is expected to identify Hezekiah whose reform is reflected in the contents of the second tablets (Exod. 34: 12–26). But since for the deuteronomic historian the second tablets again contain the Ten Commandments, there as elsewhere in the Old Testament (cp. Exod. 31: 18; Deut. 10: 4) they are written by God himself.

5. *and I put the tablets in the Ark that I had made*: cp. on 4: 13.

6. *The Israelites journeyed by stages*: verses 6–9 seem to be a

later interpolation which has some connection with the journey recorded in Num. 33, though there are marked differences both in the spelling of place names and their order. Further, in Num. 20: 22ff., part of the Priestly account, Aaron is reported to have died at Mount Hor rather than *Moserah* (cp. 32: 50). *and his son Eleazar succeeded him in the priesthood*: in spite of his role in the incident of the golden calf, Aaron's son follows him in the priesthood. As elsewhere in the ancient Near East, the priesthood in Israel was hereditary, and all priests traced their ancestry back to Aaron.

8. *At that time the LORD set apart the tribe of Levi*: the Levites were originally a secular tribe (Gen. 34), who later obtained the exclusive right to act as Israel's priests. They were also responsible for teaching the law, which is why some scholars have accredited them with the authorship of the deuteronomic literature (cp. p. 7). The Levites owned no land and were dependent on a share of the sacrifices offered at the shrine for their maintenance (18: 1–5). With the centralization of worship at Jerusalem, the country Levites, dispossessed of their means of support, became objects of charity (cp. 12: 12; 18: 1–8; 26: 12f.). Later still the Levites acted as an inferior order of priests, being denied access to the altar (Ezek. 44: 10–14), though subsequently in the period after the exile they acquired considerable importance as administrators of the temple and singers of its liturgy, and also as teachers. The mention of the Levites here is due to the incident in Exod. 32: 25–9 when, after the worship of the golden calf, they alone remained loyal to God. This is probably further polemical material directed at Jeroboam I reflecting the contention that he appointed non-levitical priests (1 Kings 12: 31; 13: 33), though in fact at that time the priesthood was not yet restricted to Levites. ✱

THE NATURE OF ISRAEL'S GOD

What then, O Israel, does the LORD your God ask of 12
you? Only to fear the LORD your God, to conform to all
his ways, to love him and to serve him with all your
heart and soul. This you will do by keeping the com- 13
mandments of the LORD and his statutes which I give you
this day for your good. To the LORD your God belong 14
heaven itself, the highest heaven, the earth and everything
in it; yet the LORD cared for your forefathers in his love 15
for them and chose their descendants after them. Out
of all nations you were his chosen people as you are this
day. So now you must circumcise the foreskin of your 16
hearts and not be stubborn any more, for the LORD 17
your God is God of gods and Lord of lords, the great,
mighty, and terrible God. He is no respecter of persons
and is not to be bribed; he secures justice for widows and 18
orphans, and loves the alien who lives among you,
giving him food and clothing. You too must love the 19
alien, for you once lived as aliens in Egypt. You must 20
fear the LORD your God, serve him, hold fast to him
and take your oaths in his name. He is your praise, your 21
God who has done for you these great and terrible
things which you have seen with your own eyes. When 22
your forefathers went down into Egypt they were only
seventy strong, but now the LORD your God has made
you countless as the stars in the sky.

* In this somewhat confused passage, part of which may be a
later interpolation of the deuteronomic historian, God is
described as the owner of the whole universe. The breadth

of his sovereign rule is then immediately contrasted with his election of insignificant Israel. Further, because he owns the universe, the welfare of individuals within that universe becomes a matter of special concern to him, especially in the case of those who had no means of protecting themselves.

12. *Only to fear the LORD your God*: cp. on 6: 13.

16. *So now you must circumcise the foreskin of your hearts*: cp. Jer. 4: 4. Originally circumcision appears to have been connected with initiation into marriage (cp. Gen. 34: 14–18; Exod. 4: 25), being performed at puberty. Since this also coincided with entry into full membership of the covenant community with the responsibilities imposed by religion, law and warfare, circumcision quickly became a sign of such membership. But because all the other peoples whom early Israel encountered practised circumcision, except the Philistines (called in the Old Testament 'the uncircumcised'), circumcision itself could not be used to distinguish the Israelites from foreign nations. This explains why no reference is made to it in the Ten Commandments. It was only in the exile among the uncircumcised Babylonians that circumcision became a distinguishing mark, and it was as a result of this that the rite was transferred by the Priestly legislators to the eighth day after birth, the story of the covenant with Abraham being adapted for this purpose (Gen. 17: 9–14). Failure to circumcise then resulted in excommunication from the elect community. Thus while in Israel after the exile circumcision acquired a new importance, it did from very early times constitute an act of purification and dedication by the young man passing into adulthood. It is this idea that is here spiritualized. Israel is not merely to purify and dedicate herself outwardly by the physical rite of circumcision: she is to do so inwardly by such a radical change of heart that it could only be described by comparison with circumcision.

17. *He is no respecter of persons and is not to be bribed*: no one was outside the scope of God's laws, not even the king, as

the incident of David and Uriah confirms (2 Sam. 12); nor could anyone avoid his responsibility should he break them.

18. *he secures justice for widows and orphans, and loves the alien*: all three classes could readily be exploited, and would have had the greatest difficulty in getting legal satisfaction through the courts. They thus had to rely on charity for their protection. On the resident alien, cp. 1: 16.

19. *for you once lived as aliens in Egypt*: as in 5: 15, the sufferings of Israel in Egypt are cited as a reason why she in her turn should exercise charity towards those who might be expected to suffer in her own society.

20. *take your oaths in his name*: cp. on 6: 13.

21. *He is your praise*: God is to be the sole object of Israel's praise.

22. *they were only seventy strong*: the full list of immigrants is given in Gen. 46: 8–27. ✻

CURSE OR BLESSING?

You shall love the LORD your God and keep for all **11** time the charge he laid upon you, the statutes, the laws, and the commandments. This day you know the disci- **2** pline of the LORD, though your children who have neither known nor experienced it do not; you know his greatness, his strong hand and outstretched arm, the **3** signs he worked and his acts in Egypt against Pharaoh the king and his country, and all that he did to the **4** Egyptian army, its horses and chariots, when he caused the waters of the Red Sea to flow over them as they pursued you. In this way the LORD destroyed them, and so things remain to this day. You know what he did for **5** you in the wilderness as you journeyed to this place, and what he did to Dathan and Abiram sons of Eliab, **6** son of Reuben, when the earth opened its mouth and swallowed them in the sight of all Israel, together with their households and their tents and every living thing

7 in their company. With your own eyes you have seen the mighty work that the LORD did.

8 You shall observe all that I command you this day, so that you may have strength to enter and occupy the

9 land into which you are crossing, and so that you may live long in the land which the LORD swore to your forefathers to give them and their descendants, a land

10 flowing with milk and honey. The land which you are entering to occupy is not like the land of Egypt from which you have come, where, after sowing your seed,

11 you irrigated it by foot like a vegetable garden. But the land into which you are crossing to occupy is a land of mountains and valleys watered by the rain of heaven.

12 It is a land which the LORD your God tends[a] and on

13 which his eye rests from year's end to year's end. If you pay heed to the commandments which I give you this day, and love the LORD your God and serve him with all

14 your heart and soul, then I will send rain for your land in season, both autumn and spring rains, and you will

15 gather your corn and new wine and oil, and I will provide pasture in the fields for your cattle: you shall

16 eat your fill. Take good care not to be led astray in your hearts nor to turn aside and serve other gods and prostrate

17 yourselves to them, or the LORD will become angry with you: he will shut up the skies and there will be no rain, your ground will not yield its harvest, and you will soon vanish from the rich land which the LORD is giving

[a] which...tends: *or* whose soil the LORD your God has made firm.

you. You shall take these words of mine to heart and 18
keep them in mind; you shall bind them as a sign on
the hand and wear them as a phylactery on the forehead.
Teach them to your children, and speak of them indoors 19
and out of doors, when you lie down and when you rise.
Write them up on the door-posts of your houses and on 20
your gates. Then you will live long, you and your 21
children, in the land which the LORD swore to your
forefathers to give them, for as long as the heavens are
above the earth.

If you diligently keep all these commandments that I 22
now charge you to observe, by loving the LORD your
God, by conforming to his ways and by holding fast
to him, the LORD will drive out all these nations before 23
you and you shall occupy the territory of nations greater
and more powerful than you. Every place where you 24
set the soles of your feet shall be yours. Your borders
shall run from the wilderness to*a* the Lebanon and from
the River, the river Euphrates, to the western sea. No 25
man will be able to withstand you; the LORD your God
will put the fear and dread of you upon the whole land
on which you set foot, as he promised you. Understand 26
that this day I offer you the choice of a blessing and a
curse. The blessing will come if you listen to the com- 27
mandments of the LORD your God which I give you this
day, and the curse if you do not listen to the command- 28
ments of the LORD your God but turn aside from the way
that I command you this day and follow other gods
whom you do not know.

When the LORD your God brings you into the land 29

[a] *Prob. rdg.; Heb.* and.

which you are entering to occupy, there on Mount
Gerizim you shall pronounce the blessing and on Mount
30 Ebal the curse. (These mountains are on the other side
of the Jordan, close to Gilgal beside the terebinth[a] of
Moreh, beyond the road to the west which lies in the
31 territory of the Canaanites of the Arabah.) You are
about to cross the Jordan to enter and occupy the land
which the LORD your God is giving you; you shall
32 occupy it and settle in it, and you shall be careful to
observe all the statutes and laws which I set before you
this day.

✻ Deut. 11: 2–32 forms the third large insertion of the
deuteronomic historian into the original introduction to
Deuteronomy. After again reminding Israel of her salvation
history, he goes on to describe the abundant fertility of the
promised land. However, Israel's prosperity there entirely
depends on her absolute loyalty to her God. For just as he
controls history, so he (and not the Canaanite fertility
deities) controls nature, and can bring about not only abundant
harvests, but also famine leading to starvation. Whether
Israel enjoys God's blessing or curse is entirely up to her.
Clearly this passage is again directed at the exilic generation
now suffering the effects of the covenant curse, but whom the
deuteronomic historian still considers may yet once again
enjoy God's blessing.

6. *and what he did to Dathan and Abiram*: cp. Num. 16
where the story of the revolt of Dathan and Abiram is combined with that of Korah, who is not mentioned here.

11. *a land of mountains and valleys watered by the rain of
heaven*: the deuteronomic historian contrasts the man-made
irrigation of Egypt with the God-given rain of Canaan. But
he makes no mention of the regular flooding of the Nile

[a] *So Sept.; Heb.* terebinths.

80

valley which secures its fertility. This comparison of Egyptian
and Canaanite agriculture is therefore artificial, and serves a
theological rather than a geographical purpose (cp. Gen.
13: 10). While in Egypt men had to work in order to achieve
agricultural prosperity, in Canaan God himself tended the
land and ensured its fertility.

14. *both autumn and spring rains*: the October rains break
the long drought of summer during which the earth has lain
parched. The spring rains are the final rains before summer,
and on their duration and quantity depends the success or
otherwise of the harvest.

17. *he will shut up the skies*: drought was interpreted as
direct divine punishment (1 Kings 17f.). Rainfall was thus a
frequent subject of both blessing and curse (Deut. 28: 12, 24).

18. *You shall take these words of mine to heart*: verses 18–19
virtually repeat 6: 6–9, and are to be regarded here as a late
intrusion, for the curse of verses 16–17 should be directly
followed by the blessing of verses 22–5. For further comment
on verses 18–19, cp. on 6: 6–9.

24. *Your borders shall run from*: these boundaries reflect
the extent of the Davidic empire which served as an ideal
for future generations (cp. 1: 6–8).

26. *this day I offer you the choice of a blessing and a curse*:
Israel's future is entirely in her own hands. She knows what
she has to do: the only question is whether she will have
sufficient faith to do it.

29. *there on Mount Gerizim...and on Mount Ebal*: it seems
that this passage preserves the memory of an ancient rite
associated with the renewal of the covenant in pre-monarchical days. This would have taken place at Shechem which
acted as the central shrine of the confederacy of tribes which
made up Israel (cp. Josh. 24), and which was situated in the
valley between the two mountains Gerizim and Ebal.
Cp. Josh. 8: 30–5, and for further discussion the commentary
on Deut. 27: 1–13; 31: 10ff.

30. *close to Gilgal beside the terebinth of Moreh*: *Gilgal,*

meaning a stone circle, was situated near Jericho, where Israel first encamped after crossing the Jordan (Josh. 4). Though it is possible that there may have been another place of the same name near Shechem, it would seem from comparison with 27: 1ff. that the deuteronomic historian deliberately conflated traditions about Israel's first day at *Gilgal* with the ceremony of the renewal of the covenant at Shechem, which he wished to stress. For other references to the well-known sacred tree at *Moreh*, near Shechem, cp. Gen. 12: 6; 35: 4; Josh. 24: 26; Judg. 9: 6. Such trees frequently marked a place of worship, and are usually described either as oaks or terebinths (turpentine tree). In fact reference is probably being made to any large-sized tree. *

God's laws delivered by Moses

* Chapters 12–26 contain the deuteronomic laws. While some scholars argue that these laws were the product of Josiah's reform, the majority still hold that they were contained in the law book found in the temple whose discovery precipitated that reform (2 Kings 22–3).

Although the deuteronomic laws cover a great variety of subjects, they are not to be thought of as a fully comprehensive law code dealing with all aspects of Israelite life at the time of Josiah. For instance it has already been noted (see the commentary on 4: 2) that the deuteronomic laws are nowhere concerned with civil wrongs leading to actions for damages such as are found in the Book of the Covenant (Exod. 21: 18 – 22: 17). Rather their overall concern is to ensure Israel's exclusive allegiance to her God, and thereby the maintenance of the covenant relationship. None the less, as in the Book of the Covenant, a number of laws seem to have been included in Deuteronomy for no other reason than a strong humanitarian concern for the weak and oppressed, which even extends to a right attitude towards animals. This concern arose from a recognition of the kind of God with whom Israel had to deal. For in the face of the great empires of the world, insignificant Israel interpreted her election as God's chosen people as evidence of his abiding concern for the underprivileged. As a result she in her turn had to respect those who found themselves in a dependent position in her own society (cp. 5: 15; 10: 19). ✳

THE LAW OF THE CENTRAL SANCTUARY

THESE ARE THE STATUTES and laws that you shall **12** be careful to observe in the land which the LORD the God of your fathers is giving you to occupy as long as you live on earth. You shall demolish all the sanctuaries 2 where the nations whose place you are taking worship their gods, on mountain-tops and hills and under every spreading tree. You shall pull down their altars and 3 break their sacred pillars, burn their sacred poles and hack down the idols of their gods and thus blot out the name of them from that place.

You shall not follow such practices in the worship of 4 the LORD your God, but you shall resort to the place 5 which the LORD your God will choose out of all your tribes to receive his Name that it may dwell there. There you shall come and bring your whole-offerings and 6 sacrifices, your tithes and contributions, your vows and freewill offerings, and the first-born of your herds and flocks. There you shall eat before the LORD your God; 7 so you shall find joy in whatever you undertake, you and your families, because the LORD your God has blessed you.

8 You shall not act as we act here today, each of us
9 doing what he pleases, for till now you have not reached
the place of rest, the patrimony which the LORD your
10 God is giving you. You shall cross the Jordan and settle
in the land which the LORD your God allots you as your
patrimony; he will grant you peace from all your
enemies on every side, and you will live in security.
11 Then you shall bring everything that I command you
to the place which the LORD your God will choose as a
dwelling for his Name – your whole-offerings and sacrifices, your tithes and contributions, and all the choice
12 gifts that you have vowed to the LORD. You shall
rejoice before the LORD your God with your sons and
daughters, your male and female slaves, and the Levites
who live in your settlements[a] because they have no
holding or patrimony among you.

* The centralization of the cult at Jerusalem with the consequent destruction of all other sanctuaries has long been
recognized as the most important single element in the
deuteronomic reform. However, the general statement of law
initiating this innovation is not original to Deuteronomy,
but as the plural form of address indicates, has been inserted
later by the deuteronomic historian. Once more he has been
conditioned by the JE narrative of the Sinai events, where the
laws of the Book of the Covenant are preceded by the law
of the altar (Exod. 20: 24–6). But whereas this earlier law
presupposes a number of different sanctuaries, the deuteronomic historian categorically lays down that there is only one
place which God has chosen for his worship.

But although Deut. 12: 1–12 is itself a later addition
of the deuteronomic historian, the law of the centralization

[a] *Lit.* gates.

of worship at one sanctuary runs right through the deuteronomic laws and is integral to them. It is therefore not to be
regarded as some later interpolation, but is a fundamental
strand around which the law book is developed. Clearly
the deuteronomists' motive was to ensure the absolute purity
of Israel's religion and her exclusive allegiance to her God.
The easiest way to achieve this was to make sure that all
worship was carried out at one sanctuary where it could be
rigorously controlled. Naturally they selected Jerusalem
whose sanctuary had long been pre-eminent in Israel through
its association with the Davidic throne and covenant (2 Sam.
7). It was this place which God had specifically chosen for
his temple. On the discovery of the law book, Josiah, recog-
nizing the threat both to himself and his kingdom, readily
accepted the necessity of one single sanctuary, and so through
his reform brought all worship under his personal supervision at Jerusalem.

Since Deuteronomy is supposed to be Moses' last will and
testament spoken in Moab on the eve of entry into the
promised land, Jerusalem is never specifically identified as
the central sanctuary. This has led some scholars to argue that
Deuteronomy is reiterating an ancient law concerned with
the central shrine of the pre-monarchical confederacy of
tribes, where the Ark was deposited and the covenant periodi-
cally renewed (cp. 31: 9ff.). But such an argument fails to
recognize that Deuteronomy is not merely concerned to
make Jerusalem Israel's central sanctuary (a position which
in fact it already held), but rather to declare it her sole
legitimate place of worship. Of such radical action there
is no earlier evidence. Consequently the law of the centralization of the cult must be interpreted as new law going far
beyond the more limited ideas contained in Hezekiah's
reform.

While in Deut. 12: 1–7 centralization appears as the result
of carrying out the demand to destroy all the Canaanite
sanctuaries and their cult apparatus, in verses 8–12 it repre-

sents the final stage in her salvation history, being consequent upon her entry into the promised land, and the idyllic and God-given peace that she would there enjoy.

1. *These are the statutes and laws*: this verse acts as the title to the deuteronomic laws which follow, obedience to which would ensure the permanent occupation of the land.

2. *You shall demolish all the sanctuaries*: Canaanite sanctuaries and their apparatus are to be utterly obliterated so that there will be nothing left which might in any way pollute Israel's religion, which is now to be installed in the promised land at the one chosen sanctuary. *under every spreading tree*: sanctuaries were frequently set up in the cool of a shady tree, which itself may have had some sacred connection, though nowhere is it indicated that such trees were worshipped.

3. *and thus blot out the name of them*: by destroying the sanctuaries of the Canaanite gods, their memory would be utterly wiped out. For the proclamation of the name of the god in worship both indicated his ownership of the sanctuary itself, and his authority over those who worshipped there. Once the sanctuary ceased to exist, the god was denied the means of making himself known, and so claiming his worshipper's allegiance.

5. *to the place which the LORD your God will choose out of all your tribes*: in contrast to the multitude of Canaanite shrines, Israel is only to have one, chosen specially by her God. This undoubtedly refers to Jerusalem, whose importance had been further enhanced by the fact that Sennacherib had been unable to capture it during his campaign in 701 B.C. (2 Kings 19: 35f.). *to receive his Name that it may dwell there*: whereas Exod. 20: 24 envisages God coming in person to his sanctuary to bless his people, Deuteronomy makes no mention of God's actual presence. This is due to the deuteronomists' desire to emphasize God's transcendence (cp. on 10: 1). He is in heaven (26: 15): it is only his Name, conceived of as an almost physical entity, which is in his chosen sanctuary, and whose proclamation mediates

the divine blessing. This distinctive deuteronomic theological position almost certainly evolved in reaction to the mistaken notion of the temple as the indestructible dwelling-place of God (cp. Jer. 7).

5f. *There you shall come and bring*: all the required sacrifices and offerings, together with any given voluntarily, are now only to be made at Jerusalem, where there would be no risk of them being devoted to any heathen god, *and the first-born of your herds and flocks*: cp. 15: 19–23.

7. *There you shall eat before the LORD your God*: many offerings culminated in a meal eaten by the worshipper and his household before his god. *so you shall find joy*: the right worship of Israel's God could only result in joy. It was the purpose of the deuteronomic laws to bring this about, which is why they are counted as a blessing.

8. *each of us doing what he pleases*: here Israel's present disorder and lack of discipline is not attributed to the influence of Canaanite religion, but to the fact that she has not yet entered the promised land. With her settlement there, an idyllic order will be ushered in.

9. *you have not reached the place of rest*: after the long years of desert wandering, Israel is to enjoy untroubled rest in Canaan (cp. 25: 19). This promise pictures Israel luxuriating in the riches of Canaan in perfect harmony with her God. Nothing was further from the truth for the generation to whom this was written.

12. *You shall rejoice before the LORD your God*: as elsewhere in the deuteronomic legislation concerning appearance at the central sanctuary (cp. 12: 18; 16: 11, 14; 29: 11, 18), *You* refers to both husbands and wives. For by the deuteronomic reform adult women were brought within the scope of the covenant community, and so made subject to the covenant law (cp. on 5: 21). But the husbands and wives are to take with them to the central sanctuary all dependent persons who were not members of the covenant community, together with the Levites. As a result of the centralization of worship

at Jerusalem, these country Levites had lost their means of support from the local sanctuaries, and having no land of their own, had become entirely dependent on charity for their survival (cp. on 10: 8; 18: 1-8; 26: 12f.). ✳

THE SLAUGHTER OF DOMESTIC ANIMALS FOR MEAT

13 See that you do not offer your whole-offerings in any
14 place at random, but offer them only at the place which the LORD will choose in one of your tribes, and there you
15 must do all I command you. On the other hand, you may freely kill for food in all your settlements, as the LORD your God blesses you. Clean and unclean alike may eat
16 it, as they would eat the meat of gazelle or buck. But on no account must you eat the blood; pour it out on the
17 ground like water. In all your settlements you may not eat any of the tithe of your corn and new wine and oil, or any of the first-born of your cattle and sheep, or any of the gifts that you vow, or any of your freewill offerings
18 and contributions; but you shall eat it before the LORD your God in the place that the LORD your God will choose – you, your sons and daughters, your male and female slaves, and the Levites in your settlements; so you shall find joy before the LORD your God in all that you
19 undertake. Be careful not to neglect the Levites in your land as long as you live.

20 When the LORD your God extends your boundaries, as he has promised you, and you say to yourselves, 'I would like to eat meat', because you have a craving for
21 it, then you may freely eat it. If the place that the LORD your God will choose to receive his Name is far away, then you may slaughter a beast from the herds or flocks

which the LORD has given you and freely eat it in your
own settlements as I command you. You may eat it as 22
you would the meat of gazelle or buck; both clean and
unclean alike may eat it. But you must strictly refrain 23
from eating the blood, because the blood is the life; you
must not eat the life with the flesh. You must not eat it, 24
you must pour it out on the ground like water. If you 25
do not eat it, all will be well with you and your children
after you; for you will be doing what is right in the eyes
of the LORD. But such holy-gifts as you may have and 26
the gifts you have vowed, you must bring to the place
which the LORD will choose. You must present your 27
whole-offerings, both the flesh and the blood, on the
altar of the LORD your God; but of your shared-offerings
you shall eat the flesh, while the blood is to be poured
on the altar of the LORD your God. See that you listen 28
and do*a* all that I command you, and then it will go well
with you and your children after you for ever; for you
will be doing what is good and right in the eyes of the
LORD your God.

* Before the deuteronomic reform, the slaughter of a domestic
animal for meat was regarded as a sacrificial act. It had to be
carried out at the local sanctuary, where the blood was
offered to God. But with the abolition of all shrines other
than the sanctuary at Jerusalem, this was no longer practicable,
and the slaughtering of such animals was secularized, though
the prohibition on eating blood was retained. This had to be
poured out on the ground before the meat could be enjoyed.
But this secularization of the law concerning the slaughter
of domestic animals did not affect other sacrificial require-

[a] and do: *so Sam.; Heb. om.*

ments which now could only be carried out at the sole sanctuary in Jerusalem. While the Holiness Code (Lev. 17–26), probably written just before the exile, attempted to reverse this deuteronomic innovation by requiring that all domestic animals should be slaughtered at the central sanctuary (Lev. 17: 1ff.), in fact the totally changed conditions of life in post-exilic Israel prevented this.

Deut. 12: 13–19 is virtually restated in verses 20–8, though there it is assumed that from the first Israel only had one sanctuary at which slaughter of domestic animals took place. It is the possible expansion of her territory which might threaten this arrangement.

13. *See that you do not offer your whole-offerings in any place at random*: before setting out the change in the law relating to the slaughter of domestic animals, Deuteronomy makes it quite clear that Israel's sacrificial rites can only be carried out at the sanctuary at Jerusalem, for all other shrines have been rendered illegal by the reform. This is further reiterated in verses 17f., 26f.

15. *On the other hand, you may freely kill for food in all your settlements*: the slaughter of domestic animals is no longer regarded as part of Israel's sacrificial rites, but is secularized. Since there was now nothing sacral about the eating of meat which necessitated admission to a sanctuary, those doing so did not have to be ritually clean (cp. Lev. 7: 20f.). Indeed all meat is now treated like game (*gazelle or buck*) which, although it could have been freely eaten, could not have been offered in sacrifice, and therefore was never ritually killed before eating (cp. 14: 5).

16. *But on no account must you eat the blood*: all life was regarded as the gift of God to whom it belonged as of right. Since life was thought to be controlled by the blood (verse 23), in no circumstances could this be appropriated by man (Gen. 9: 4). Hence before the deuteronomic reform it was offered to God in the local sanctuary at the time of the slaughter of the animal for food. The new law in no way

alters this attitude to blood: it must still be returned to God by being poured out on the ground in an irretrievable way. It will thus be absorbed into the earth like water.

19. *Be careful not to neglect the Levites*: cp. on 12: 12.

20. *When the LORD your God extends your boundaries*: this may reflect Josiah's invasion of the former northern kingdom (2 Kings 23: 15–20). *

A WARNING AGAINST APOSTASY

When the LORD your God exterminates, as you 29 advance, the nations whose country you are entering to occupy, you shall take their place and settle in their land. After they have been destroyed, take care that you are 30 not ensnared into their ways. Do not inquire about their gods and say, 'How do these nations worship their gods? I too will do the same.' You must not do for the LORD 31 your God what they do, for all that they do for their gods is hateful and abominable to the LORD. As sacrifices for their gods they even burn their sons and their daughters.

See that you observe everything I command you: you must not add anything to it, nor take anything away 32[a] from it.

* After her entry into the land, Israel is warned not to be inquisitive about the religious practices of the former inhabitants, lest she should be tempted into the same abominable actions, of which child sacrifice is one example.

31. *As sacrifices for their gods they even burn their sons and their daughters*: this refers to the sacrifice to Molech practised

[a] *13: 1 in Heb.*

in the valley of Ben-hinnom just outside Jerusalem during the last years of the Davidic monarchy (Lev. 20: 1–5; Jer. 7: 31; 32: 35). It is not to be confused with the exceptional sacrifice of a child in time of national danger (2 Kings 3: 27). The fact that Lev. 18: 21 refers to the sacrifice to Molech in a list of sexual offences may indicate that the children involved were the sons and daughters of the cult prostitutes (cp. Ezek. 16: 20ff.; 23: 37ff.). Molech is a combination of the consonants of the Hebrew for 'king', with the vowels of the word for 'shame'. It is probable that originally this sacrifice was offered to Israel's God (Jer. 7: 31; 19: 5; 32: 35), though later it was thought of as so abhorrent that it was specifically regarded as a Canaanite practice. This resulted in Baal being specifically identified as the God involved (Jer. 19: 5; 32: 35). Cp. further on 18: 10.

32. *you must not add anything to it*: cp. on 4: 2. ✳

INSTANCES OF APOSTASY

13 When a prophet or dreamer appears among you and
2 offers you a sign or a portent and calls on you to follow other gods whom you have not known and worship
3 them, even if the sign or portent should come true, do not listen to the words of that prophet or that dreamer. God is testing you through him to discover whether you love the LORD your God with all your heart and soul.
4 You must follow the LORD your God and fear him; you must keep his commandments and obey him, serve
5 him and hold fast to him. That prophet or that dreamer shall be put to death, for he has preached rebellion against the LORD your God who brought you out of Egypt and redeemed you from that land of slavery; he has tried to lead you astray from the path which the

LORD your God commanded you to take. You must rid yourselves of this wickedness.

If your brother, your father's son or*ᵃ* your mother's 6 son, or your son or daughter, or the wife of your bosom or your dearest friend should entice you secretly to go and worship other gods – gods whom neither you nor your fathers have known, gods of the people round 7 about you, near or far, at one end of the land or the other – then you shall not consent or listen. You shall have no 8 pity on him, you shall not spare him nor shield him, you shall put him to death; your own hand shall be 9 the first to be raised against him and then all the people shall follow. You shall stone him to death, because he 10 tried to lead you astray from the LORD your God who brought you out of Egypt, out of the land of slavery. All Israel shall hear of it and be afraid; never again will 11 anything as wicked as this be done among you.

When you hear that miscreants*ᵇ* have appeared in any 12–13 of the cities which the LORD your God is giving you to occupy, and have led its inhabitants astray by calling on them to serve other gods whom you have not known, then you shall investigate the matter carefully. If, after 14 diligent examination, the report proves to be true and it is shown that this abominable thing has been done among you, you shall put the inhabitants of that city to 15 the sword; you shall lay the city under solemn ban together with everything in it.*ᶜ* You shall gather all its 16 goods into the square and burn both city and goods as a complete offering to the LORD your God; and it shall

[a] your father's son or: *so Sam.; Heb. om.*　　　[b] *Lit.* sons of Belial.
[c] *So Sept.; Heb. adds* and the cattle to the sword.

17 remain a mound of ruins, never to be rebuilt. Let nothing
out of all that has been laid under the ban be found in
your possession, so that the LORD may turn from his
anger and show you compassion; and in his compassion
he will increase you as he swore to your forefathers,
18 provided that you obey the LORD your God and keep
all his commandments which I give you this day, doing
only what is right in the eyes of the LORD your God.

* Having frequently warned against apostasy, Deuteronomy
gives three examples of concrete situations in which it might
arise, namely through cult officials, within the family, or
through the conversion of an entire city. In all cases it is to be
forthwith eradicated by the most drastic action. These
examples, formed as legal precedents, once more reflect the
deuteronomic ideal of what ought to have occurred. Instead
apostasy had been allowed to exist unchecked, and had so
polluted the whole religious life of the nation, that God had
been forced to implement the threat implicit in the covenant
relationship, and judge Israel.

1. *When a prophet or dreamer appears among you*: dreams
acted as a frequent means of divine revelation. Though the
precise distinction between the prophet and dreamer is
unclear (cp. Jer. 23: 25–32), both claimed that they had
access to information not available to ordinary men. They
therefore exercised considerable power.

2. *even if the sign or portent should come true*: at a time when
the prophets were by no means united in their advice (cp.
Jer. 28), the problem of identifying a false prophet was a
serious practical issue. In order to assert their legitimacy,
the prophets resorted to self-authenticating proofs (cp. Matt.
12: 38; John 6: 30). But Deuteronomy points out that no
matter how good a prophet's credentials might appear to be,
if he encouraged the worship of any god other than Yahweh,

he was apostate, and his message must be ignored. The problem of false prophecy is again tackled in 18: 21f. In fact there was no ready criterion for establishing the authenticity of a prophet's message. The hearers had to make up their own minds.

3. *God is testing you through him*: this is offered as an explanation of the unsatisfactory position of false prophets apparently being able to prove their authenticity. Comparison should be made with the case of Micaiah ben Imlah (1 Kings 22: 22f.) where God is described as deliberately misleading Israel through false prophets in order to punish her.

5. *That prophet or that dreamer shall be put to death*: the apostate must be executed forthwith as he has broken the first and fundamental commandment. *You must rid yourselves of this wickedness*: a deuteronomic formula (much stronger in the Hebrew than in this English translation) always used in connection with a breach of the criminal law requiring the death penalty to be exacted (cp. 17: 7, 12; 19: 19; 21: 21; 22: 21, 22, 24; 24: 7). Only through the death of the offender could the community cleanse itself from the pollution of his act. Thus the execution acted as a means of propitiating God.

6. *or daughter*: female relations are to be equally liable as male (cp. on 5: 21).

8. *You shall have no pity on him*: relatives are to be encouraged to see that even members of their own families and close friends are successfully prosecuted and executed if they commit apostasy. Loyalty to God is more important than loyalty to family or friends.

9. *your own hand shall be the first to be raised against him*: execution was by stoning. This method was chosen as the easiest way by which all members of the community could join together in the execution and so jointly share responsibility for it. But the deuteronomic law (cp. 17: 7) recognized that the chief responsibility for the conviction rested on the witnesses. Accordingly they are made to start the stoning,

and so become personally responsible for any miscarriage of justice. Cp. further on 17: 6f.

11. *All Israel shall hear of it and be afraid*: the deuteronomic law adopts a deterrent theory of punishment (17: 13; 19: 20; 21: 21). Its hope is that the rigorous enforcement of capital punishment will check the general breakdown in law and order, and so avoid God's at present inevitable judgement on Israel.

12. *When you hear that miscreants*: literally 'sons of Belial'. While it is clear that in the Old Testament Belial is not used as a proper name, its precise etymological explanation is uncertain. One recent suggestion connects it with the abyss and understands this phrase colloquially as referring to those whose actions or words bring a man to ultimate ruin (cp. 15: 9). It could then be rendered 'infernal fellows'. Cp. 2 Cor. 6: 15 where it is used as a synonym for Satan.

15f. *you shall lay the city under solemn ban together with everything in it*: for the ban cp. on 2: 34. Because of the gravity of the offence everything in the city has become polluted, and must be destroyed. Indeed even the ground remains contaminated so that no rebuilding can take place.

17. *Let nothing out of all that has been laid under the ban be found in your possession*: if anything is stolen from the city, then it brings under the ban all with which it comes in contact, and so necessitates further destruction. Cp. the case of Achan (Josh. 7). Only when the city and its entire contents have been destroyed can God show mercy on those who have remained loyal. Until then they can only expect his wrath for all Israel is collectively responsible for the apostasy within her borders. ✳

LAWS ON MOURNING RITES

14 You are the sons of the LORD your God: you shall not gash yourselves nor shave your forelocks[a] in mourning

[a] *Lit.* between your eyes.

for the dead. You are a people holy to the LORD your 2
God, and the LORD has chosen you out of all peoples on
earth to be his special possession.

☀ Certain well-known mourning rites are forbidden to
Israel probably because of their pagan associations (cp. Lev.
19: 27f.). She had been especially chosen by God, and her
exclusive relationship with him could all too easily be im-
paired unless she was careful to maintain her distinctiveness
from the cultic practices of other peoples.
    1. *you shall not gash yourselves nor shave your forelocks*:
the object of these rites was probably to make the mourner
unrecognizable, and so free him from any attention which
the dead man's spirit might pay him.
    2. *You are a people holy to the LORD your God*: cp. on
7: 6. ☀

FOOD LAWS

You shall not eat any abominable thing. These are the 3, 4
animals you may eat: ox, sheep, goat, buck, gazelle, 5
roebuck, wild-goat, white-rumped deer, long-horned
antelope, and rock-goat. You may eat any animal which 6
has a parted foot or a cloven hoof and also chews the cud;
those which only chew the cud or only have a parted or 7
cloven hoof you may not eat. These are: the camel, the
hare, and the rock-badger,[a] because they chew the cud
but do not have cloven hoofs; you shall regard them as
unclean; and the pig, because it has a cloven hoof but 8
does not chew the cud, you shall regard as unclean. You
shall not eat their flesh or even touch their dead carcasses.
Of creatures that live in water you may eat all those that 9
have fins and scales, but you may not eat any that have 10

[a] *Or* rock-rabbit.

neither fins nor scales; you shall regard them as unclean.

11, 12 You may eat all clean birds. These are the birds you may not eat: the griffon-vulture,[a] the black vulture, the

13, 14 bearded vulture,[b] the kite,[c] every kind of falcon,[d] every

15 kind of crow,[e] the desert-owl, the short-eared owl, the

16 long-eared owl, every kind of hawk, the tawny owl,

17 the screech-owl, the little owl, the horned owl, the osprey,

18 the fisher-owl, the stork,[f] every kind of cormorant, the hoopoe, and the bat.

19 All teeming winged creatures you shall regard as

20 unclean; they may not be eaten. You may eat every clean insect.

21 You shall not eat anything that has died a natural death. You shall give it to the aliens who live in your settlements, and they may eat it, or you may sell it to a foreigner; for you are a people holy to the LORD your God.

You shall not boil a kid in its mother's milk.

✴ These laws, which are very similar to those in Lev. 11: 2–23 and clearly come from the same source, carefully distinguish between animal food which Israel may eat and that which is prohibited to her. The criteria on which this distinction is made cannot now be recovered. No doubt some of the reasons are quite simple such as natural aversion, superstition, or the fact that certain food invariably caused illness. But the desire to differentiate Israel from the cultic and magical practices of her neighbours, and particularly the Canaanites (see verse 21), may also have influenced the

[a] Or eagle. [b] Or ossifrage.
[c] So Sam., cp. Lev. 11: 14; Heb. has an unknown word.
[d] So some MSS.; others add kite. [e] Or raven. [f] Or heron.

final formation of the list in which a number of the animals and birds can now no longer be identified with certainty.

3. *You shall not eat any abominable thing*: that is, anything displeasing to God. This is the general law which is then particularized by the examples which follow, first of animals, then fish, birds and insects.

4. *These are the animals you may eat*: external factors determine which animals are clean.

8. *You shall not eat their flesh or even touch their dead carcasses*: a dead unclean animal had simply to be left where it was as food for the birds of prey, themselves regarded as unclean. Cp. on verse 21 below.

9. *Of creatures that live in water*: in general the Israelites could eat fish.

12. *These are the birds you may not eat*: the list consists almost entirely of birds of prey.

19. *All teeming winged creatures you shall regard as unclean*: flying insects cannot be eaten.

20. *You may eat every clean insect*: this is probably a late note referring to the exception to the general law about insects contained in Lev. 11: 21–2, whereby permission was given for the eating of locusts and grasshoppers.

21. *You shall give it to the aliens*: even animals regarded as clean cannot be eaten if they die naturally, presumably because the regulations concerning the draining of blood could not be properly carried out (cp. on 12: 16). Instead the carcass is either to be given to resident aliens, or sold to foreigners, neither of whom were as yet subject to this law. Later it was extended to resident aliens (Lev. 17: 15), who were generally made equally responsible as Israelites under the law (Lev. 20: 2), and given the same legal rights (Deut. 1: 16). But Deut. 1: 16 is the work of the deuteronomic historian and reflects the legislation contained in the Holiness Code (Lev. 17–26) formulated after Josiah's reform but before the deuteronomic historian published his Work. The deuteronomic laws themselves (Deut. 12–26) nowhere

give the resident alien the same rights as the Israelite, but continually treat him as an object of charity. Cp. on 1: 16. *You shall not boil a kid in its mother's milk*: in contrast to Exod. 23: 19; 34: 26, where this injunction forms part of an appendix to a feast calendar, here it is understood as another food law. This indicates that at the time the deuteronomic laws were compiled, its original purpose was lost. Probably, as one of the Ugaritic texts indicates, it reflected a Canaanite fertility rite connected with a spring festival. If so, then the Passover laws concerning the roasting of the Passover animal (Exod. 12: 1–27) may consciously seek to differentiate Israelite practice from the indigenous Canaanite ritual with which it must on no account be associated. ✳

TITHING LAWS

22 Year by year you shall set aside a tithe of all the produce
23 of your seed, of everything that grows on the land. You shall eat it in the presence of the LORD your God in the place which he will choose as a dwelling for his Name – the tithe of your corn and new wine and oil, and the first-born of your cattle and sheep, so that for all time
24 you may learn to fear the LORD your God. When the LORD your God has blessed you with prosperity, and the place which he will choose to receive his Name is far from you and the journey too great for you to be able to
25 carry your tithe, then you may exchange it for silver. You shall tie up the silver and take it with you to the
26 place which the LORD your God will choose. There you shall spend it as you will on cattle or sheep, wine or strong drink, or whatever you desire; you shall consume it there with rejoicing, both you and your family, in the
27 presence of the LORD your God. You must not neglect

the Levites who live in your settlements; for they have
no holding or patrimony among you.

At the end of every third year you shall bring out all 28
the tithe of your produce for that year and leave it in
your settlements so that the Levites, who have no holding 29
or patrimony among you, and the aliens, orphans, and
widows in your settlements may come and eat their fill.
If you do this the LORD your God will bless you in
everything to which you set your hand.

* Every year Israelites offered a tithe of their crops at the
local sanctuary and joined in a festal meal which reminded
them that the earth was God's and that it was he who had
provided the harvest. But the concentration of all worship
at Jerusalem with the consequent abolition of the local
sanctuaries meant that this custom could no longer be easily
carried out by those living at some distance from Jerusalem.
Consequently a new deuteronomic law directed that the
tithe of the crops was to be sold, and the money received
offered instead at the Jerusalem sanctuary, where the festal
meal would now be eaten. Further new regulations provided
for the welfare of the country Levites and those who were
dependent on charity for their sustenance.

23. *You shall eat it in the presence of the LORD your God*:
this is not to be understood as meaning that all the tithe was
eaten by the worshipper. While he enjoyed a harvest meal at
the sanctuary, the bulk of his tithe went to support the clergy
over the coming year. *and the first-born of your cattle and sheep*:
the tithing provisions only concern agricultural crops. The
insertion of the first-born here is probably due to the fact
that they would also have been offered at the same time
(cp. on 15: 19–25).

26. *There you shall spend it as you will*: only a portion of the
tithe money would have been spent on food and wine for the

festal meal, the remainder going to the support of the sanctuary. The meal was to be an occasion of general family rejoicing.

27. *You must not neglect the Levites who live in your settlements*: through the abolition of the local sanctuaries, the country Levites had lost their means of support (cp. on 10: 8; 12: 12; 18: 1-8). They now had to depend on charity alone for their sustenance.

28. *At the end of every third year*: because of the large number in the community who had no means of supporting themselves, once every three years an Israelite was absolved from his duty of taking the tithe money to the sanctuary at Jerusalem. Instead he was to give the tithe of the crops to those who, possessing no land, had no harvest of their own. Clearly this tithe-year (cp. 26: 12) was not intended to be observed simultaneously throughout Israel since it sought to provide a regular harvest for those in need (cp. 24: 19). ✶

THE RELEASE OF DEBTS

15 At the end of every seventh year you shall make a
2 remission of debts. This is how the remission shall be made: everyone who holds a pledge shall remit the pledge of anyone indebted to him. He shall not press a fellow-countryman for repayment, for the LORD's
3 year of remission has been declared.[a] You may press foreigners; but if it is a fellow-countryman that holds anything of yours, you must remit all claim upon it.
4-5 There will never be any poor among you if only you obey the LORD your God by carefully keeping these commandments which I lay upon you this day; for the LORD your God will bless you with great prosperity in the land which he is giving you to occupy as your

[a] *Or* has come.

patrimony. When the LORD your God blesses you, as he 6
promised, you will lend to men of many nations, but
you yourselves will not borrow; you will rule many
nations, but they will not rule you.

When one of your fellow-countrymen in any of your 7
settlements in the land which the LORD your God is
giving you becomes poor, do not be hard-hearted or
close-fisted with your countryman in his need. Be open- 8
handed towards him and lend him on pledge as much as
he needs. See that you do not harbour iniquitous 9
thoughts*a* when you find that the seventh year, the year
of remission, is near, and look askance at your needy
countryman and give him nothing. If you do, he will
appeal to the LORD against you, and you will be found
guilty of sin. Give freely to him and do not begrudge 10
him your bounty, because it is for this very bounty that
the LORD your God will bless you in everything that you
do or undertake. The poor will always be with you in the 11
land, and for that reason I command you to be open-
handed with your countrymen, both poor and distressed,
in your own land.

* All debts of fellow-Israelites, as opposed to foreigners, are
to be cancelled every seventh year, the year of release. The
type of loan envisaged here involved the pledge of a person
as security, who, on non-payment of the debt, was taken by
the creditor, who used his services as compensation. As a
result of this deuteronomic law not only would the enforcement of repayment have been prohibited, but anyone who
had been seized as pledge would also have been freed. Further,
the law commanded the Israelites to be generous in their

[a] *Lit.* thoughts of Belial.

attitude to their poor, and even if the year of release was imminent, they were still to lend to those in need. But while Israel might freely lend to foreign nations, she was not to borrow from them. Such action would indicate dependence on them, and not on Yahweh, who would not only richly provide for her, but even wipe out poverty altogether if she kept his law.

1. *At the end of every seventh year*: the law of the release of debts should not automatically be connected with the law of fallowing in Exod. 23: 10f., at any rate in the form in which that law is now set out in the Book of the Covenant. For since the purpose of letting the land lie fallow was clearly to provide permanent sustenance for the poor and wild animals, fallowing cannot have taken place simultaneously throughout Israel, but must have been staggered by a system of rotation. No mention of this law of fallowing is made in Deuteronomy, which may indicate that the practice had lapsed. Its social benefits appear to have been taken over by 14: 28ff.; 24: 19ff. However, through the creation of the sabbatical year, the Holiness Code did ordain a universal year of fallowing, though no attempt was made to connect this with provision for the poor and wild animals.

3. *You may press foreigners*: the law does not apply to non-Israelites. Whether resident aliens, as opposed to other foreigners, were protected by this provision is unclear, but is perhaps unlikely (cp. 14: 21).

4–5. *There will never be any poor among you*: apparently contradicts the more realistic statement in verse 11. For the truly obedient community, blessing will be universal; poverty is here seen as a consequence of disobedience.

6. *you will lend to men of many nations*: it would seem very unlikely that Israel was ever in a position to make economic loans to her neighbours. But the deuteronomists' chief concern is that she in her turn should never be dependent on other nations as an economic vassal, for this would imply dependence on those nations' gods who ensured their pros-

perity. To borrow from another nation therefore amounted
to apostasy.

8. *as much as he needs*: there is to be no limit to the amount
which a fellow Israelite might be asked to lend. If he has
sufficient wealth, then his poor neighbour has every right
to ask for whatever he needs. But the borrower was expected
to pay back his loan (Ps. 37: 21).

9. *See that you do not harbour iniquitous thoughts*: even
though to lend money will inevitably result in loss, as there
will be insufficient time before the year of release to allow for
repayment, the loan must still be made. It in effect amounts
to a gift. For the literal rendering 'thoughts of Belial' (N.E.B.
footnote), cp. p. 96.

11. *The poor will always be with you*: this verse stresses the
proper concern for the needy and makes a quite different
point from verses 4–5. *

THE RELEASE OF SLAVES

When a fellow-Hebrew, man or woman, sells himself 12
to you as a slave, he shall serve you for six years and in the
seventh year you shall set him free. But when you set 13
him free, do not let him go empty-handed. Give to him 14
lavishly from your flock, from your threshing-floor
and your winepress. Be generous to him, because the
LORD your God has blessed you. Do not take it amiss 18
when you have to set him free, for his six years' service
to you has been worth twice*a* the wage of a hired man.
Then the LORD your God will bless you in everything
you do. Remember that you were slaves in Egypt and the 15
LORD your God redeemed you; that is why I am giving
you this command today.

If, however, a slave is content to be with you and 16

[a] worth twice: *or* equivalent to.

says, 'I will not leave you, I love you and your family',
17 then you shall take an awl and pierce through his ear to
the door, and he will be your slave for life. You shall
treat a slave-girl in the same way.

✳ All Israel's slaves are to be released after six years' service,
and generous provision is to be made for them. A slave may,
however, elect to remain with his master for life. This
provision constitutes a complete reworking of the original
law of release of slaves in the Book of the Covenant (Exod.
21: 2–11), with which it should be compared. While foreign
prisoners of war were used as slaves, sale of fellow-Israelites
for debt formed the chief source (2 Kings 4: 1).

12. *When a fellow-Hebrew, man or woman*: whatever the
word *Hebrew* originally meant, here it refers to Israelites as
opposed to foreigners who have no right to release. As
elsewhere, the deuteronomists extend the application of this
law to include women as well as men (cp. on 5: 21).

13. *do not let him go empty-handed*: Exod. 21: 2–11 makes
no provision for the departing slave. This no doubt deterred
many from exercising their rights. Provided a slave felt
well treated, there was no point in exchanging security
without freedom, for freedom without security. In addition
Exod. 21: 4 enacts that any wife whom the master had given
the slave (in order to increase his slave holdings through
birth), together with the children of the marriage, were not
allowed to go away with him, but remained his master's
property. The deuteronomic revision now actively encourages
the slave to claim his freedom. Generous provision is to be
made for him to start a new life. Further the omission of any
mention of his family probably indicates that this part of the
law was repealed, the master no longer having any control
over the slave's private life.

18. *twice the wage of a hired man*: as the N.E.B. footnote
indicates with its alternative reading 'equivalent to', the

Hebrew here is uncertain. If *twice* is the correct rendering, then the normal three-year contract of hire (Isa. 16: 14) is being contrasted with the six-year period of slavery. The nineteenth-century B.C. Babylonian Code of Lipit-Ishtar provided for the release of a debtor once he had given services equivalent to twice the amount of his debt, while the Code of Hammurabi more than a century-and-a-half later granted release after three years.

15. *Remember that you were slaves in Egypt*: because God had shown mercy to the Israelites by delivering them from slavery in Egypt, they in their turn are to show pity to the less fortunate in their midst (cp. 5: 15). The great experiences of Israel's salvation history were directly to influence the day-to-day conduct of her affairs.

16. *If, however, a slave is content to be with you*: in contrast to Exod. 21: 6, no mention is made of bringing the slave to *'elohim* ('God' in the N.E.B.), that is the household gods or *teraphim* before whom the ceremony was performed (cp. Gen. 31: 19–35). These had been rendered illegal objects under Josiah's reform (2 Kings 23: 24). But essentially the same ceremony is referred to in the deuteronomic revision, though the law is now extended to include women (cp. on 5: 21). Like divorce (Hos. 2: 2, N.E.B. footnote), this ceremony is an example of family law which was administered not through the courts but in the home by the head of the household acting on his own initiative without recourse to any other authority or person.

17. *pierce through his ear*: the pierced ear would have indicated to the general public the slave's legal position. This would explain why, in contrast to divorce (24: 1), no document was ever needed to certify the position. ✶

THE LAW OF THE FIRST-BORN

19^a You shall dedicate to the LORD your God every male first-born of your herds and flocks. You shall not plough with the first-born of your cattle, nor shall you shear the
20 first-born of your sheep. Year by year you and your family shall eat them in the presence of the LORD your
21 God, in the place which the LORD will choose. If any animal is defective, if it is lame or blind, or has any other serious defect, you must not sacrifice it to the LORD your
22 God. Eat it in your settlements; both clean and unclean alike may eat it as they would the meat of gazelle or buck.
23 But you must not eat the blood; pour it out on the ground like water.

✻ It had long been the custom to offer the first-born of animals to God in recognition that all life belonged to him (cp. Exod. 13: 2, 11–16; 22: 29f.; 34: 19f.). But because of the centralization of worship at Jerusalem, the law had to be amended. However, in contrast to animals, Deuteronomy nowhere mentions any provision concerning the first-born of men.

19. *You shall not plough...nor shall you shear*: since the first-born are dedicated to God, they cannot be used for secular purposes, nor is their owner to derive any gain from them.

20. *Year by year*: Exod. 22: 30 provided that the animal was to be kept seven days for the welfare of the mother, and then slaughtered in sacrifice on the eighth. Centralization of worship made such a regulation impracticable as it would have necessitated frequent journeys to Jerusalem. Consequently the law is amended to allow the animal to be offered

[a] *Verse 18 transposed to follow verse 14.*

to God at any time during the first year of its life. This would usually have taken place during the time of the annual pilgrimage to Jerusalem for the offering of tithes (cp. 14: 23).

21–3. *If any animal is defective*: any physical deformity made the animal impure and therefore unfit for offering to God. Instead it could be eaten by the owner at his home in accordance with the new deuteronomic provisions for the eating of meat (cp. 12: 20–5). Mal. 1: 7f. reproaches the Israelites for breaking this law after the return from exile. ✲

THE FESTAL CALENDAR

Observe the month of Abib and keep the Passover to the **16** LORD your God, for it was in that month that the LORD your God brought you out of Egypt by night. You shall 2 slaughter a lamb, a kid, or a calf as a Passover victim to the LORD your God in the place which he will choose as a dwelling for his Name. You shall eat nothing leavened 3 with it. For seven days you shall eat unleavened cakes, the bread of affliction. In urgent haste you came out of Egypt, and thus as long as you live you shall commemorate the day of your coming out of Egypt. No leaven 4 shall be seen in all your territory for seven days, nor shall any of the flesh which you have slaughtered in the evening of the first day remain overnight till morning. You may 5 not slaughter the Passover victim in any of the settlements which the LORD your God is giving you, but 6 only in the place which he will choose as a dwelling for his Name; you shall slaughter the Passover victim in the evening as the sun goes down, the time of your coming out of Egypt. You shall boil it and eat it in the place 7 which the LORD your God will choose, and then next morning you shall turn and go to your tents. For six 8 days you shall eat unleavened cakes, and on the seventh day there shall be a closing ceremony in honour of the LORD your God; you shall do no work.

9 Seven weeks shall be counted: start counting the seven weeks from the time when the sickle is put to the standing
10 corn; then you shall keep the pilgrim-feast of Weeks to the LORD your God and offer a freewill offering in proportion to the blessing that the LORD your God has
11 given you. You shall rejoice before the LORD your God, with your sons and daughters, your male and female slaves, the Levites who live in your settlements, and the aliens, orphans, and widows among you. You shall rejoice in the place which the LORD your God will choose
12 as a dwelling for his Name and remember that you were slaves in Egypt. You shall keep and observe all these statutes.

13 You shall keep the pilgrim-feast of Tabernacles*a* for seven days, when you bring in the produce from your
14 threshing-floor and winepress. You shall rejoice in your feast, with your sons and daughters, your male and female slaves, the Levites, aliens, orphans, and widows
15 who live in your settlements. For seven days you shall keep this feast to the LORD your God in the place which he will choose, when the LORD your God gives you his blessing in all your harvest and in all your work; you shall keep the feast with joy.

16 Three times a year all your males shall come into the presence of*b* the LORD your God in the place which he will choose: at the pilgrim-feasts of Unleavened Bread, of Weeks, and of Tabernacles. No one shall come into

[a] *Or* Booths *or* Arbours.   [b] *Lit.* see the face of.

the presence of the LORD empty-handed. Each of you 17
shall bring such a gift as he can in proportion to the
blessing which the LORD your God has given you.

✳ On entry into Canaan, the Israelites took over the three
main agricultural festivals of Unleavened Bread, with which
Passover came to be associated, Weeks and Tabernacles.
These marked the three stages of the harvest from the cutting
of the first cereal crops, to their complete harvest, and ending
with the gathering-in of the fruit. Initially they were celebrated at the local sanctuary, but as a result of Josiah's reform
came to be celebrated at the one sanctuary in Jerusalem. In
consequence earlier practice had to be amended, and the
festal calendar reworked (cp. Exod. 23: 14–17; 34: 18,
22–4). It is, however, possible that, as indicated in Exod. 34:
24, there had already been an attempt to centralize these
festivals. Like much of Exod. 32–4, this probably reflects
Hezekiah's reform, which certainly attempted some measure
of centralization (2 Kings 18: 4), though it did not result in
the destruction of all ancient places of worship, and which
culminated in the celebration of the Passover in Jerusalem to
which men were summoned from all over Israel (2 Chron.
30: 5).

   1. *Observe the month of Abib and keep the Passover*: originally
Passover was a festival of semi-nomadic shepherds celebrated
on the night before they struck camp to move off to their
summer pastures. It included the sprinkling of blood on the
tent poles to ward off evil spirits, and so protect the flocks,
and particularly the new-born lambs. This rite, with its
dominant feature of an imminent departure, naturally served
as a suitable model for a regular reminder of the exodus
event, and the term Passover came to be explained from the
tradition that God 'passed over' the blood-daubed houses of
the Israelites when he struck dead the first-born in Egypt.
But while the name Passover does seem to have been derived

from a verb meaning 'limp' (1 Kings 18: 21, R.S.V. 'How long will you go limping?'), its origin is better explained from a kind of limping dance associated with the original shepherds' rite. The combination of Passover with the feast of Unleavened Bread is not, as some scholars have asserted, to be understood as a deuteronomic innovation. While Deut. 16: 1–8 clearly shows that two originally independent religious observances are being dealt with (verses 1, 2, 4*b*–7 refer to Passover; verses 3, 4*a*, 8 to Unleavened Bread), this fragmentary approach has arisen simply through the centralization of worship at Jerusalem, which necessitated new regulations for Passover. The fact that both feasts had from the first been celebrated in the same Spring month, *Abib* ('fresh ears', 'green shoots'), and associated with the exodus tradition (Exod. 23: 15), indicates that their connection is much older than the deuteronomic reform. Further Exod. 23: 18 specifically refers to the Passover ritual (cp. Exod. 34: 25). If the eating of unleavened bread was from the first an integral part of the Passover ceremony, then this no doubt facilitated the early combination of the two observances. But it is possible that the eating of unleavened bread in the Passover ritual in fact owes its origin to this combination which resulted in the elaboration of the exodus story by the tradition that in their haste to leave Egypt, the Israelites had to take their dough unleavened (Exod. 12: 34).

2. *You shall slaughter a lamb, a kid, or a calf*: the feast of Passover–Unleavened Bread can now only be celebrated at the central sanctuary. Any sacrificial animal can be offered, and not merely the lamb or kid of the original rite (Exod. 12: 5). Further, since the worshippers will now be some distance from home, the practice of daubing the house with the blood of the Passover animal is dropped (Exod. 12: 7).

3. *For seven days you shall eat unleavened cakes*: originally the feast of Unleavened Bread celebrated the cutting of the first new cereal and the consequent end of dependence on the previous year's crops. To mark this continuance of life,

the first of the new cereal was taken and baked without the addition of any leaven. But even in the festal calendar of the Book of the Covenant, the feast of Unleavened Bread has already lost its simple agricultural connection, and has been associated with the exodus tradition (Exod. 23: 15).

4. *No leaven shall be seen in all your territory for seven days*: generally leaven was supplied from the kept-over fermented dough of the previous baking. With the advent of the new crop, this must be destroyed and a new start made.

7. *You shall boil it*: this was specifically forbidden in Exod. 12: 9. The change in practice probably reflects the method of cooking meat at the Jerusalem sanctuary (cp. 1 Sam. 2: 12–17). *then next morning you shall turn and go to your tents*: the Passover meal was still eaten at night. *to your tents* usually means 'to go home' (1 Sam. 4: 10; 1 Kings 12: 16: translated 'homes' in the N.E.B.). But here it must be understood literally, as referring to the tents in which the pilgrims to Jerusalem would be encamped during the combined festival.

8. *on the seventh day there shall be a closing ceremony*: only after the final ceremony could the pilgrims return home.

9. *Seven weeks shall be counted*: the second of the three agricultural festivals marked the end of the cereal harvest. Originally it would have had no precise date, but later it was fixed at seven weeks after the first cereal cutting. Hence its new name of Weeks (cp. Exod. 23: 16). Nowhere in the Old Testament is the festival given an historical explanation, although in later Judaism it was associated with the giving of the Ten Commandments at Horeb.

10. *offer a freewill offering*: no amount is laid down, but each individual is left to assess this for himself in accordance with the success or otherwise of his harvest.

11. *You shall rejoice before the LORD your God*: as elsewhere in the deuteronomic legislation about worship at the central sanctuary, *You* refers to both husbands and wives (cp. on 12: 12), adult women now being treated as members of the covenant community, and therefore subject to the covenant

law (cp. on 5: 21). But the festival is to be an occasion of general rejoicing – so too in verse 14 – throughout the whole population, including dependent persons who were not members of the covenant community, because the Israelites themselves were once in a similar dependent social position (cp. 5: 15; 15: 15).

13. *You shall keep the pilgrim-feast of Tabernacles*: the third of the agricultural festivals marked the gathering-in of the fruit, mainly olives and grapes, and took place in the early autumn. In early Israel this marked the end of the year, and with the coming of the first rains, the beginning of the new one. Although the feast is now named Tabernacles or Booths, it is not until the Holiness Code (Lev. 23:43) that this name is given an historical interpretation and associated with the wandering in the desert where the Israelites had no permanent houses. It is probable that originally Tabernacles referred to the temporary dwellings in which the farmers lived during the harvest.

16. *all your males*: this reflects the earlier legislation of the Book of the Covenant which was addressed solely to males (Exod. 23: 17), and clearly contradicts the new deuteronomic legislation (Deut. 16: 11, 14) which assumes that the law applies to all adults whether male or female. It was this earlier legislation which the deuteronomist worked over in the light of centralization of worship. *No one shall come into the presence of the LORD empty-handed*: a general regulation that whenever a worshipper attends at the sanctuary, he must bring with him an offering (Exod. 23: 16). Its value is left to the worshipper to determine. The phrase *come into the presence of* means literally 'see the face of' and originally referred to the face of an idol which the worshipper would see at the sanctuary. Although Israel prohibited images of her God (5: 8), and consequently the Ark on which Yahweh manifested himself remained empty, she none the less retained the use of this phrase. So personal was her relationship with her God that she could only speak of him in human terms. ✳

114

THE APPOINTMENT OF JUDGES

You shall appoint for yourselves judges and officers, 18 tribe by tribe, in every settlement which the LORD your God is giving you, and they shall dispense true justice to the people. You shall not pervert the course of 19 justice or show favour, nor shall you accept a bribe; for bribery makes the wise man blind and the just man give a crooked answer. Justice, and justice alone, you shall 20 pursue, so that you may live and occupy the land which the LORD your God is giving you.

✷ Originally the elders, that is the male heads of every household, had administered justice, meeting in the gate of their town. Consequently every local community determined its own legal cases on a strictly democratic basis, each family having a say in every judgement. Later, probably under Jehoshaphat's reform (2 Chron. 19: 5ff.), professional judges were appointed in all the fortified cities who had the support of officers by whom their judgements could be enforced. Cp. on 1: 9ff.

18. *judges and officers*: the courts were no longer to be in the hands of the local community, but administered by royal appointees responsible to the king for the district under their control. How many judges were appointed for each city, whether they were drawn from the local community, and the precise area of their jurisdiction cannot be ascertained. While a number of deuteronomic provisions still mention the elders as administering justice (19: 12; 21: 2–9, 19f.; 22: 15–21; 25: 7f.), quite clearly Deuteronomy as a whole considers the local administration of justice to be in the hands of professional judges. Accordingly these provisions, while still current law at the time Deuteronomy was promulgated, must antedate Josiah's reform, and indeed are probably older than Jehoshaphat's.

19. *You shall not pervert the course of justice*: a manual for judges which could originally have been addressed to the elders (cp. Exod. 23: 1–3, 6–9).

20. *Justice, and justice alone, you shall pursue*: Israel's occupation of the land depends entirely on her obedience to God's law, which includes ensuring that no one is hampered from securing his proper rights. It is only through the maintenance of justice that the community will be able to guarantee right relations between man and God and man and his neighbour. ✶

LAWS CONCERNING THE CULT

21 You shall not plant any kind of tree as a sacred pole[a] beside the altar of the LORD your God which you shall
22 build. You shall not set up a sacred pillar, for the LORD your God hates them.

17   You shall not sacrifice to the LORD your God a bull or sheep that has any defect or serious blemish, for that would be abominable to the LORD your God.

✶ Yahweh's altar is to be kept pure from all forms of contamination.

21f. *You shall not plant any kind of tree*: two cult objects normally found at every Canaanite shrine, the sacred tree (*asherah*), named after the female consort of Baal, and the stone pillar (*massebah*) representing a male deity, are not to be erected beside Yahweh's altar (cp. 7: 5).

17: 1. *a bull or sheep that has any defect*: the same point about defective sacrificial animals appears at 15: 21. ✶

NORMAL CRIMINAL PROCEDURE

2 If so be that, in any one of the settlements which the LORD your God is giving you, a man or woman is found

[a] sacred pole: *Heb*. asherah.

among you who does what is wrong in the eyes of the
LORD your God, by breaking his covenant and going to 3
worship other gods and prostrating himself before them
or before the sun and moon and all the host of heaven – a
thing that I have forbidden – then, if it is reported to 4
you or you hear of it, make thorough inquiry. If the report
proves to be true, and it is shown that this abominable
thing has been done in Israel, then bring the man or 5
woman who has done this wicked deed to the city gate[a]
and stone him to death. Sentence of death shall be 6
carried out on the testimony of two or of three witnesses:
no one shall be put to death on the testimony of a single
witness. The first stones shall be thrown by the witnesses 7
and then all the people shall follow; thus you shall rid
yourselves of this wickedness.

* This precedent, modelled by way of example on a case of
apostasy, indicates how a criminal is to be dealt with by the
court of first instance. Once the judges become aware that a
crime may have been committed, they are to bring the accused
before them, and try the case: on conviction they must
secure his immediate execution. But in order for the accused
to be found guilty, there must be corroboratory evidence.
The witnesses themselves begin the execution.

2. *a man or woman*: under Josiah's reform, women became
equally liable as men for breach of the covenant law (cp. on
5: 21).

3. *before the sun and moon and all the host of heaven*: the
worship of astral powers in Israel appears to have arisen late
(cp. on 4: 19).

4. *make thorough inquiry*: the judges are to bring the accused
before them, but he will only be convicted if there is sufficient
evidence against him.

[a] *So Sept.; Heb. adds* the man or the woman.

5. *to the city gate*: with the exception of 22: 21, execution by communal stoning always took place outside the city gate as this was the only practical place both as regards space and materials.

6. *the testimony of two or of three witnesses*: no longer can a man simply be convicted on the evidence of his accuser. There must be corroboration (cp. on 19: 15). The phrase *of two or of three witnesses* may mean two witnesses other than his accuser, that is three witnesses in all.

7. *The first stones shall be thrown by the witnesses*: by making the witnesses begin the execution, responsibility for any miscarriage of justice is placed upon them. This law sought to deter not only the false witness, who was in any event liable as a criminal under the ninth commandment (cp. on 5: 20), but the careless or irresponsible witness. Only if a man was very sure of his facts would he risk giving evidence. *you shall rid yourselves of this wickedness*: for comment on this strong Hebrew phrase, cp. commentary on 13: 5. ✻

THE HIGHER COURT

8 When the issue in any lawsuit is beyond your competence, whether it be a case of blood against blood, plea against plea, or blow against blow, that is disputed in your courts,[a] then go up without delay to the place

9 which the LORD your God will choose. There you must go to the levitical priests or to the judge then in office; seek their guidance, and they will pronounce the sentence.

10 You shall act on the pronouncement which they make from the place which the LORD will choose. See that

11 you carry out all their instructions. Act on the instruction which they give you, or on the precedent that they cite; do not swerve from what they tell you, either to right

12 or to left. Anyone who presumes to reject the decision

[a] *Lit.* in your gates.

either of the priest who ministers there to the LORD your God, or of the judge, shall die; thus you will rid Israel of wickedness. Then all the people will hear of it and be 13 afraid, and will never again show such presumption.

* Cases which cannot be determined by the local judiciary are to be resolved by a central appeal court in Jerusalem presided over by clerical and lay judges. Deut. 19: 16–21 constitutes an example of a case being referred to this court, whose establishment may again reflect Jehoshaphat's reform (2 Chron. 19: 8–11). As drawn, this deuteronomic provision only envisages reference to the higher court by the local judiciary, and not by the accused. The reason for this is that if the accused was found guilty he would have been executed forthwith (17: 5). Whether in non-criminal cases this court replaced the right of appeal to the king or his appointed deputy (2 Sam. 15: 2–4; 1 Kings 7: 7) is nowhere stated, but should probably be assumed. Deuteronomy makes no mention of civil law cases or civil law procedure: its prime concern is the criminal law, the breach of which threatened the whole covenant relationship.

8. *blow against blow*: indicates a case in which it is uncertain whether there has been murder (a crime) or merely assault (a civil wrong for which the injured party sued for damages) (cp. Exod. 21: 18–27).

9. *the levitical priests or to the judge*: a clumsy combination probably indicating that the original legislation dealing only with appeal to a single lay judge has been subsequently amended. Cp. verse 12 and 2 Chron. 19: 11.

13. *and be afraid*: the deuteronomists adopted a deterrent theory of punishment (cp. 19: 20; 21: 21). Their hope was that the execution of the criminal would prevent others following suit, and so prevent such a widespread breach of the law that God would have to intervene and sever the covenant relationship once and for all. *

THE KING

14 When you come into the land which the LORD your God is giving you, and occupy it and settle in it, and you then say, 'Let us appoint over us a king, as all the sur-
15 rounding nations do', you shall appoint as king the man whom the LORD your God will choose. You shall appoint over you a man of your own race; you must not appoint
16 a foreigner, one who is not of your own race. He shall not acquire many horses, nor, to add to his horses, shall he cause the people to go back to Egypt, for this is what the LORD said to you, 'You shall never go back that way.'
17 He shall not acquire many wives and so be led astray; nor shall he acquire great quantities of silver and gold for
18 himself. When he has ascended the throne of the kingdom, he shall make a copy of this law in a book at the dictation
19 of the levitical priests. He shall keep it by him and read from it all his life, so that he may learn to fear the LORD his God and keep all the words of this law and observe
20 these statutes. In this way he shall not become prouder than his fellow-countrymen, nor shall he turn from these commandments to right or to left; then he and his sons will reign long over his kingdom in Israel.

* Unlike other ancient Near Eastern countries, the king in Israel was not an absolute monarch, but, alongside those whom he ruled, was subject to the covenant law (2 Sam. 12), which it was his duty to uphold. Failure to do so could only result in Israel's misfortune. While the deuteronomists recognized that the monarchy could bring divine blessing, it was the failure of her kings which secured God's ultimate judgement. This law does not condemn the institution of monarchy as such, but takes it for granted. After 400 years, life in Israel without a king was inconceivable.

14. *Let us appoint over us a king*: on the one hand the Deuteronomic Work (cp. 1 Sam. 8–15) sees the appointment of a king as an act of defiance against God, and on the other recognizes the monarchy as a divinely ordained institution. Opposition to the monarchy centred on fear that it would lead to widespread exploitation (1 Sam. 8: 11–18), and a contempt for the law (1 Kings 21). The institution of monarchy would have been well known to Israel both from the Canaanite city-states (Judg. 1: 5) and her neighbouring territories (Gen. 36: 31–9).

15. *a man of your own race*: there is no recorded instance of any attempt to place a foreigner on the throne of either the northern or southern kingdoms. Even in the last years of the monarchy, when kings were both deposed and appointed by Israel's suzerains (2 Kings 23: 34; 24: 15–17), no such attempt was made. Perhaps this clause is simply stressing that Israel's king must be a man familiar with and subject to her law, though it is possible that reference is being made to the half-Canaanite Abimelech whose story is told in Judg. 9.

16f. *He shall not acquire many horses*: clearly Solomon has served as a model for the deuteronomic polemic. He was famous for his trading in horses (1 Kings 10: 28f.), his harem (1 Kings 11: 1–8) and his wealth (1 Kings 10: 23–5, 27). Probably reference is being made to the practice of selling mercenaries for foreign armies, in this case to Egypt, in exchange for goods. For the deuteronomists, to allow members of the covenant community to return to Egypt amounted to a direct repudiation of God's plans for Israel's salvation. The source of the quotation is unknown. The inference here is that the king ought not to get involved in foreign affairs for this will inevitably lead to apostasy. 2 Kings 23: 13 records that it was Josiah who first dared to destroy the shrines which Solomon had built for his foreign wives.

18. *he shall make a copy of this law in a book*: cp. 1 Sam. 10: 25.

It is possible that on his accession, the king was handed a copy of the covenant law which he was to uphold, and which was to be regularly recited (cp. on 31: 10f.). Evidence for this is found in the *'eduth* ('warrant') given to Joash on his enthronement (2 Kings 11: 12). Cp. Ps. 132: 12 where the same word (there translated 'teaching') is used as a parallel to 'covenant'. The fact that it is the levitical priests who dictate the deuteronomic law has been seen as evidence that they were not merely its guardians but its authors (cp. p. 7).

20. *then he and his sons*: probably a reference to the Davidic covenant under which God promised that David and his successors would rule for ever (2 Sam. 7: 8–16). But most scholars understand that this covenant was itself subject to the earlier Mosaic covenant, obedience to which determined the continuance of the nation, and so of the Davidic line. ✻

THE PRIESTS

18 The levitical priests, the whole tribe of Levi, shall have no holding or patrimony in Israel; they shall eat the
2 food-offerings of the LORD, their patrimony. They shall have no patrimony among their fellow-countrymen; the LORD is their patrimony, as he promised them.

3 This shall be the customary due of the priests from those of the people who offer sacrifice, whether a bull or a sheep: the shoulders, the cheeks, and the stomach shall
4 be given to the priest. You shall give him also the first-fruits of your corn and new wine and oil, and the first
5 fleeces at the shearing of your flocks. For it was he whom the LORD your God chose from all your tribes to attend on the LORD*a* and to minister in the name of the LORD, both he and his sons for all time.

[a] on the LORD: *so Sam.; Heb. om.*

When a Levite comes from any settlement in Israel 6
where he may be lodging to the place which the LORD
will choose, if he comes in the eagerness of his heart and 7
ministers in the name of the LORD his God, like all his
fellow-Levites who attend on the LORD there, he shall 8
have an equal share of food with them, besides what he
may inherit from his father's family.

* The Levites, regarded by Deuteronomy as the only
legitimate priests, were to own no land. Instead for their
keep they were to rely on their share of the sacrificial offerings
(cp. on 10: 8). As a result of the centralization of worship
at Jerusalem, country Levites were permitted to officiate there,
and take their appropriate share in the revenues. In fact this
provision appears to have been rejected by the Jerusalem
priesthood (2 Kings 23: 9), and country Levites were forced
to depend for their sustenance on charity alone (cp. 10: 8;
12: 12, 19; 14: 27; 26: 12f.).
    4. *and the first fleeces at the shearing of your flocks*: the means
for clothing as well as food were to be supplied.
    8. *besides what he may inherit from his father's family*: an
obscure clause which apparently indicates that while a Levite
might not own land, he could inherit personal property. *

THE PROPHETS

When you come into the land which the LORD your 9
God is giving you, do not learn to imitate the abominable
customs of those other nations. Let no one be found 10
among you who makes his son or daughter pass through
fire, no augur or soothsayer or diviner or sorcerer, no 11
one who casts spells or traffics with ghosts and spirits,
and no necromancer. Those who do these things are 12
abominable to the LORD, and it is because of these

abominable practices that the LORD your God is driving
13 them out before you. You shall be whole-hearted in your
service of the LORD your God.

14 These nations whose place you are taking listen to
soothsayers and augurs, but the LORD your God does not
15 permit you to do this. The LORD your God will raise up a
prophet from among you like myself, and you shall
16 listen to him. All this follows from your request to the
LORD your God on Horeb on the day of the assembly.
There you said, 'Let us not hear again the voice of the
LORD our God, nor see this great fire again, or we shall
17 die.' Then the LORD said to me, 'What they have said is
18 right. I will raise up for them a prophet like you, one of
their own race, and I will put my words into his mouth.
19 He shall convey all my commands to them, and if
anyone does not listen to the words which he will speak
20 in my name I will require satisfaction from him. But the
prophet who presumes to utter in my name what I have
not commanded him or who speaks in the name of other
21 gods – that prophet shall die.' If you ask yourselves, 'How
shall we recognize a word that the LORD has not uttered?',
22 this is the answer: When the word spoken by the prophet
in the name of the LORD is not fulfilled and does not
come true, it is not a word spoken by the LORD. The
prophet has spoken presumptuously; do not hold him[a]
in awe.

* These provisions render illegal every type of divination
and occult practice. Although no penalty is laid down, it
may be assumed that anyone found guilty of any of these

[a] *Or* it.

practices would have been executed. The scope of the law is here being greatly extended, for while sorcery (Exod. 22: 18) and necromancy (1 Sam. 28: 3–19) had been earlier prohibited, this was not so of divination in general (Isa. 3: 2; Mic. 3: 7). The reason for this absolute deuteronomic prohibition was that the deuteronomists interpreted such acts as infringing Yahweh's essential freedom from man's control, guaranteed by the covenant relationship and reflected in both the second and third commandments of the Decalogue. Men were only to be informed of what lay in the future as and when Yahweh decided. Then this would be disclosed by his own medium, his chosen prophet, and not by diviners typical of heathen religions. But even among the prophets there could be charlatans. If in fact a prophecy did not come true, then this was clear indication that the prophet had not been inspired by God, but had spoken of his own accord.

10. *who makes his son or daughter pass through fire*: this refers to the sacrifice to Molech (cp. on 12: 31), regarded here as a type of magical practice. While Josiah did destroy the high place in the valley of Ben-hinnom where this ritual was performed (2 Kings 23: 10), its practice was revived after his death. *no augur*: the Hebrew word used here is the collective term for divining. It is then followed by a list of different kinds of activity which fell under this general head. It is not always precisely clear what is the difference between the various terms used, though the intention of the law is plain. Every form of divination whether from cultic or natural objects, as well as communion with the dead, and all forms of magic are to be utterly ruled out. In fact resort to magic had already been prohibited under the third commandment (cp. on 5: 11), and exceptionally (cp. on 5: 21) women had been brought within the scope of this prohibition by the Book of the Covenant (Exod. 22: 18). In effect the deuteronomic law interprets divination as yet another magical practice, and as such abhorrent to God.

15. *a prophet from among you like myself*: the thought here is not of one single prophet to arise at some time in the future, but of a succession of faithful prophets who will continue to fulfil Moses' role as covenant mediator (cp. on 5: 22 – 6: 3). By regarding Moses as the first prophet, the deuteronomists made it clear that the function of his successors was to confirm the truth of his law, and seek its enforcement. So on the discovery of the book of the law in the temple, Josiah immediately sought prophetic confirmation of its authenticity (2 Kings 22: 14–20), before proceeding to implement its provisions.

16. '*Let us not hear again...or we shall die*': the people's refusal at Sinai to listen to God (Exod. 20: 19–21) is reinterpreted by the deuteronomists as the reason for the inauguration of the prophetic office. Since God is not allowed to speak to the people direct, he has to have intermediaries who will proclaim the divine word.

20. *But the prophet who presumes to utter in my name*: both the prophet who speaks when he has received no message from God, and the prophet who speaks in the name of another god (cp. on 13: 1–18), are to be executed as false prophets. They have committed apostasy.

21. '*How shall we recognize a word that the LORD has not uttered?*': as the dispute between Jeremiah and Hananiah indicates (Jer. 28), false prophecy was an important contemporary issue. Here it is laid down that if the prophecy is not fulfilled, then it is clearly false, and the prophet is no longer to be feared. But the fact that now no mention is made of execution indicates the very great difficulty in deciding categorically that a certain prophecy was false, for the law imposes no time-limit on possible fulfilment. This was Jeremiah's dilemma, for although he consistently prophesied Judah's doom, it was forty years before it came about. In fact there was no adequate means of assessing false prophecy, and the hearers had to come to their own conclusion as to a prophet's credentials. It was for them to decide whether or not the prophet's message was in the true tradition. *

THE CITIES OF REFUGE

When the LORD your God exterminates the nations whose **19**
land he is giving you, and you take their place and settle
in their cities and houses, you shall set apart three cities 2
in the land which he is giving you to occupy. Divide into 3
three districts the territory which the LORD your God
is giving you as patrimony, and determine where each
city shall lie. These shall be places in which homicides
may take sanctuary.

This is the kind of homicide who may take sanctuary 4
there and save his life: the man who strikes another
without intent and with no previous enmity between
them; for instance, the man who goes into a wood with 5
his mate to fell trees, and, when cutting a tree, he relaxes
his grip on the axe,[a] the head glances off the tree, hits
the other man and kills him. The homicide may take
sanctuary in any one of these cities, and his life shall be safe.
Otherwise, when the dead man's next-of-kin who had 6
the duty of vengeance pursued him in the heat of
passion, he might overtake him if the distance were great,
and take his life, although the homicide was not
liable to the death-penalty because there had been no
previous enmity on his part. That is why I command 7
you to set apart three cities.

If the LORD your God extends your boundaries, as he 8
swore to your forefathers, and gives you the whole land
which he promised to them, because you keep all the 9
commandments that I am laying down today and carry
them out by loving the LORD your God and by conform-

[a] when...axe: *or* as he swings the axe to cut a tree.

ing to his ways for all time, then you shall add three
10 more cities of refuge to these three. Let no innocent blood
be shed in the land which the LORD your God is giving
you as your patrimony, or blood-guilt will fall on you.
11   When one man is the enemy of another, and he lies in
wait for him, attacks him and strikes him a blow so that
he dies, and then takes sanctuary in one of these cities,
12 the elders of his own city shall send to fetch him; they
shall hand him over to the next-of-kin, and he shall die.
13 You shall show him no mercy, but shall rid Israel of the
guilt of innocent blood; then all will be well with you.

* The cities of refuge replaced the earlier right of the killer
who claimed that he had acted unintentionally to seek
asylum at the local sanctuary (Exod. 21: 13). Their establishment guaranteed that his claim would be treated impartially,
for under the earlier legislation the local elders could still
remove the killer from the altar and execute him if they
considered his act premeditated (Exod. 21: 14). Now the
elders of the cities of refuge determined the killer's responsibility. These cities, originally six, were set up in the period
of the united monarchy of David and Solomon (cp. on 4: 41–3)
on a geographical rather than a tribal basis to cover all parts
of the country. Deut. 19: 1–13, however, assumes that
Transjordan is no longer in Israelite hands, and therefore
initially only orders the establishment of three cities. Probably
the establishment of a court of appeal to hear homicide cases
(cp. on 17: 8–13), though it did not abolish the right to
asylum at the cities of refuge (cp. the later Priestly legislation
in Num. 35: 9–15), ended the judicial role of their elders.
Deut. 19: 1–13 would then reflect earlier legislation.
It finds its way into the deuteronomic laws because of its
humanitarian concern that innocent blood should not be
shed.

4f. *the man who strikes another without intent*: whereas in Exod. 21: 13 the unpremeditated killing is treated as a direct act of God, in Deuteronomy it is regarded as a pure accident.

6. *the dead man's next-of-kin who had the duty of vengeance*: the Hebrew phrase *go'el haddam*, literally 'the redeemer of blood', has usually been interpreted as in the N.E.B. translation. Yet the Old Testament supplies no evidence that blood vengeance was practised in ancient Israel. On the contrary, the Book of the Covenant (Exod. 21: 12) treats murder like any other crime for which the criminal had to suffer execution (cp. Exod. 21: 15, 16, 17). And Exod. 21: 14 certainly implies that this would have been at the community's hands. Indeed Deut. 21: 1–9 indicates that whenever a murder occurred, God had to be propitiated either by the execution of the murderer or, if he was unknown, by an animal substitute. This confirms that murder was the concern of the community at large, and not merely of the individual family which had suffered loss. Indeed the dead man's blood was never considered the property of his family to be recovered by his next-of-kin, but of God, frequently described as 'the Seeker' of blood (Gen. 9: 5; 42: 22; Ps. 9: 12; Ezek. 3: 18, 20; 33: 6, 8), to whom all blood belonged (cp. on Deut. 12: 16), and to whom it would be released from the murderer's control following his execution (cp. Gen. 4: 9f.). While the term *go'el* is frequently used of a family's accredited agent charged with recovering property, the fact that in the one case of murder the phrase has been expanded would in any event seem to indicate that a different person from the family *go'el* was being described. Since the *go'el haddam* is not mentioned in the Book of the Covenant, but with one exception appears solely in connection with the legislation establishing the cities of refuge, it would seem probable that this term indicated someone with a specific function to perform in connection with those cities. Now clearly under the new procedure the elders of the local community would have needed an authorized agent to act on

their behalf at the city of refuge in order to recover a man whom they considered ought to be executed as a murderer. Deut. 19: 12 and Josh. 20: 5 indicate that this was the *go'el haddam*, who was sent by the elders of the murderer's city to recover the killer (Deut. 19: 12), and to whom the elders of the city of refuge handed him on being satisfied that he had acted intentionally (Josh. 20: 5). *in the heat of passion*: as the representative of the local community which had found the killer guilty of murder, the *go'el haddam* was entitled to execute the murderer if through his zealousness he encountered him before he reached the city of refuge. This verse illustrates the tension that existed as a result of the establishment of the cities of refuge whose elders could overrule a decision of the local elders that the murderer ought to be executed. It was, therefore, imperative that the man who claimed asylum should have every opportunity of gaining access to a city of refuge in order to put his case. Otherwise innocent blood would be shed.

9. *then you shall add three more cities of refuge*: the editors have forgotten that this legislation is part of a speech by Moses made in Transjordan. Cp. on 4: 41–3.

12. *they shall hand him over to the next-of-kin*: comparison with Josh. 20: 5 clearly indicates that *they* refers to the elders of the city of refuge. It is possible that rather than bring the murderer back to his own city for execution, the *go'el haddam* carried out the execution himself at the city of refuge, no doubt under the supervision of the elders. As the officer appointed by the local community to act on their behalf, he would have been regarded as the representative of that local community, and so death at his hands would have been entirely appropriate.

13. *You shall show him no mercy*: cp. the purging formula in 13: 5. ✷

FALSE WITNESS

Do not move your neighbour's boundary stone, fixed 14
by the men of former times in the patrimony which
you shall occupy in the land the LORD your God gives
you for your possession.

A single witness may not give evidence against a man 15
in the matter of any crime or sin which he commits:
a charge must be established on the evidence of two or
of three witnesses.

When a malicious witness comes forward to give false 16
evidence against a man, and the two disputants stand 17
before the LORD, before the priests and the judges then
in office, if, after careful examination by the judges, he 18
be proved to be a false witness giving false evidence against
his fellow, you shall treat him as he intended to treat his 19
fellow, and thus rid yourself of this wickedness. The rest 20
of the people when they hear of it will be afraid: never
again will anything as wicked as this be done among
you. You shall show no mercy: life for life, eye for eye, 21
tooth for tooth, hand for hand, foot for foot.

* Two general provisions, one forbidding the moving of
boundary stones and the other conviction on the evidence of
a single witness, are followed by an example of false witness
in a case before the central appeal court in Jerusalem.

14. *Do not move your neighbour's boundary stone*: boundary
stones acted as witnesses to the ownership of land. Hence
their very great importance. It was easy enough to move
these and so acquire additional land illegally (cp. 27: 17).
This practice is roundly condemned in the prophetic teaching
of Isaiah (5: 8) and Micah (2: 2).

15. *A single witness may not give evidence*: cp. on 17: 6f. The fact that this law appears twice in Deuteronomy and is again stressed in the later Priestly legislation (Num. 35: 30) may indicate that it is new legislation. If so, then the deuteronomic historian has made the trial of Naboth conform to this later requirement by having two witnesses (1 Kings 21: 10, 13). Frequent reference to this important rule is found in the New Testament (cp. Matt. 18: 16).

16. *When a malicious witness comes forward*: the witness is clearly seeking to secure the death of another through a miscarriage of justice. This is confirmed by verse 19, for the purging formula (cp. on 13: 5) is only used in cases involving capital punishment. The precedent is thus an elaboration of the ninth commandment (cp. on 5: 20).

17. *before the priests and the judges*: the case has proved too difficult for the local judiciary, who have referred it to the central appeal court in Jerusalem for decision (cp. on 17: 8–13).

20. *The rest of the people...will be afraid*: another reference to the deuteronomic deterrent theory of punishment (cp. on 17: 13).

21. *life for life*: one of the three examples of the *lex talionis* (the law of retaliation) in the Old Testament (cp. Exod. 21: 23ff.; Lev. 24: 17–22). While the opening talionic provision seems at first sight appropriate, there is no indication that physical injury of the type described in the other provisions was ever inflicted in ancient Israel (cp. on 25: 11f.). They thus have no relevance to the case of false witness. But since the actual death of the prospective victim did not have to occur for the false witness to be convicted and executed, even the first provision is literally inappropriate. In fact in all three places where the *lex talionis* appears it will be found on examination to be a later addition. Since the *lex talionis* has been inserted in all three major legal strands of the Old Testament, the Book of the Covenant (Exod. 21: 23ff.), Deuteronomy, and the Priestly legislation (Lev. 24: 17ff.),

its insertion is clearly late, and most probably to be attributed
to the pentateuchal editor who brought these legal strands
together to form the Torah. Deut. 19: 21 is probably
the original formula which is expanded in Exodus and
Leviticus. But the origin of the *lex talionis* is not to be sought
in Israel's legal history which shows no knowledge of punishment by literal retaliation, but among foreign legal systems,
probably Babylonian. Nor should it be assumed that post-
exilic Israel adopted literal retaliation as its method of punishment. Rather the formula is used in the Old Testament as a
shorthand expression to indicate that in every case due
compensation is to be made to the injured party, whether an
individual or, as in the case of murder (cp. on 19: 6), God
himself. The *life for life* formula has then no retaliatory basis
and the phrase *lex talionis* results from a misunderstanding of
its purpose. ✳

LAWS CONCERNING WARFARE

When you take the field against an enemy and are faced **20**
by horses and chariots and an army greater than yours,
do not be afraid of them; for the LORD your God, who
brought you out of Egypt, will be with you. When you 2
are about to join battle, the priest shall come forward
and address the army in these words: 'Hear, O Israel, 3
this day you are joining battle with the enemy; do not
lose heart, or be afraid, or give way to panic in face of
them; for the LORD your God will go with you to fight 4
your enemy for you and give you the victory.' Then the 5
officers shall address the army in these words: 'Any man
who has built a new house and has not dedicated it shall
go back to his house; or he may die in battle and another
man dedicate it. Any man who has planted a vineyard and 6
has not begun to use it shall go back home; or he may die

7 in battle and another man use it. Any man who has pledged himself to take a woman in marriage and has not taken her shall go back home; or he may die in

8 battle and another man take her.' The officers shall further address the army: 'Any man who is afraid and has lost heart shall go back home; or his comrades will

9 be discouraged as he is.' When these officers have finished addressing the army, commanders shall be appointed to lead it.

10 When you advance on a city to attack it, make an

11 offer of peace. If the city accepts the offer and opens its gates to you, then all the people in it shall be put to

12 forced labour and shall serve you. If it does not make

13 peace with you but offers battle, you shall besiege it, and the LORD your God will deliver it into your hands. You

14 shall put all its males to the sword, but you may take the women, the dependants, and the cattle for yourselves, and plunder everything else in the city. You may enjoy the use of the spoil of your enemies which the LORD your

15 God gives you. That is what you shall do to cities at a great distance, as opposed to those which belong to

16 nations near at hand. In the cities of these nations whose land the LORD your God is giving you as a patrimony,

17 you shall not leave any creature alive. You shall annihilate them – Hittites, Amorites, Canaanites, Perizzites, Hivites,

18 Jebusites – as the LORD your God commanded you, so that they may not teach you to imitate all the abominable things that they have done for their gods and so cause you to sin against the LORD your God.

19 When you are at war, and lay siege to a city for a long time in order to take it, do not destroy its trees by taking

the axe to them, for they provide you with food; you shall not cut them down. The trees of the field are not men that you should besiege them. But you may destroy 20 or cut down any trees that you know do not yield food, and use them in siege-works against the city that is at war with you, until it falls.

✻ Deuteronomy lays considerable stress on laws concerning warfare (20: 1–20; 21: 10–14; 23: 9–14; 24: 5; 25: 17–19). These laws, although now brought up to date and incorporating typically deuteronomic humanitarian ideas, none the less reflect the ancient concept of the holy war particularly associated with the period of the conquest and settlement. Since Israel's wars were understood as the wars of her God, those who fought in them were considered to be performing a religious function. In consequence in order to take part in God's holy war, the combatants had themselves to be holy, that is ritually clean (cp. 23: 14). Two important elements in the holy war were the part played by the Ark, the throne of God, in the actual battle (Num. 10: 35f.; 1 Sam. 4; 2 Sam. 11: 11), and the infliction of the ban following victory. With the establishment of the monarchy war became the business of the state, and its sacral character was lost. For the deuteronomists faced with vassaldom to heathen empires the holy war through which Israel had been brought into existence was a most useful concept, and their revival of its ideals no doubt fostered her nationalistic resurgence under Josiah.

1. *horses and chariots*: the initial military superiority of the Canaanites was due to their chariotry (Josh. 11: 4; Judg. 1: 19). Yet in spite of this Yahweh enabled Israel to defeat them and take possession of their land. In consequence, for Israel to pin her hopes on *horses and chariots* became symbolic of a total lack of faith in his saving power, and therefore inevitably would result in her defeat (cp. Isa. 31: 1–3).

for the LORD your God...will be with you: although the deuteronomists revive the idea of the holy war, no mention is made of the Ark. None the less, the transcendent God will be present with his troops, and no matter what the odds, secure their victory. In all probability the omission of the Ark is not due to deuteronomic theology (cp. on 10: 1), but indicates that its presence in battle had long been abandoned. It is last mentioned at the battle-front in David's war with Ammon (2 Sam. 11: 11).

5ff. *Then the officers shall address the army*: the term *officers* refers to royal officials entrusted with the task of recruiting an army. Cp. 1: 15; 16: 18 where the same term is used of those responsible for the administration of the courts. Those who have recently entered into a new domestic commitment, but have not had time to enjoy it, are to be excused military service. They would in any event make poor fighting material for their minds would be elsewhere. This is another example of deuteronomic humanitarianism.

8. *Any man who is afraid*: in addition to those who have a legitimate reason for not wanting to fight, those who are frightened of the coming battle are discharged. Clearly this is a prudent measure for their presence could be expected to affect the fighting morale of the whole army. However, the overall impression left by these exemptions is that in any event numbers are immaterial to the final outcome: the victory is assured by God's presence. Cp. Judg. 7 where the two themes are interwoven; those who are afraid go home from the battle, and God saves Israel by Gideon's three hundred.

10f. *make an offer of peace*: the Israelites are not to engage in unnecessary bloodshed. If the enemy city will surrender without fighting, then the lives of its inhabitants are to be spared. Such action will also prevent loss of life by the invading Israelites.

12ff. *If it does not make peace*: should the besieged city refuse to surrender, then all its males are to be put to the ban (cp. on 2: 34), but everything else can be taken and enjoyed by the Israelites. The women and children would be absorbed into the Israelite community and lose their original identity. It would be as if the foreign city had never existed.

15ff. *cities at a great distance...nations near at hand*: the foregoing legislation does not, however, apply to *nations near at hand*, that is the inhabitants of Canaan, here listed without reference to the Girgashites (cp. on 7: 1). In their case the Israelites are specifically directed to show no mercy, but put to the ban every man, woman, child and animal. This measure reflects the deuteronomic theological standpoint that failure to exterminate the Canaanites had led Israel into adopting their practices, and so to commit apostasy.

19f. *do not destroy its trees*: a practical measure again typical of Deuteronomy's humane outlook. The law ensured that after the siege there should still be a regular supply of food.   *

THE UNKNOWN MURDERER

When a dead body is found lying in open country, **21** in the land which the LORD your God is giving you to occupy, and it is not known who struck the blow, your 2 elders and your judges shall come out and measure the distance to the surrounding towns to find which is nearest. The elders of that town shall take a heifer that 3 has never been mated*a* or worn a yoke, and bring it down 4 to a ravine where there is a stream that never runs dry and the ground is never tilled or sown, and there in the ravine they shall break its neck. The priests, the sons of 5 Levi, shall then come forward; for the LORD your God has chosen them to minister to him and to bless in the name of the LORD, and their voice shall be decisive in

[a] *Prob. rdg.; Heb.* put to work.

6 all cases of dispute and assault. Then all the elders of the town nearest to the dead body shall wash their hands over the heifer whose neck has been broken in
7 the ravine. They shall solemnly declare: 'Our hands did not shed this blood, nor did we witness the bloodshed.
8 Accept expiation, O LORD, for thy people Israel whom thou hast redeemed, and do not let the guilt of innocent blood rest upon thy people Israel: let this bloodshed be
9 expiated on their behalf.' Thus, by doing what is right in the eyes of the LORD, you shall rid yourselves of the guilt of innocent blood.

* Normally where a murder occurred the murderer would be executed to propitiate God (Exod. 21: 12). But where the murderer remained undetected, the local community had to resort to an animal substitute in order to ward off any direct divine action against them. This ancient practice with its almost magical overtones shows conclusively that murder was always the concern of the community as a whole, and not simply the responsibility of the murdered man's family (cp. on 19: 6).

1f. *When a dead body is found lying in open country*: the city responsible for propitiating God has first to be identified. Proximity to the corpse determines this duty.

2. *your elders and your judges*: the mention of professional judges reflects Jehoshaphat's reform under which the administration of justice passed out of the hands of the local elders to royally appointed judges sitting in the fortified cities (cp. on 1: 9-18; 16: 18). But the duty of propitiating God in the case of an unknown murderer remained a local responsibility, for it was upon the local community that God was expected to vent his wrath.

3. *a heifer that has never been mated or worn a yoke*: although the killing of the heifer is not strictly undertaken as a sacrifice

(cp. Lev. 4: 1ff.), none the less the animal is to be of such a nature as suitable for propitiating God. Consequently it must be so young as never to have been used for any profane purpose (cp. Num. 19: 2).

4. *a ravine where there is a stream that never runs dry*: the place of execution is to be a wild and remote spot where men do not normally go, and where the blood of the heifer may sink into the uncultivated soil and remain undisturbed. For the primitive intention of the ritual is to transfer the guilt which rests on the local community, and which is thought of in materialistic terms, from the local town to this desert place. This compares with the driving out of the scapegoat into the wilderness on the Day of Atonement (cp. Lev. 16: 22).

5. *The priests, the sons of Levi*: another addition reflecting later judicial practice under which difficult homicide cases were heard at a central appeal court in Jerusalem presided over by priests (identified in Deuteronomy as Levites) and lay judges (cp. 17: 8–13). In fact the priests play no part in this ritual which remains a matter of local secular responsibility.

6f. *shall wash their hands*: by the ritual washing and declaration of innocence, the elders absolve themselves from all responsibility for the murder. They neither had committed it nor knew the murderer's identity.

8f. *Accept expiation, O LORD*: by killing another, the murderer obtained control of his blood which by right belonged to God (cp. 12: 23f.), who sought its recovery (Gen. 9: 5; 42: 22; Ps. 9: 12; Ezek. 3: 18, 20; 33: 6, 8), and to whom it would have been restored on the execution of the murderer (cp. Gen. 4: 9f.). The fact that it has been found necessary to add this prayer to the original declaration of innocence indicates the deuteronomists' recognition that such restoration could not in fact be achieved by this primitive rite. None the less it was to be considered effective in absolving Israel from guilt. ✶

139

MARRIAGE WITH A FEMALE CAPTIVE

10 When you wage war against your enemy and the
LORD your God delivers them into your hands and you
11 take some of them captive, then if you see a comely
woman among the captives and take a liking to her,
12 you may marry her. You shall bring her into your house,
13 where she shall shave her head, pare her nails, and discard
the clothes which she had when captured. Then she shall
stay in your house and mourn for her father and mother
for a full month. After that you may have intercourse
with her; you shall be her husband and she your wife.
14 But if you no longer find her pleasing, let her go free.
You must not sell her, nor treat her harshly, since you
have had your will with her.

✶ This is another provision recalling the conditions of the
holy war (cp. on ch. 20). Whereas for the deuteronomists
marriage with Canaanite women, who in any event ought to
have been put to the ban (20: 16), was utterly forbidden
(cp. 7: 3), marriage with other foreign captives was permitted.
Only later were the dangers of such marriages recognized,
and foreign marriage entirely prohibited (Ezra 9–10; Neh.
10: 30; 13: 23). The final provision dealing with the treatment
of the foreign wife on the dissolution of the marriage is again
typical of the deuteronomic humanitarian outlook.

12f. *shave her head, pare her nails, and discard the clothes*:
these actions are usually explained as mourning rites. But
they may instead symbolize the foreign woman's complete
renunciation of her country of origin. It is with new hair,
nails and clothes that she enters on her new life as a married
woman in Israel. This would explain why these practices are
regarded as quite innocuous by the deuteronomists, as
opposed to the mourning rites mentioned in 14: 1.

14. *let her go free*: since the woman has been legally the wife of a free Israelite, she cannot be treated as a chattel and disposed of for gain. She is therefore allowed the same right to leave her husband on the dissolution of the marriage as any free Israelite woman. Cp. Exod. 21: 7–11 for the protection afforded to a slave whom the master marries. *nor treat her harshly*: the Hebrew verb used here which occurs again in 24: 7 is difficult to translate. In both instances it should probably be understood as a commercial term the precise meaning of which has now been lost. *

THE RIGHT OF PRIMOGENITURE

When a man has two wives, one loved and the other 15 unloved, if they both bear him sons, and the son of the unloved wife is the elder, then, when the day comes 16 for him to divide his property among his sons, he shall not treat the son of the loved wife as his first-born in contempt of his true first-born, the son of the unloved wife. He shall recognize the rights of his first-born, the 17 son of the unloved wife, and give him a double share of all that he possesses; for he was the firstfruits of his manhood, and the right of the first-born is his.

* No whim of the father can set aside his eldest son's privileged position as the major heir to his father's estate. By virtue of his birth, the law guarantees him a set portion of the estate, which cannot be disposed of otherwise. The purpose of this right was probably as far as possible to keep family property intact in one holding.

15f. *When a man has two wives*: polygamy was permitted in Israel, though in fact only those with considerable wealth could afford the luxury of a number of wives. A harem was thus a sign of a considerable personal fortune. This law envisages only two wives. Naturally the later and presumably younger wife could easily become her husband's favourite, and, as in the case of Bathsheba (1 Kings 1:17), try to influence him in the disposition of his property. In fact the law takes this out of his hands. Only in the period after the exile were daughters given the right to inherit their father's estate where there were no sons (Num. 27:1-11).

17. *a double share of all that he possesses*: the Hebrew here means two-thirds of the estate (cp. Zech. 13:8). ✶

THE DISOBEDIENT SON

18 When a man has a son who is disobedient and out of control, and will not obey his father or his mother, or
19 pay attention when they punish him, then his father and mother shall take hold of him and bring him out to the
20 elders of the town, at the town gate. They shall say to the elders of the town, 'This son of ours is disobedient and out of control; he will not obey us, he is a wastrel
21 and a drunkard.' Then all the men of the town shall stone him to death, and you will thereby rid yourselves of this wickedness. All Israel will hear of it and be afraid.

✶ This provision is an extension of the fifth commandment to honour, that is submit to the authority of, one's parents. While its original purpose was to give children no option but to accept their parents' faith (cp. on 5:16), it was later extended to include any form of disobedience from physical assault (Exod. 21:15) to generally dissolute behaviour.

19. *bring him out to the elders of the town*: being a crime, repudiation of parental authority was a matter for the community as a whole. Parents could not take the law into their own hands, but had to prove their case before the local court. Since this is envisaged as made up of the elders, this

provision must be older than the deuteronomic reform
(cp. on 1: 9–18; 16: 18).

20. *a wastrel and a drunkard*: cp. Prov. 23: 19–21. But this
is only an example of the kind of action which would be
accepted as evidence of the son's rejection of parental authority.

21. *all the men of the town*: although Deuteronomy brought
women within the scope of the law, it specifically provided
that execution should still be carried out by men alone
(cp. 22: 21). This verse refers both to the deuteronomic
purging formula (cp. on 13: 5), and also to Deuteronomy's
deterrent theory of punishment (cp. on 17: 13). ✳

EXPOSURE OF A CORPSE

When a man is convicted of a capital offence and is 22
put to death, you shall hang him on a gibbet; but his 23
body shall not remain on the gibbet overnight; you
shall bury it on the same day, for a hanged man is
offensive*[a]* in the sight of God. You shall not pollute the
land which the LORD your God is giving you as your
patrimony.

✳ Although stoning, not hanging, was the method of execution in Israel (cp. Gen. 40: 22; 41: 13 of Egypt), none the less
the criminal's corpse might still be exhibited. Yet the purpose
for this is not entirely clear. Since in any event the whole
male population would have joined in the execution it is
unlikely to have been for deterrent purposes, nor even for
publicity as in the case of enemies killed in battle (cp. Josh.
8: 29; 10: 26f.). It may, however, be connected with an
ancient custom whereby, where the land was already thought
of as suffering divine punishment, the corpse of the man whose
action was considered to have provoked God was exposed
until the suffering stopped. Then God would be seen to have

[a] *Or* accursed.

143

been appeased. There is some indication of this practice in the account of the execution of the seven sons of Saul by the Gibeonites, when the bodies of those who were executed were exhibited until the drought ceased (2 Sam. 21: 1-14). This would explain their execution in the first days of the barley harvest, which had failed for the third time, and Rizpah's watch over their bodies until the rains came. If this is so, then the deuteronomists evidently considered such a practice not only improper, but positively harmful, preventing the very thing it was designed to achieve – the prosperity of the land. This could then represent a further deuteronomic rejection of customs associated with Canaan.

23. *offensive in the sight of God*: as the N.E.B. footnote indicates, the Hebrew phrase has been the subject of some scholarly debate. It is perhaps best understood as indicating actual repudiation of God, rather than simply referring to action which he finds invidious. *

HELP FOR DOMESTIC ANIMALS

22 When you see a fellow-countryman's ox or sheep
2 straying, do not ignore it but take it back to him. If the owner is not a near neighbour and you do not know who he is, take the animal into your own house and keep it with you until he claims it, and then give it
3 back to him. Do the same with his ass or his cloak or anything else that your fellow-countryman has lost, if you find it. You may not ignore it.
4   When you see your fellow-countryman's ass or ox lying on the road, do not ignore it; you must help him to lift it to its feet again.

* An Israelite is not to ignore a lost domestic animal, but is himself to look after it until claimed by its owner. Other-

wise some harm might befall the animal. This principle is
then extended to lost property in general, whether animate
or inanimate. Further, if a domestic animal has fallen in the
road, the owner is to be helped to get it up. No doubt these
laws were originally designed simply to protect the property
of a fellow-Israelite, but they would have also appealed to the
deuteronomists from a humanitarian standpoint for they
ensured that animals should not be allowed to suffer unnecessarily (cp. 25: 4).

1. *a fellow-countryman's*: in Exod. 23: 4f. this obligation is
specifically applied to the animals of 'your enemy', which
in the context indicates an opponent in a law suit. Even
such a situation does not absolve an Israelite from his duty
to protect his neighbour's property. ✻

TRANSVESTISM

No woman shall wear an article of man's clothing, 5
nor shall a man put on woman's dress; for those
who do these things are abominable to the LORD your
God.

✻ Neither sex is to wear clothing appropriate to the other.
This is another example of anti-Canaanite legislation and
reflects certain sexual practices in the cult. Its purpose is
then not to prohibit what is considered improper from the
secular standpoint, but rather, as the phrase *abominable to
the LORD your God* indicates, what might contaminate the
purity of the Israelite faith. ✻

MISCELLANEOUS LAWS

When you come across a bird's nest by the road, in a 6
tree or on the ground, with fledglings or eggs in it and
the mother-bird on the nest, do not take both mother and

7 young. Let the mother-bird go free, and take only the young; then you will prosper and live long.

8 When you build a new house, put a parapet along the roof, or you will bring the guilt of bloodshed on your house if anyone should fall from it.

9 You shall not sow your vineyard with a second crop, or the full yield will be forfeit, both the yield of the seed you sow and the fruit of the vineyard.

10 You shall not plough with an ox and an ass yoked together.

11 You shall not wear clothes woven with two kinds of yarn, wool and flax together.

12 You shall make twisted tassels on the four corners of your cloaks which you wrap round you.

* It is difficult to be certain of any connecting link between these apparently very varied laws. Following verse 5, a desire to prevent unnatural mixing and so keep different species distinct has been noted, as has an obviously humanitarian concern reminiscent of verses 1–4. Further verses 9–11 probably refer to ancient taboos associated with alien religious practices. Perhaps this miscellaneous collection is best explained as a series of laws indicating what action is or is not prudent. This could be the work of the scribes or the wise (cp. p. 7).

6. *do not take both mother and young*: an environmental law. By allowing the mother to live, she can lay again, and so provide further food.

8. *put a parapet along the roof*: roofs were generally flat and used for all kinds of purposes (cp. Josh. 2: 6; 1 Sam. 9: 25; Jer. 19: 13). The owner of a house who failed to take this obvious safety precaution would have no defence against a charge of constructive murder. He ought to have foreseen what were the likely consequences of his negligence.

9. *You shall not sow your vineyard with a second crop*: cp. Lev. 19: 19, where the provision applies simply to a field.

10. *an ox and an ass yoked together*: this method of ploughing is still practised in Palestine today.

11. *woven with two kinds of yarn*: cp. Lev. 19: 19.

12. *You shall make twisted tassels*: the explanation given for this provision in Num. 15: 37–40 is clearly a later rationalization. Perhaps this custom originally reflected some magical connotation, but the tassels may simply have acted as weights for the cloak. ✳

LOSS OF VIRGINITY BEFORE MARRIAGE

When a man takes a wife and after having intercourse 13 with her turns against her and brings trumped-up 14 charges against her, giving her a bad name and saying, 'I took this woman and slept with her and did not find proof of virginity in her', then the girl's father and 15 mother shall take the proof of her virginity to the elders of the town, at the town gate. The girl's father shall say 16 to the elders, 'I gave my daughter in marriage to this man, and he has turned against her. He has trumped 17 up a charge and said, "I have not found proofs of virginity in your daughter." Here are the proofs.' They shall then spread the garment before the elders of the town. The elders shall take the man and punish him: 18 they shall fine him a hundred pieces of silver because he 19 has given a bad name to a virgin of Israel, and hand them to the girl's father. She shall be his wife: he is not free to divorce her all his life long. If, on the other hand, the 20 accusation is true and no proof of the girl's virginity is found, then they shall bring her out to the door of her 21 father's house and the men of her town shall stone her to death. She has committed an outrage in Israel by playing the prostitute in her father's house: you shall rid yourselves of this wickedness.

* The situation envisaged here is not a petition for divorce which the husband could obtain without recourse to the courts (cp. on 24: 1–4), but an action by the husband to recover from his father-in-law the bride-price paid on marriage. His alleged grounds are that the wife had already lost her virginity by the time she married him. Should he fail in his action, the law prescribes the payment of punitive damages to his father-in-law, and prevents him from ever divorcing his wife: if he succeeds, his wife is treated as an adulteress, and executed forthwith. Though it is not stated, the husband would, of course, have received back the bride-price. In fact verses 20–1, which include the characteristic deuteronomic purging formula (cp. on 13: 5), are a later addition to a pre-deuteronomic piece of legislation as the reference to the elders, and not professional judges, makes plain (cp. on 1: 9–18; 16: 18). These later verses were necessitated by the fact that under the deuteronomic reform for the first time the adulteress was made criminally liable with her lover (cp. on 22: 22), and in consequence she too had to be executed. Thus 22: 20f. unequivocally asserts that 'adulteress' includes a woman who on marriage was found to have lost her virginity, no matter whether this occurred before or after betrothal. Before the deuteronomic reform the husband would simply have recovered the bride-price and divorced his wife.

15. *the proof of her virginity*: in order to defeat the husband's claim, the parents present the court with the matrimonial bed-covering stained with their daughter's blood. This primitive means is taken as decisive evidence as to whether or not the girl had had previous sexual intercourse.

18. *and punish him*: the Hebrew has usually been understood

as indicating the infliction of corporal punishment (cp. 21: 18). If this is so, then this is the only example of an actual situation in which beating was specifically prescribed, though its occurrence was clearly not infrequent (cp. on 25: 1–3).

19. *they shall fine him a hundred pieces of silver*: the translation *fine* is technically incorrect for fines are a penalty of the criminal law imposed by the state to whom they are payable. Here the money is paid to the father-in-law by way of damages for slander. He has been falsely accused of taking the bride-price for a daughter who was not in fact marriageable. The damages are excessively severe, being double those laid down for seduction of an unbetrothed virgin (cp. 22: 29). Since these (fifty pieces of silver) seem to represent an average bride-price, the husband probably has to pay his father-in-law twice the amount which he himself hoped to recover. While the general principle of Israelite civil law was that the damages should restore the injured to the position he was in before his loss (Exod. 21: 36), as early as the Book of the Covenant punitive damages were prescribed as a deterrent measure (Exod. 22: 1–4). A further deterrent in this case is the absolute ban on the exercise of the husband's normally unfettered right to divorce his wife at will for whatever reason he chose.

21. *to the door of her father's house*: if the parents cannot prove their daughter's virginity at the time of her marriage, she is treated like an adulteress and executed by the normal method of stoning. But exceptionally this takes place not outside the city, but outside her father's house as a sign of community displeasure over his fraud, whether or not he was aware of the facts. He should have proved a better guardian of his property. By accepting the bride-price, he had in effect given a warranty on what would be his daughter's condition on marriage, and this had proved false. *an outrage in Israel*: the Hebrew word *nebalah* indicates conduct resulting in crass disorder. It is particularly used of sexual practices which Israel with her high standard of sexual morality regarded as particularly abhorrent (cp. Gen. 34: 7). ✳

ADULTERY

22 When a man is discovered lying with a married woman, they shall both die, the woman as well as the man who lay with her: you shall rid Israel of this wickedness.

* In ancient Israel, adultery was defined as sexual intercourse with a married or betrothed woman. But it would seem that before the deuteronomic reform only the man was held criminally liable and executed on conviction. As Hos. 2: 2 (N.E.B. footnote) and Jer. 3: 8 confirm, the husband's remedy for his wife's adultery was to divorce her. Indeed it seems from Hos. 2: 3 that a custom known elsewhere was adopted whereby the wife was stripped naked and driven from the home as if she were a common prostitute. But in accordance with the general deuteronomic practice of making women equally liable with men (cp. on 5: 21), the deuteronomists made the adulteress jointly liable with her lover, and so ordered her execution as well.

When a man is discovered: in general a prosecution could only have been successfully brought if there were actual eyewitnesses. Otherwise, if the husband suspected that his wife had committed adultery but had no actual evidence to enable him to bring a prosecution, he could take her to the sanctuary where a ritual was performed which would confirm or allay his suspicions (cp. Num. 5: 11–31). *you shall rid Israel of this wickedness*: for this deuteronomic purging formula, cp. 13: 5. *

SEXUAL INTERCOURSE WITH A BETROTHED AND UNBETROTHED GIRL

23 When a virgin is pledged in marriage to a man and another man comes upon her in the town and lies with
24 her, you shall bring both of them out to the gate of that

town and stone them to death; the girl because, although
in the town, she did not cry for help, and the man because
he dishonoured another man's wife: you shall rid yourselves of this wickedness. If the man comes upon such a 25
girl in the country and rapes her, then the man alone
shall die because he lay with her. You shall do nothing 26
to the girl, she has done nothing worthy of death: this
deed is like that of a man who attacks another and
murders him, for the man came upon her in the country 27
and, though the girl cried for help, there was no one to
rescue her.

When a man comes upon a virgin who is not pledged 28
in marriage and forces her to lie with him, and they are
discovered, then the man who lies with her shall give the 29
girl's father fifty pieces of silver, and she shall be his wife
because he has dishonoured her. He is not free to divorce
her all his life long.

* By making the woman equally liable with the man for
the crime of adultery, the new deuteronomic legislation
immediately raised two issues: (i) if the woman was not a
virgin on marriage, was she to be executed as an adulteress?;
(ii) if the woman was forced, was she still to be regarded as
criminally liable? The first problem is dealt with by 22: 20-1,
the second by 22: 23-7. This provides (at any rate in the case
of a betrothed girl) that if the sexual act took place in the
town, the girl is liable since, by failing to summon help, she
is deemed to have consented: but if it took place in the country,
she is to be acquitted, as even if she had called for aid, it
could not be assumed that anyone would have heard her.
But where the girl was neither married nor betrothed, sexual
intercourse with her does not constitute the crime of adultery
but the civil wrong of seduction. To stress this, 22: 28-9

reiterates the earlier law of the Book of the Covenant (Exod. 22: 16f.) that the father must be compensated with damages for the injury suffered to his property.

23. *When a virgin is pledged in marriage*: the contract of marriage was established at the time of the betrothal when the bride-price was paid to the girl's father. A considerable interval might elapse before the marriage itself was consummated.

24. *you shall rid yourselves of this wickedness*: cp. on 13: 5.

25. *such a girl*: though this law only refers to the betrothed girl, it seems probable that it was also intended to cover the married woman.

29. *the girl's father*: even though Deuteronomy brought women within the scope of the law, they still remained entirely subject to the authority of men, first of their father, and then of their husband, to whom damages had to be paid. *fifty pieces of silver*: in contrast to Exod. 22: 16f., damages are now fixed. *fifty pieces of silver* was probably considered an average bride-price. Thus in accordance with the general principles of Israelite civil law, the father was restored to the position he would have been in had he made a marriage for his daughter in the normal manner. In addition the seducer must marry the girl, and is prevented from divorcing her. Clearly these provisions served as a deterrent, particularly in the case of a poor girl. However, Exod. 22: 16f. reserved the right of the father to withhold his daughter from her seducer. Apparently this is now abandoned, perhaps to ensure that the father would not be tempted at a later date to try and pass off his daughter as a virgin (cp. 22: 13–21). ✳

AN UNNATURAL RELATIONSHIP

30[a] A man shall not take his father's wife: he shall not bring shame on his father.

[a] *23: 1 in Heb.*

* By prohibiting marriage or sexual relations with one's father's wife as an unnatural sexual offence (cp. 27: 20–3), the deuteronomists brought to an end the ancient right of the heir to inherit his father's wives and concubines (cp. 2 Sam. 16: 22). Since a son by a first marriage would often be of the same age as one of his father's later wives, sexual relations between them could be expected. Though no penalty is prescribed, the position of this law at the conclusion of detailed legislation on the crime of adultery would seem to indicate that it is itself to be understood as an extension of this crime. This is confirmed by the later Priestly legislation, which, drawing on ancient customary family law forbidding casual sexual relations outside marriage with women normally found in one's home (Lev. 18: 6–18), built on this deuteronomic extension, and, in reaction to what was thought of as the immorality of Canaan, reinterpreted the crime of adultery to include all unnatural sexual unions. So in Lev. 18: 6–18; 20: 10–21 there is worked out a fully comprehensive code of all sexual crimes for the post-exilic period. Thus the word used in the Septuagint for fornication or adultery includes even marriage within the prohibited degrees. *

EXCLUSION FROM THE CULTIC ASSEMBLY

No man whose testicles have been crushed or whose **23** organ has been severed shall become a member of the assembly of the LORD.

No descendant of an irregular union, even down to the 2 tenth generation, shall become a member of the assembly of the LORD.

No Ammonite or Moabite, even down to the tenth 3 generation, shall become a member of the assembly of the LORD. They shall never become members of the assembly of the LORD, because they did not meet you 4

with food and water on your way out of Egypt, and
because they hired Balaam son of Beor from Pethor in
5 Aram-naharaim*a* to revile you. The LORD your God
refused to listen to Balaam and turned his denunciation
into a blessing, because the LORD your God loved you.
6 You shall never seek their welfare or their good all your
life long.
7 You shall not regard an Edomite as an abomination,
for he is your own kin; nor an Egyptian, for you were
8 aliens in his land. The third generation of children born
to them may become members of the assembly of the
LORD.

✻ Certain classes of persons are to be totally disqualified from
playing any part in the Israelite cult.

1. *whose testicles have been crushed*: in post-exilic Israel,
this prohibition was revoked, and eunuchs were specifically
brought within the cult (Isa. 56: 3–5). Cp. Lev. 21: 16–23
where any physical defect rules out membership of the
priesthood.

2. *No descendant of an irregular union*: the Hebrew word
used here probably indicates the child of an incestuous
relationship (cp. 22: 30). *even down to the tenth generation*:
that is, in effect, for ever.

3ff. *No Ammonite or Moabite*: as ancient enemies, neither
Ammonites nor Moabites living in Israel are ever to be allowed
any part in the cult (cp. Gen. 19: 30–8). No mention of the
historical explanation for this prohibition is found in 2: 9,
19. Reliance on this law led to Nehemiah's policy of
rigorous exclusivism (Neh. 13). It is probably no accident
that in reaction to this policy a Moabitess, Ruth, was made
the heroine of a parable actively encouraging mission to
non-Jews. For the story of Balaam see Num. 22–4.

[a] *That is* Aram of Two Rivers.

7f. *You shall not regard an Edomite as an abomination...nor an Egyptian*: in contrast to the Ammonites and Moabites, after two generations, Edomites and Egyptians living in Israel are no longer to be regarded as ritually unclean, and therefore repugnant to God, but can instead take their place in the Israelite cult. Why they are given such preferential treatment by the deuteronomists is unclear. In the case of Edom reference is apparently being made to the tradition that Esau was the father of the Edomites (Gen. 36: 1–8). Besides the settlement of Jacob and his sons in Goshen (Gen. 47), Abraham had also dwelt as a foreigner in Egypt (Gen. 12: 10–20). ✳

PURITY OF THE CAMP

When you are encamped against an enemy, you shall 9 be careful to avoid any foulness. When one of your 10 number is unclean because of an emission of seed at night, he must go outside the camp; he may not come within it. Towards evening he shall wash himself in water, and at 11 sunset he may come back into the camp. You shall have a 12 sign outside the camp showing where you can withdraw. With your equipment you will have a trowel,[a] and when 13 you squat outside, you shall scrape a hole with it and then turn and cover your excrement. For the LORD your 14 God goes about in your camp, to keep you safe and to hand over your enemies as you advance, and your camp must be kept holy for fear that he should see something indecent and go with you no further.

✳ Under the concept of the holy war upon which the deuteronomists laid considerable stress (cp. 20: 1–18), Israel's God was thought of as actually present with his forces.

[a] *Lit.* peg.

Consequently her army camps had to be in a ritually clean state to allow God to remain there. Thus men who in the night had emitted semen were to be temporarily excluded from the camp (cp. Lev. 15: 1–18), and all excrement was to be carefully buried outside it. There must be nothing found in the camp which could be considered offensive to God. ✻

THE RUNAWAY SLAVE

15 You shall not surrender to his master a slave who has
16 taken refuge with you. Let him stay with you anywhere he chooses in any one of your settlements, wherever suits him best; you shall not force him.

✻ In contrast to 15: 12, no mention is made of the slave's nationality. But in all probability this law related to foreign slaves for whom extradition was sought. An example of such extradition may be detected in 1 Kings 2: 39f. Special provision was made for this both in ancient Near Eastern law codes, and also in state treaties. Now on humanitarian grounds, Deuteronomy authorizes the rejection of an extradition request. The runaway slave is to be allowed to remain *in any one of your settlements*, that is in Israel. ✻

CULTIC PROSTITUTION

17 No Israelite woman shall become a temple-prostitute, and no Israelite man shall prostitute himself in this way.
18   You shall not allow a common prostitute's fee, or the pay of a male prostitute, to be brought into the house of the LORD your God in fulfilment of any vow, for both of them are abominable to the LORD your God.

✻ Prostitution was widely practised throughout the ancient Near East as part of the fertility cult to ensure the prosperity of the land, and prostitutes of both sexes would be found at the sanctuaries. From time to time it even found a place in Israelite worship (cp. 1 Kings 14: 24; Hos. 4: 14) until as part of the deuteronomic anti-Canaanite legislation it was specifically rendered illegal, and direct action taken against the prostitutes (2 Kings 23: 7). Secular prostitution was never prohibited, though those who resorted to prostitutes were frowned upon (Prov. 23: 27).

18. *a common prostitute's fee*: though the Hebrew word used here could indicate a secular as opposed to a cultic prostitute, the fact that a cultic term is used for the *male prostitute* probably shows that in both cases reference is being made to sanctuary officials. The *male prostitute* is described in Hebrew as 'a dog'. But this usage, which is not restricted to Israel, is not to be understood in a derogatory sense, but indicates quite generally a relationship of humble service by the prostitute on behalf of his god. ✲

USURY

You shall not charge interest on anything you lend to a 19 fellow-countryman, money or food or anything else on which interest can be charged. You may charge 20 interest on a loan to a foreigner but not on a loan to a fellow-countryman, for then the LORD your God will bless you in all you undertake in the land which you are entering to occupy.

✲ An Israelite with sufficient for his own needs had a duty to help his fellow-countrymen (cp. on 15: 8). But he was not to charge interest on any loan made by him. Indeed the very high interest rates then prevailing would have made such loans prohibitive. This provision probably reiterates Exod. 22: 25 which lays down that interest is not to be exacted in advance. Since interest was normally paid in this way by deduction from the amount of the loan, Exod. 22: 25 apparently forbids the charging of any interest at all (cp. Lev. 25: 35–7). But this humanitarian concern for fellow-Israelites does not extend to foreigners who may quite properly be charged with interest. ✶

VOWS

21 When you make a vow to the LORD your God, do not put off its fulfilment; otherwise the LORD your God will require satisfaction of you and you will be guilty of
22 sin. If you choose not to make a vow, you will not be
23 guilty of sin; but if you voluntarily make a vow to the LORD your God, mind what you say and do what you have promised.

✶ Once a vow has been made, it must be promptly undertaken. Like an oath (cp. Num. 30: 2) it has a force of its own, and there can be no drawing back. But there is no obligation to make such a vow: it is undertaken quite voluntarily, and no stigma attaches to the man who fails to make one.

21. *guilty of sin*: this phrase indicates that this provision is not a law to be enforced by sanctions, but rather a piece of good advice typical of the wise or the scribes (cp. p. 7). Indeed very similar advice is given in Eccles. 5: 4–6. ✶

PROVISION FOR THE TRAVELLER

24 When you go into another man's vineyard, you may eat as many grapes as you wish to satisfy your hunger, but you may not put any into your basket.
25 When you go into another man's standing corn, you may pluck ears to rub in your hands, but you may not put a sickle to his standing corn.

✻ An Israelite passing through another's property is given the right to satisfy his hunger from the fruit and cereal growing there. But he is forbidden to take any produce away with him. These provisions are a further example of the humane outlook of the deuteronomists, being aimed at providing sustenance for travellers (cp. Matt. 12: 1). But they also protected the farmer's property from robbery. ✻

REMARRIAGE WITH A FORMER WIFE

When a man has married a wife, but she does not win **24** his favour because he finds something shameful in her, and he writes her a note of divorce, gives it to her and dismisses her; and suppose after leaving his house she 2 goes off to become the wife of another man, and this next 3 husband turns against her and writes her a note of divorce which he gives her and dismisses her, or dies after making her his wife – then in that case her first husband who dis- 4 missed her is not free to take her back to be his wife again after she has become for him unclean. This is abominable to the LORD; you must not bring sin upon the land which the LORD your God is giving you as your patrimony.

✻ This law prohibits a husband from remarrying his divorced wife when she becomes free from her second husband either through death or divorce (cp. Jer. 3: 1). The ritual terminology indicates that in contrast to whatever may have been pagan practice, the deuteronomists considered such action totally taboo.

1. *something shameful in her*: this Hebrew expression, literally 'the nakedness of a thing', does not refer to the wife's adultery for which she would in any event have been executed following the deuteronomic extension of the law (cp. on 22: 22). Rather it indicates anything else which the husband

found distasteful in his wife, and which might lead him to divorce her. That the phrase has no moral connotation is confirmed from 23 : 14 where it is used of what is unbecoming, but not of what is immoral. *a note of divorce*: while a wife could never divorce her husband, the latter had an absolute right to divorce his wife at any time and for any reason. Probably childlessness was the chief ground for divorce. Being part of family law (cp. 15: 16f.), there was no recourse to the courts, the husband acting entirely unilaterally. After pronouncing the recognized divorce formula: 'She is not my wife and I am not her husband' (cp. Hos. 2: 2, N.E.B. footnote), all the husband had to do to put the divorce into effect was to dismiss his wife from the matrimonial home. Henceforth she was known as *gerushah*, 'the expelled'. But later it became customary to supply the wife with a bill of divorce, literally called 'deed of cutting', in order that she should have proof that her marriage had been terminated. Clearly this was important where to have sexual intercourse with a married woman could lead to a prosecution on a capital charge of adultery. But even after the introduction of the giving of bills of divorce, a practice which is taken for granted in this deuteronomic enactment, divorce itself continued to remain an entirely domestic affair, and no resort was made to the courts. ✲

FURTHER EXEMPTION FROM MILITARY SERVICE

5 When a man is newly married, he shall not be liable for military service or any other public duty. He shall remain at home exempt from service for one year and enjoy the wife he has taken.

✲ The newly married man is to be allowed one year free from any claims which the state might make upon him, whether military or civic. For further examples of those excused military service, cp. 20: 5–9. ✲

MILLSTONES AS A PLEDGE

No man shall take millstones, or even the upper one 6
alone, in pledge; that would be taking a life in pledge.

* An absolute prohibition is placed on taking millstones,
or even one stone, in pledge. Since they were used in the
daily process of grinding and baking, to deprive a household
of them meant in effect depriving it of one of the necessities
of life. This is another example of Deuteronomy's humanitarian outlook, for naturally the law only materially affected
the poor. *

MAN-THEFT

When a man is found to have kidnapped a fellow- 7
countryman, an Israelite, and to have treated him harshly
and sold him, he shall die: you shall rid yourselves of
this wickedness.

* The man-thief, called in Hebrew 'the stealer of life',
is to be executed as a criminal in accordance with the eighth
commandment (cp. on 5: 19). His aim would have been to
sell the Israelite into foreign slavery (cp. Gen. 37). Even in
deuteronomic times this commandment retained its importance with Israel continually subject to foreign invasion.
    treated him harshly: this Hebrew phrase is probably best
understood as a commercial term, the precise meaning of
which has now been lost (cp. on 21: 14). In Exod. 21: 16
the law is extended to include the possibility that the stolen
man might still be found in the thief's possession. *you shall
rid yourselves of this wickedness*: for this deuteronomic purging
formula, cp. 13: 5. *

LEPROSY

8 Be careful how you act in all cases of malignant skin-disease; be careful to observe all that the levitical priests tell you; I gave them my commands which you must
9 obey. Remember what the LORD your God did to Miriam, on your way out of Egypt.

* An original injunction to be careful to avoid leprosy has, as the plural form of address indicates, been changed by the deuteronomic historian into a caution to act in accordance with priestly regulations (cp. Lev. 13f.). It seems that what is feared is an outbreak of plague.

9. *Remember what the LORD your God did to Miriam*: cp. Num. 12: 9–15. Both the breaking out of leprosy and its cure are entirely in the control of God whose accredited agents, the priests, are to be responsible for its treatment. The term 'leprosy' does not describe the disease known especially in the Middle Ages, but some as yet not adequately defined skin-complaint. *

PLEDGES

10 When you make a loan to another man, do not enter
11 his house to take a pledge from him. Wait outside, and the man whose creditor you are shall bring the pledge
12 out to you. If he is a poor man, you shall not sleep in the
13 cloak he has pledged. Give it back to him at sunset so that he may sleep in it and bless you; then it will be counted to your credit in the sight of the LORD your God.

* Two further laws on loans supported by a pledge again stress the basic humanitarianism of the deuteronomists (cp. 24: 6). Those in need are neither to be abused nor unnecessarily deprived by those more fortunate than themselves.

10f. *do not enter his house*: under customary law, it is probable that uninvited entry into another's house on any pretext was absolutely forbidden. Evidence of this custom is found in other ancient Near Eastern law codes. Within his house, the owner was entitled to absolute privacy, which was never to be abused, no matter what the ground.

12f. *you shall not sleep in the cloak he has pledged*: a man's cloak in which he would wrap himself at night was his most necessary possession: he would only pledge it when he had nothing else left to offer. But a man in such a condition is to be treated with charity, which will itself be rewarded for, in so acting, the more fortunate Israelite mirrors God's own compassionate nature (cp. Exod. 22: 26f.). The Israelites' attitude to their neighbours was a direct result of their understanding of the character of their God. ✶

DAILY WAGES

You shall not keep back the wages of a man*[a]* who is 14 poor and needy, whether a fellow-countryman or an alien living in your country in one of your settlements. Pay him his wages on the same day before sunset, for 15 he is poor and his heart is set on them: he may appeal to the LORD against you, and you will be guilty of sin.

✶ Those labourers working on a day-to-day basis for their keep are not to have their wages withheld (cp. Lev. 19: 13). Otherwise they would go hungry. This provision applies to both the full Israelite and also the resident alien (cp. on 1: 16). Both are entitled to the same humanitarian concern. Failure to observe this law can only result in condemnation by Israel's compassionate God (cp. Exod. 22: 26f.). ✶

[a] keep...man: *so Scroll; Heb.* oppress a hired man.

CRIMINAL RESPONSIBILITY

16 Fathers shall not be put to death for their children, nor children for their fathers; a man shall be put to death only for his own sin.

✻ Only the actual individual guilty of committing the crime is to suffer execution. In general this had long been the practice of Israelite criminal law. But where the criminal action amounted to a total repudiation of Israel's God, then in this one case the ban (cp. on 2: 34) was enforced involving the death of the culprit's family also. Thus exceptionally the Book of the Covenant prescribes this drastic action in the case of a man who sacrifices to other gods (Exod. 22: 20), and it was also exacted on Naboth and his sons (2 Kings 9: 26). Further 2 Kings 14: 6, which anachronistically refers to this deuteronomic provision, indicates that normally regicides received similar treatment. As a result of the Davidic covenant (2 Sam. 7), by which the king was thought of as God's adopted son (Ps. 2: 7), to murder the king could only be interpreted as a clear renunciation of the God who had chosen him. Now by the deuteronomic revision, the general position of Israel's criminal law was to be extended to include even cases of blatant apostasy (cp. 13: 2–11; 17: 2–7). But in spite of this measure governing human punishment, the deuteronomists did not alter their understanding of the nature of divine punishment (5: 9), which could fall quite indiscriminately on all or any of the community. It was to avoid such punishment that the community sought to appease God by the execution of the criminal. No one else would do (cp. 21: 1–9). Only in the period after the exile, when Israel no longer understood her relationship to her God in terms of the suzerainty treaties (cp. pp. 4f.), were the principles of human punishment applied to the divine sphere as well. While Jeremiah prophesied of a time when it would no longer be

said that 'The fathers have eaten sour grapes and the
children's teeth are set on edge' (Jer. 31: 29f.), it was Ezekiel
who saw its fulfilment (Ezek. 18). *

LAWS OF CHARITY

You shall not deprive aliens and[a] orphans of justice 17
nor take a widow's cloak in pledge. Remember that you 18
were slaves in Egypt and the LORD your God redeemed
you from there; that is why I command you to do this.

When you reap the harvest in your field and forget a 19
swathe, do not go back to pick it up; it shall be left for
the alien, the orphan, and the widow, in order that the
LORD your God may bless you in all that you undertake.

When you beat your olive-trees, do not strip them 20
afterwards; what is left shall be for the alien, the orphan,
and the widow.

When you gather the grapes from your vineyard, do 21
not glean afterwards; what is left shall be for the alien,
the orphan, and the widow. Remember that you were 22
slaves in Egypt; that is why I command you to do this.

* Having no one to protect them, widows, orphans and
aliens had to rely on the charity of the community for legal
protection and economic survival. As the weakest members
of society, they were of special concern to God (cp. on
10: 18) whose own compassionate nature was to be reflected
in Israel's attitude to the underprivileged members in her
society. The eighth-century prophets had continually to
remind Israel of their rights (e.g. Amos 2: 6–8).

17. *You shall not deprive aliens and orphans of justice*: although
neither aliens (cp. on 1: 16) nor orphans had legal status,

[a] *So Sept.; Heb. om.*

none the less their rights were to be protected by the community. *nor take a widow's cloak in pledge*: here an absolute prohibition is placed on taking the cloak (cp. 24: 12f.).

18. *you were slaves in Egypt*: Israel is to show the same generosity to the deprived in her community as God had shown to her (cp. 5: 15; 15: 15).

19ff. *do not go back to pick it up*: once there may have been a custom of leaving behind a sheaf for the god of the field: but all trace of this practice has now lapsed. Instead what is overlooked in the harvest is to be left for those in need. ✶

CORPORAL PUNISHMENT

25 When two men go to law and present themselves for judgement, the judges shall try the case; they shall acquit 2 the innocent and condemn the guilty. If the guilty man is sentenced to be flogged, the judge shall cause him to lie down and be beaten in his presence; the number of strokes shall correspond to the gravity of the offence. 3 They may give him forty strokes, but not more; otherwise, if they go further and exceed this number, your fellow-countryman will have been publicly degraded.

✶ Even a man who has been judged worthy of a flogging is entitled to humanitarian treatment. A limit is set on the number of strokes which can be given in order that he should not be abused. As this precedent indicates, the infliction of corporal punishment was not uncommon. Most probably it was ordered for any activity which had caused or was likely to cause a breach of the peace (cp. on Deut. 22: 18). It was certainly not the normal penalty of the criminal law, breach of which automatically resulted in the execution of the criminal. But the criminal law only dealt with a limited number of offences and contained no provisions for the maintenance of law and order in the community. Evidently discretionary powers were given to the judges to order a flogging when they deemed it necessary. Thus Paul tells the Corinthians that he had received 'the thirty-nine strokes' five times (2 Cor. 11: 24). Alternatively a man likely to cause a breach of the peace could be detained in the stocks (2 Chron. 16: 10). Both punishments acted as strong deterrents to disorderly conduct.

1ff. *the judges shall try the case*: reflects the change in the administration of justice from the elders to professional judges (cp. on 1: 9–18; 16: 18). ✳

THE WORKING OX

You shall not muzzle an ox while it is treading out the 4 corn.

✳ This law is yet a further example of deuteronomic humanitarianism. An ox engaged in threshing is not to be prevented from feeding itself from the grain its hooves have beaten out. This provision was used by Paul to justify the maxim that a labourer is worthy of his hire (1 Cor. 9: 9). ✳

LEVIRATE MARRIAGE

When brothers live together and one of them dies 5 without leaving a son, his widow shall not marry outside the family. Her husband's brother shall have intercourse with her; he shall take her in marriage and do his duty by her as her husband's brother. The first son she bears shall 6 perpetuate the dead brother's name so that it may not be blotted out from Israel. But if the man is unwilling to 7 take his brother's wife, she shall go to the elders at the town gate and say, 'My husband's brother refuses to

perpetuate his brother's name in Israel; he will not do
8 his duty by me.' At this the elders of the town shall
summon him and reason with him. If he still stands his
9 ground and says, 'I will not take her', his brother's
widow shall go up to him in the presence of the elders;
she shall pull his sandal off his foot and spit in his face
and declare: 'Thus we requite the man who will not
10 build up his brother's family.' His family shall be known
in Israel as the House of the Unsandalled Man.

* This provision deals with refusal to undertake the ancient
custom of levirate marriage (from Latin, *levir* = husband's
brother). Under this, the brother of a man who died without
a son to inherit his name and property had a duty to marry
the widow, and to provide his dead brother with an heir.
Its purpose was both to perpetuate the family name and keep
the family property together. But since this custom was part
of family law, strictly speaking, like making slavery permanent (cp. 15: 16f.) or divorce (cp. 24: 1), it was of no concern
to the courts. Though the widow could have her brother-in-
law brought into court, and could publicly humiliate him
there, the court itself could take no further action either to
enforce the marriage or punish the unwilling brother-in-law.
It is probable that even by the time of Deuteronomy the
custom was unpopular, and it was apparently abolished by the
Holiness Code (Lev. 20: 21). This in turn led the later Priestly
legislation to allow daughters to inherit property, and so
continue the name of their deceased and sonless father (Num.
27: 1–11).

5. *When brothers live together*: until a younger brother
married and had children of his own, he would have remained
in his father's or elder brother's house. Originally the duty of
levirate marriage extended beyond brothers to include the
father (Gen. 38), but here it seems to be restricted to brothers

alone. The position in Ruth, where the duty is apparently again extended beyond brothers, is, however, very confused. Indeed it is probable that the author has set his story against a legal background which he did not entirely understand. The Sadducees used an example of levirate marriage to ridicule the idea of resurrection (Matt. 22: 24–30).

6. *perpetuate the dead brother's name*: the Israelites believed that after death their personalities were perpetuated in the lives of their sons who bore their name, while they themselves went to the shadowy half-life of Sheol. To have no son, and therefore have one's name blotted out, was the ultimate misfortune. It was as if one had never existed.

7. *she shall go to the elders*: since this provision takes no account of the change in the administration of justice from the elders to professional judges (cp. 1: 9–18; 16: 18), it indicates that the widow's right to have the brother-in-law brought to court is older than the deuteronomic reform.

9. *she shall pull his sandal off his foot*: a sandal was used symbolically to indicate transfer of rights over property (cp. Amos 2: 6). Hence the widow's action indicates that the brother-in-law has surrendered his right to marry her and honour his dead brother by giving him a son. It is a deliberately ironical act, for by his failure, the brother-in-law (assuming the father to be dead) naturally inherits the family property. Instead of acquiring property by having a sandal handed to him to mark the conveyance, as was the general custom (Ruth 4: 7), he acquires it through having a sandal taken from him. ✻

INDECENT ASSAULT

When two men are fighting and the wife of one of 11 them comes near to drag her husband clear of his opponent, if she puts out her hand and catches hold of the man's genitals, you shall cut off her hand and show her no 12 mercy.

✻ A woman who seizes a man's genitals, even in defence of her husband, is to have her hand cut off. In contrast to other ancient Near Eastern law, this is the only example in Israelite law of mutilation being ordered. Normally assault is treated as a civil offence for which damages are paid to the injured party (Exod. 21: 18ff.). But here the assault is treated as a crime, for which the community inflicts a specific penalty. But the mutilation is not ordered simply for the woman's immodesty, but rather because by her action she may have damaged the man's testicles, and thereby affected his ability to have children. He could consequently be left in the position of being unable to father a son, and therefore of having his name blotted out (cp. on Deut. 25: 6). This accounts for the position of this law after the provision on levirate marriage. The Assyrian laws contain a similar provision which could have become known to the deuteronomists. ✻

UNEQUAL WEIGHTS

13 You shall not have unequal weights in your bag, one
14 heavy, the other light. You shall not have unequal measures[a] in your house, one large, the other small.
15 You shall have true and correct weights and true and correct measures, so that you may live long in the land
16 which the LORD your God is giving you. All who commit these offences, all who deal dishonestly, are abominable to the LORD.

✻ In commercial dealings the same weights are to be used in both purchasing and selling. Dishonest traders would resort to a light weight when selling and heavy weight when buying (cp. Amos 8: 5).

14. *You shall not have unequal measures*: in Hebrew '*ephah*

[a] *Heb*. ephah.

and *ephah'* (cp. N.E.B. footnote). The *ephah* was a dry measure for grain whose exact size cannot now be determined with any certainty. ✴

THE AMALEKITES

Remember what the Amalekites did to you on your 17 way out of Egypt, how they met you on the road when 18 you were faint and weary and cut off your rear, which was lagging behind exhausted: they showed no fear of God. When the LORD your God gives you peace from 19 your enemies on every side, in the land which he is giving you to occupy as your patrimony, you shall not fail to blot out the memory of the Amalekites from under heaven.

✴ The Amalekites were a tough Bedouin tribe living in the Sinai desert. Tradition asserts that in their journey to Canaan, the Israelites inflicted a severe defeat on the Amalekites which led to perpetual hostility between the two peoples (Exod. 17: 8–13). In the time of David, Amalekite raids could cause considerable suffering to those living in the south of Judah (1 Sam. 30). But after that time no encounter with the Amalekites is mentioned in Israel's history, nor is the incident referred to here, and alluded to in 1 Sam. 15: 2, known from elsewhere. The deuteronomists have apparently used an ancient tradition of a cowardly act by the Amalekites as a reminder that in the promised land pagan enemies of Israel's God are to be utterly exterminated (cp. 20: 15–18). ✴

THE OFFERING OF FIRSTFRUITS

When you come into the land which the LORD your God **26** is giving you to occupy as your patrimony and settle in

2 it, you shall take the firstfruits of all the produce of the
soil, which you gather in from the land which the LORD
your God is giving you, and put them in a basket.
Then you shall go to the place which the LORD your
3 God will choose as a dwelling for his Name and come to
the priest, whoever he shall be in those days. You shall
say to him, 'I declare this day to the LORD your God
that I have entered the land which the LORD swore to
4 our forefathers to give us.' The priest shall take the basket
from your hand and set it down before the altar of the
5 LORD your God. Then you shall solemnly recite before
the LORD your God: 'My father was a homeless*a* Aramaean who went down to Egypt with a small company
and lived there until they became a great, powerful, and
6 numerous nation. But the Egyptians ill-treated us,
7 humiliated us and imposed cruel slavery upon us. Then
we cried to the LORD the God of our fathers for help,
and he listened to us and saw our humiliation, our hard-
8 ship and distress; and so the LORD brought us out of
Egypt with a strong hand and outstretched arm, with
9 terrifying deeds, and with signs and portents. He brought
us to this place and gave us this land, a land flowing with
10 milk and honey. And now I have brought the firstfruits
of the soil which thou, O LORD, hast given me.' You shall
then set the basket before the LORD your God and bow
11 down in worship before him. You shall all rejoice,
you and the Levites and the aliens living among you,
for all the good things which the LORD your God has
given to you and to your family.

[a] *Or* wandering.

✻ An Israelite coming to the central sanctuary at Jerusalem to make his annual obligatory offering of the firstfruits must formally acknowledge his utter dependence on Yahweh who has given Israel her land, and blessed it by its harvest. At no time is the worshipper to be allowed to think that he is self-reliant.

2. *the firstfruits of all the produce of the soil*: part of these were due to the priest (cp. 18: 4). Whether the firstfruits were additional to the tithe or included in it is not clear (cp. 14:22–9). *the place which the LORD your God will choose*: cp. on 12: 5.

3. *which the LORD swore to our forefathers to give us*: cp. on 1: 8. The worshipper acknowledges his total debt to Yahweh the nature of which is elaborated in verses 5ff.

4. *The priest shall take the basket from your hand*: this does not agree with verse 10, and indicates that this section has been elaborated.

5. *My father was a homeless Aramaean*: refers to the patriarch Jacob, whose mother Rebecca was from Aramnaharaim in Mesopotamia (Gen. 24: 10) where Jacob himself spent many years in the service of her brother, Laban (Gen. 29–31). The Hebrew word translated *homeless* or, as in the N.E.B. footnote, 'wandering' indicates the lost position of a man who has abandoned citizenship in his own country, but has not acquired a new one.

8. *and so the LORD brought us out of Egypt*: the fact that no mention is made of the Sinai events has led some scholars to argue that originally the exodus–conquest traditions existed separately from those of Sinai, being experienced by different clans, and were only later combined after entry into Canaan (cp. on 6: 21). But the solemn recital which the worshipper bringing the firstfruits to the sanctuary is to make is not to be understood as a formal creed of Israelite belief. Indeed its sole interest is in Israel's possession of the land in contrast to the position obtaining in the period of the patriarchs and the slavery in Egypt. All the response seeks to do is to obtain from the worshipper the unequivocable assertion that he

recognizes that the land is the gift of God, and in consequence so are his crops. Without God's deliverance from Egypt, he would not be enjoying the abundant fruits of Canaan. He thus asserts that Yahweh is both lord of history and lord of nature, and blesses Israel through both. Indeed far from being an ancient creed, the solemn recital may be the work of the deuteronomists themselves who thereby give the ceremony of the firstfruits an historical explanation by specifically connecting it with the exodus experience. Cp. Deut. 16. *

THE TRIENNIAL TITHE

12 When you have finished taking a tithe of your produce in the third year, the tithe-year, you shall give it to the Levites and to the aliens, the orphans, and the widows. They shall eat it in your settlements and be well fed. 13 Then you shall declare before the LORD your God: 'I have rid my house of the tithe that was holy to thee and given it to the Levites, to the aliens, the orphans, and the widows, according to all the commandments which thou didst lay upon me. I have not broken or forgotten 14 any of thy commandments. I have not eaten any of the tithe while in mourning, nor have I rid myself of it for unclean purposes,[a] nor offered any of it to[b] the dead. I have obeyed the LORD my God: I have done all that thou 15 didst command me. Look down from heaven, thy holy dwelling-place, and bless thy people Israel and the ground which thou hast given to us as thou didst swear to our forefathers, a land flowing with milk and honey.'

* As a result of the centralization of all worship at Jerusalem, the triennial tithe (14: 28f.) was no longer offered at the

[a] nor have I...purposes: *mng. of Heb. obscure.*   [b] *Or* for.

local sanctuary, but instead given direct to those in need. But the donor, who would in consequence appear at the central sanctuary empty-handed, had still to declare that even though he had not actually offered the tithe to God at the sanctuary, he had none the less complied with cultic requirements of cleanliness.

12. *to the Levites*: as a result of the abolition of local sanctuaries the country Levites lost their means of support (cp. on 10: 8; 12: 12; 18: 1–8), and so are included at the head of those who were dependent on community charity for their maintenance (cp. 24: 17ff.).

13. *the tithe that was holy to thee*: the tithe was still considered an offering to God, and as such had to be *holy*, that is fit for his use.

14. *I have not eaten any of the tithe while in mourning*: by means of this short confessional formula the donor asserts that he has not distributed unclean food as tithe. Had he eaten part of the tithe while in mourning or any other unclean state (cp. Hos. 9: 4; Hag. 2: 13), or placed any of it in the grave of a dead man, he would have polluted the whole of the tithe, which could no longer be accepted by God. The tithe thus retained its sacral character. ✶

CONCLUSION TO THE LAWS

This day the LORD your God commands you to keep 16 these statutes and laws: be careful to observe them with all your heart and soul. You have recognized the LORD 17 this day as your God; you are to conform to his ways, to keep his statutes, his commandments, and his laws, and to obey him. The LORD has recognized you this day 18 as his special possession, as he promised you, and to keep his commandments; he will raise you high above all 19 the nations which he has made, to bring him praise and fame and glory, and to be a people holy to the LORD your God, according to his promise.

* As covenant-mediator, Moses concludes his delivery of the laws by reminding Israel of the basic nature of the covenant relationship. She has acknowledged Yahweh as her God, and in consequence must obey his law: in return he has recognized Israel as his specially elected people whom he will bless abundantly (cp. Exod. 19: 5f.). But the blessing remains conditional on Israel's obedience. *

Concluding charge of Moses to the people

* As in the suzerainty-treaty form, the original book of Deuteronomy concluded with a list of blessings and curses which would fall on Israel in the event of her obedience or disobedience to God's laws (28). But this conclusion has now been considerably supplemented by the deuteronomic historians anxious to point out that although the covenant curse had fallen on defeated and exiled Israel, yet through repentance she might again enjoy God's blessing (29–30). This material is now set in the context of an ancient rite of blessing and curses, associated with the renewal of the covenant in pre-monarchical days (27), and which had already been referred to by the deuteronomic historians (cp. on 11: 29ff.). Finally, again drawing on the suzerainty-treaty form, this section concludes with regulations concerning the writing down and deposit of the laws, and their future public recitation (31: 1–13). *

THE FIRST DAY IN CANAAN

MOSES, WITH THE ELDERS of Israel, gave the people **27** this charge: 'Keep all the commandments that I lay upon you this day. On the day that you cross the Jordan 2 to the land which the LORD your God is giving you, you shall set up great stones and plaster them over. You 3 shall inscribe on them all the words of this law, when you have crossed over to enter the land which the LORD your God is giving you, a land flowing with milk and honey, as the LORD the God of your fathers promised you. When you have crossed the Jordan you 4 shall set up these stones on Mount Ebal,[a] as I command you this day, and cover them with plaster. You shall build 5 an altar there to the LORD your God: it shall be an altar of stones on which you shall use no tool of iron. You shall build the altar of the LORD your God with 6 blocks of undressed stone, and you shall offer whole-offerings upon it to the LORD your God. You shall 7 slaughter shared-offerings and eat them there, and rejoice before the LORD your God. You shall inscribe on the stones 8 all the words of this law, engraving them with care.'

Moses and the levitical priests spoke to all Israel, 'Be 9 silent, Israel, and listen; this day you have become a people belonging to the LORD your God. Obey the 10 LORD your God, and observe his commandments and statutes which I lay upon you this day.'

That day Moses gave the people this command: 11 'Those who shall stand for the blessing of the people on 12 Mount Gerizim when you have crossed the Jordan are

[a] Gerizim *in Sam.*

these: Simeon, Levi, Judah, Issachar, Joseph, and Benja-
13 min. Those who shall stand on Mount Ebal for the curse
are these: Reuben, Gad, Asher, Zebulun, Dan, and
Naphtali.'

✳ On the very day that Israel crosses the Jordan and enters
the promised land, she is to set up stones inscribed with the
laws which Moses has given her, and erect a suitable altar
for sacrifice. Then follows the ritual of blessings and curses.
In contrast to the rest of Deuteronomy which only envisages
a single sanctuary at Jerusalem, here clear reference is being
made to Shechem beneath Mounts Gerizim and Ebal, once
the cult-centre of the confederacy of tribes which made up
Israel. It was here that in pre-monarchical times the covenant
was renewed (Josh. 24). But as in 11: 29–32, it would seem
that traditions of Israel's first day in Canaan, originally
associated with Gilgal near Jericho (Josh. 4), have come to be
attached to Shechem, with the result that it now appears
that Shechem was reached on that first day – a journey from
the Jordan of nearly 20 miles (about 32 kilometres). The
deuteronomic historians have deliberately inserted these
ancient traditions as a reminder that if ever again exiled Israel
was to cross over the Jordan, then she must immediately
accord to the law the central place which had always been
envisaged for it. It was obedience to the law which not only
determined Israel's physical welfare, but ultimately possession
of the land itself.

2f. *you shall set up great stones and plaster them over*: stones
were regularly used as witnesses of the covenant, though in
neither Exod. 24: 4 nor Josh. 24: 26 is it clear that they were
inscribed with its terms. (Josh. 8: 32 is dependent on this
passage.) This method of writing on plastered walls is,
however, known from Egypt, though, in the different
climatic conditions of Israel, the inscriptions would have
had to be rewritten. Perhaps this formed part of the covenant-

renewal festival. Alternatively it is possible that reference is being made to the Hittite custom of writing on tiles which were then embedded into the wall of the sanctuary, though no evidence of this practice has so far been found in Palestine itself.

4. *Mount Ebal*: it is curious that the stones are to be set on the mount of curse (verse 13) rather than Gerizim, the mount of blessing (verse 12). But as the N.E.B. footnote indicates, the Samaritan Pentateuch does read Gerizim, which to this day remains the Samaritan sanctuary. It is therefore possible that for polemical purposes following the Samaritan schism Gerizim was changed to Ebal. The date of this schism remains uncertain, though it probably occurred shortly after the ministry of Ezra. It is perhaps reflected in the theology of the books of Chronicles, and was still a live issue at the time of Jesus (cp. John 4).

5f. *it shall be an altar of stones*: naturally the new sanctuary had to have an altar for sacrifice. This must be made of stones in their natural state in accordance with ancient law (Exod. 20: 25). For man to have worked at the stones would have destroyed their God-created wholeness, and so rendered them unfit for his service. Unlike Exod. 20: 25, the possibility of an earthen altar is no longer envisaged. In virtually reiterating the law of the altar, the deuteronomic historians were no doubt looking ahead to the restoration of the Jerusalem sanctuary.

9f. *Moses and the levitical priests spoke to all Israel*: these two verses are best understood as a continuation of 26: 16–19, and again set out the basic terms of the covenant relationship. While God has graciously elected Israel to be his people, that election is dependent on her obedience to his law. God takes the initiative, but without Israel's response that initiative will be set at nought.

11ff. *That day Moses gave the people this command*: as in 11: 29–32 reference is being made to a ceremony of blessing and cursing which followed the renewal of the covenant in

7   179   P D Y

the ancient pre-monarchical ritual at Shechem. The tribes are drawn up in liturgical formation opposite each other, and the liturgy itself is set out in sixfold form in 28: 3–6, 16–19. Significantly the children of Jacob's concubines are placed on the mount of curse, together with the first-born Reuben who had forfeited his position (Gen. 49: 3f.), and Zebulun, Leah's youngest son, while the remainder of his wives' sons stand on the mount of blessing. ✴

A CURSING LITURGY

14 The Levites, in the hearing of all Israel, shall intone[a] these words:

15 'A curse upon the man who carves an idol or casts an image, anything abominable to the LORD that craftsmen make, and sets it up in secret': the people shall all respond and say, 'Amen.'

16 'A curse upon him who slights his father or his mother': the people shall all say, 'Amen.'

17 'A curse upon him who moves his neighbour's boundary stone': the people shall all say, 'Amen.'

18 'A curse upon him who misdirects a blind man': the people shall all say, 'Amen.'

19 'A curse upon him who withholds justice from the alien, the orphan, and the widow': the people shall all say, 'Amen.'

20 'A curse upon him who lies with his father's wife, for he brings shame upon his father': the people shall all say, 'Amen.'

21 'A curse upon him who lies with any animal': the people shall all say, 'Amen.'

[a] *Lit.* recite in a high-pitched voice.

'A curse upon him who lies with his sister, his father's 22 daughter or his mother's daughter': the people shall all say, 'Amen.'

'A curse upon him who lies with his wife's mother': 23 the people shall all say, 'Amen.'

'A curse upon him who strikes another man in secret': 24 the people shall all say, 'Amen.'

'A curse upon him who takes reward to kill a man with 25 whom he has no feud': the people shall all say, 'Amen.'

'A curse upon any man who does not fulfil this law by 26 doing all that it prescribes': the people shall all say, 'Amen.'

* As the entirely different liturgical setting shows, this passage is a late insertion. The blessings and curses expected by 27: 11–13 are in fact found in 28. Thus in contrast to verse 13, the cursing liturgy is recited by the Levites alone, and responded to by all the people. Clearly the connecting factor in the liturgy is the man who secretly breaks the law. Its purpose is to deter him from improperly taking part in the cult. If despite his secret act, which may range from a serious criminal offence to mere callous behaviour, he should seek to worship at the sanctuary, he would through the liturgy be forced into condemning himself. For by assenting to the curse, he immediately laid himself open to direct divine punishment. Thus this cursing liturgy is closely related to the so-called entrance liturgies found in Ps. 15 (cp. Isa. 33: 14–16) and Ps. 24: 3–6 which were recited before admission to the sanctuary in order to encourage proper self-examination and confession by the would-be worshipper. While an early date has often been argued for Deut. 27: 15–26, its subject-matter, particularly with its stress on unnatural sexual offences, is in fact most closely connected with the Holiness Code whose legislation it seems to reflect. Its position in a part of

Deuteronomy already amplified by the deuteronomic historians indicates very late insertion.

15. *who carves an idol or casts an image*: cp. on 4: 15–24; 5: 8f. The thought here is of any image whether of Yahweh or any other god in either human or animal form. *Amen*: signifies total assent. It could be translated 'certainly', 'assuredly'.

16. *who slights his father or his mother*: cp. on 5: 16. The Hebrew word rendered *slights* indicates actual repudiation of parental authority (Exod. 21: 17; Lev. 20: 9), which, whatever form it took, resulted in the execution of the rebellious son (Exod. 21: 15; Deut. 21: 18–21).

17. *who moves his neighbour's boundary stone*: cp. on 19: 14.

18. *who misdirects a blind man*: cp. Lev. 19: 14. One was never to take advantage of the misfortune of another.

19. *who withholds justice*: cp. on 24: 17.

20. *who lies with his father's wife*: cp. on 22: 30. As the following verses indicate, sexual intercourse with one's step-mother is now regarded as unnatural.

21. *who lies with any animal*: bestiality had already been prohibited under the Book of the Covenant (Exod. 22: 19). There is evidence from Hittite law of a belief that sexual intercourse with a sacral animal could lead to physical union with the deity. Perhaps such an idea was also prevalent in Canaan, which would account for the early prohibition of bestiality by the Book of the Covenant which otherwise is uninterested in sexual offences. In Lev. 18: 23; 20: 15 it appears as one of many unnatural sexual acts.

22. *who lies with his sister*: under customary family law, sexual intercourse would have been prohibited with any woman normally found in the patriarchal family of three or four generations living together under one roof. While this would have included a full sister, and a half-sister through one's father, it would not cover a half-sister through one's mother who would have remained with her father or his family and not entered her mother's new home. But under

the Holiness Code the old customary law was extended to include any near relative whether found in the home or not (Lev. 18: 6–18; 20: 11–21). This extension is reflected here in the specific reference to the daughter of either parent.

23. *who lies with his wife's mother*: similarly under old customary family law sexual intercourse with one's mother-in-law was not prohibited, as she would not have been found in the family home. This verse also reflects the extension of the law under the Holiness Code to include any near relative wherever she lived (Lev. 18: 17).

24. *who strikes another man in secret*: that is murders him. Cp. on 21: 1–9 for the ritual which had to be performed in the case of murder by an unknown person.

25. *who takes reward to kill a man*: the hired assassin is cursed even if the assassination has not yet taken place. The N.E.B. translation implies that the blood feud was practised in ancient Israel. Of this there is no evidence (cp. on 19: 6). In fact the Hebrew phrase used in this verse, 'innocent blood', is the normal biblical expression indicating an individual whose death would amount to murder and so bring blood guilt on the community (cp. Jer. 26: 15).

26. *who does not fulfil this law*: as it now stands this curse refers to the preceding deuteronomic laws. But originally it was probably a general proviso against any law-breaker who might be worshipping at the sanctuary, and whose offence had not yet been detected. ✲

THE BLESSINGS AND CURSES

If you will obey the LORD your God by diligently **28** observing all his commandments which I lay upon you this day, then the LORD your God will raise you high above all nations of the earth, and all these blessings shall 2 come to you and light upon you, because you obey the LORD your God:

3   A blessing on you in the city; a blessing on you in the country.

4   A blessing on the fruit of your body, the fruit of your land and of your cattle, the offspring of your herds and of your lambing flocks.

5   A blessing on your basket and your kneading-trough.

6   A blessing on you as you come in; and a blessing on you as you go out.

7   May the LORD deliver up the enemies who attack you and let them be put to rout before you. Though they come out against you by one way, they shall flee before you by seven ways.

8   May the LORD grant you a blessing in your granaries and in all your labours; may the LORD your God bless you in the land which he is giving you.

9   The LORD will set you up as his own holy people, as he swore to you, if you keep the commandments of the

10 LORD your God and conform to his ways. Then all people on earth shall see that the LORD has named you

11 as his very own, and they shall go in fear of you. The LORD will make you prosper greatly in the fruit of your body and of your cattle, and in the fruit of the ground in the land which he swore to your forefathers to give

12 you. May the LORD open the heavens for you, his rich treasure house, to give rain upon your land at the proper time and bless everything to which you turn your hand. You shall lend to many nations, but you shall not borrow;

13 the LORD will make you the head and not the tail: you shall be always at the top and never at the bottom, when you listen to the commandments of the LORD your God, which I give you this day to keep and to fulfil.

You shall turn neither to the right nor to the left from 14
all the things which I command you this day nor shall
you follow after and worship other gods.

But if you do not obey the LORD your God by diligently 15
observing all his commandments and statutes which I
lay upon you this day, then all these maledictions shall
come to you and light upon you:

A curse upon you in the city; a curse upon you in the 16
country.

A curse upon your basket and your kneading-trough. 17

A curse upon the fruit of your body, the fruit of your 18
land, the offspring of your herds and of your lambing
flocks.

A curse upon you as you come in; and a curse upon 19
you as you go out.

May the LORD send upon you starvation, burning 20
thirst, and dysentery,[a] whatever you are about, until you
are destroyed and quickly perish for your evil doings,
because you have forsaken me.

May the LORD cause pestilence to haunt you until he 21
has exterminated you out of the land which you are
entering to occupy; may the LORD afflict you with wasting 22
disease and recurrent fever, ague and eruptions; with
drought, black blight and red; and may these plague
you until you perish. May the skies above you be bronze, 23
and the earth beneath you iron. May the LORD turn the 24
rain upon your country into fine sand, and may dust
come down upon you from the sky until you are blotted
out.

[a] *Or* cursing, confusion, and rebuke.

25   May the LORD put you to rout before the enemy.
Though you go out against them by one way, you shall
flee before them by seven ways. May you be repugnant
26 to all the kingdoms on earth. May your bodies become
food for the birds of the air and the wild beasts, with no
man to scare them away.

27   May the LORD strike you with Egyptian boils and with
tumours,[a] scabs, and itches, for which you will find no
28 cure. May the LORD strike you with madness, blindness,
29 and bewilderment; so that you will grope about in broad
daylight, just as a blind man gropes in darkness, and you
will fail to find your way. You will also be oppressed and
30 robbed, day in, day out, with no one to save you. A
woman will be pledged to you, but another shall ravish
her; you will build a house but not live in it; you will
31 plant a vineyard but not enjoy its fruit. Your ox will be
slaughtered before your eyes, but you will not eat any
of it; and before your eyes your ass will be stolen and
will not come back to you; your sheep will be given to
the enemy, and there will be no one to recover them.
32 Your sons and daughters will be given to another
people while you look on; your eyes will strain after
33 them all day long, and you will be powerless. A nation
whom you do not know shall eat the fruit of your land
and all your toil, and your lot will be nothing but brutal
34, 35 oppression. The sights you see will drive you mad. May
the LORD strike you on knee and leg with malignant
boils for which you will find no cure; they will spread
from the sole of your foot to the crown of your head.
36 May the LORD give you up, you and the king whom you

[a] *Or, as otherwise read*, haemorrhoids.

have appointed, to a nation whom neither you nor your
fathers have known, and there you will worship other
gods, gods of wood and stone. You will become a 37
horror, a byword, and an object-lesson to all the peoples
amongst whom the LORD disperses you.

You will carry out seed for your fields in plenty, but 38
you will harvest little; for the locusts will devour it.
You will plant vineyards and cultivate them, but you 39
will not drink the wine or gather the grapes; for the
grub will eat them. You will have olive-trees all over 40
your territory, but you will not anoint yourselves with
their oil; for your olives will drop off. You will bear 41
sons and daughters, but they will not remain yours
because they will be taken into captivity. All your trees 42
and the fruit of the ground will be infested with the mole-
cricket. The alien who lives with you will raise himself 43
higher and higher, and you will sink lower and lower.
He will lend to you but you will not lend to him: he 44
will be the head and you the tail.

All these maledictions will come upon you; they will 45
pursue you and overtake you until you are destroyed
because you did not obey the LORD your God by keeping
the commandments and statutes which he gave you.
They shall be a sign and a portent to you and your 46
descendants for ever, because you did not serve the 47
LORD your God with joy and with a glad heart for all
your blessings. Then in hunger and thirst, in nakedness 48
and extreme want, you shall serve your enemies whom
the LORD will send against you, and they will put a yoke
of iron on your neck when they have subdued you.
May the LORD raise against you a nation from afar, from 49

the other end of the earth, who will swoop upon you like a vulture, a nation whose language you will not
50 understand, a nation of grim aspect with no reverence
51 for age and no pity for the young. They will devour the young of your cattle and the fruit of your land, when you have been subdued. They will leave you neither corn, nor new wine nor oil, neither the offspring of your herds nor of your lambing flocks, until you are annihi-
52 lated. They will besiege you in all your cities*a* until they bring down your lofty impregnable walls, those city walls throughout your land in which you trust. They will besiege you within all your cities, throughout the
53 land which the LORD your God has given you. Then you will eat your own children,*b* the flesh of your sons and daughters whom the LORD your God has given you, because of the dire straits to which you will be reduced
54 when your enemy besieges you. The pampered, delicate man will not share with his brother, or the wife of his
55 bosom, or his remaining children, any of the meat which he is eating, the flesh of his own children. He is left with nothing else because of the dire straits to which you will be reduced when your enemy besieges you within your
56 cities. The pampered, delicate woman, the woman who has never even tried to put a foot to the ground, so delicate and pampered she is, will not share with her own
57 husband or her son or her daughter the afterbirth which she expels, or any boy or girl that she may bear. She will herself eat them secretly in her extreme want, because of the dire straits to which you will be reduced when your enemy besieges you within your cities.

[a] *Lit.* gates.   [b] *Lit.* the fruit of your body.

If you do not observe and fulfil all the law written 58
down in this book, if you do not revere this honoured
and dreaded name, this name 'the LORD*a* your God',
then the LORD will strike you and your descendants 59
with unimaginable plagues, malignant and persistent,
and with sickness, persistent and severe. He will bring upon 60
you once again all the diseases of Egypt which you dread,
and they will cling to you. The LORD will bring upon 61
you sickness and plague of every kind not written down
in this book of the law, until you are destroyed. Then 62
you who were countless as the stars in the sky will be
left few in number, because you did not obey the LORD
your God. Just as the LORD took delight in you, prosper- 63
ing and increasing you, so now it will be his delight to
destroy and exterminate you, and you will be uprooted
from the land which you are entering to occupy. The 64
LORD will scatter you among all peoples from one end
of the earth to the other, and there you will worship
other gods whom neither you have known nor your
forefathers, gods of wood and stone. Among those 65
nations you will find no peace, no rest for the sole of
your foot. Then the LORD will give you an unquiet
mind, dim eyes, and failing appetite. Your life will 66
hang continually in suspense, fear will beset you night
and day, and you will find no security all your life long.
Every morning you will say, 'Would God it were even- 67
ing!', and every evening, 'Would God it were morning!',
for the fear that lives in your heart and the sights that
you see. The LORD will bring you sorrowing back to 68
Egypt by that very road of which I said to you, 'You

[a] *See note on Exod. 3: 15.*

shall not see that road again'; and there you will offer
to sell yourselves to your enemies as slaves and slave-girls,
but there will be no buyer.

⁂ After the covenant terms have been accepted (27: 9–10),
in accordance with the suzerainty-treaty form (cp. Lev. 26),
the recitation of the blessings and curses follows. Deut.
28: 3–6, 16–19 contains the original sixfold formula which has
now been considerably expanded. This was probably undertaken at different times, from the writing of the original book
of Deuteronomy to its later editing by the deuteronomic
historians as the introduction to their Work. Certainly the
curses draw on the horrors of the Babylonian conquest which
resulted in exile for the leading citizens, and abject poverty for
those left behind. By remaining within the covenant relationship, Israel would automatically enjoy God's blessing. But
once his laws were broken, then curse inevitably followed.
The covenant relationship itself was thus the source of
Israel's prosperity in her day-to-day life: its breach the reason
for any misfortune which afflicted her.

5. *your basket and your kneading-trough*: that is fruit, usually
grapes and olives, gathered in baskets, and grain, which
through kneading becomes bread.

6. *you come in...you go out*: that is, in all you undertake,
your daily round (Ps. 121: 8; Isa. 37: 28).

11. *which he swore to your forefathers to give you*: cp. on
1: 8.

12f. *You shall lend to many nations*: cp. on 15: 6. Israel is
to be the dominant international power, dependent on no
other nation because she enjoys Yahweh's protection.

14. *nor shall you follow after and worship other gods*: for
the deuteronomists the first commandment guaranteeing
Israel's exclusive allegiance to her God had virtually become
the sole criterion of covenant obedience.

15ff. *then all these maledictions shall come to you*: the six
curses are the reverse of the six blessings in verses 3–6.

24. *turn the rain upon your country into fine sand*: as a consequence of the drought (verse 23), the winds bring sand and dust instead of rain.

26. *May your bodies become food for the birds*: to be left unburied, a prey to the birds and wild beasts, was considered a particularly awful fate to be prevented at all costs (cp. 2 Sam. 21: 10). Since the Israelites did not separate man into body and soul, anything done to a man's physical remains after death was understood to affect his whole person, which descended to the shadowy half-life of Sheol.

30ff. *A woman will be pledged to you*: these verses give a graphic description of the results of foreign conquest.

36. *and there you will worship other gods*: expulsion from Israel would result in the people being cut off from the true faith and condemned to a loss of relationship with Yahweh. Religion was so closely bound up with the whole life of the community and connected to possession of its land, that it could not be practised outside it, for there would be no legitimate shrine at which worship could take place (cp. 1 Sam. 26: 19). Consequently the exiled Israelites would be forced to worship heathen gods represented by images of wood and stone. It was part of Ezekiel's task to stop such apostasy by proclaiming that even in exile, in unclean Babylon, Israel could still know her God and enjoy his grace.

43f. *The alien who lives with you*: as one of those who did not possess any land in Israel, the resident alien was largely dependent on charity for his rights (cp. on 1: 16). Now his role is to be reversed, and it will be the Israelite who will seek his help in order to survive.

47. *serve the LORD your God with joy*: Israel's law was not meant to be a burden but a blessing. It ensured her well-being, and to obey should therefore have been an occasion for joy.

48. *a yoke of iron on your neck*: cp. Jer. 28: 13. This passage has a number of contacts with Jeremiah (cp. Jer. 4: 13; 5: 15, 17; 19: 9). But this is not surprising when it is remem-

bered that the deuteronomic historians also edited his work (cp. p. 2).

49. *whose language you will not understand*: neither the Assyrians (Isa. 28: 11; 33: 19) nor the Babylonians could be understood by the Israelites, though their language was Semitic and related to Hebrew. Instead Aramaic, another Semitic language, served in Assyrian and Persian times as the international language for commerce and diplomacy, though in the time of Isaiah it was not yet understood by uneducated people (Isa. 36: 11). Later it was to become the normal language of Palestine, in which Jesus spoke and taught.

53ff. *Then you will eat your own children*: as a result of the siege, even those accustomed to gracious living will be forced into secret eating of their own children, whose flesh they will refuse to share with their nearest relatives. Such terrible happenings may indeed have occurred in the final siege of Jerusalem (Lam. 4: 10), as they had earlier in Elisha's time (2 Kings 6: 24–31).

58. *all the law written down in this book*: clearly indicates that the laws, originally conceived as a speech of Moses, have now been codified. It is this written collection which the deuteronomic historian edits. *this name 'the LORD your God'*: the account in Exod. 3: 14 of the revelation of the divine name to Moses connects it with the verb 'to be'. 'Yahweh' is thus interpreted as 'he who is' or 'he who causes to be'. But it is by no means certain that this etymological explanation is correct. More probably it owes its origin to an author seeking to explain by a similar Hebrew word what had long been quite inexplicable. On the significance of knowing God's name, see commentary on 5: 11, and on the pronunciation of Yahweh, see commentary on 5: 6.

62. *you who were countless as the stars in the sky*: cp. 1: 10. Once-populous Israel is to be decimated by plague.

65ff. *you will find no peace*: the Israelites understood peace as a state of perfect harmony, complete equilibrium, when everything was all of a piece. Instead, if they fail to keep the law, they are to be consigned to endless wandering and never-ceasing anxiety. In other words, they are to experience again the conditions of the desert period when they could call no place their own, but had continually to move on in the hope that one day they would be able to settle and find peace.

68. *The LORD will bring you sorrowing back to Egypt*: this is probably not to be understood historically as referring to some actual contemporary possibility, but rather theologically as indicating a complete reversal of the history of salvation through God's call and deliverance of his chosen people Israel. Thus after a return to wandering in the desert, Israel comes back to Egypt itself. But her situation there is very different from that in the time of Moses. Then the Israelites were in slavery, but as slaves were assured of their maintenance. Now no one will buy them, and as a result they are doomed to perish. For *sorrowing* the Hebrew reads 'in ships', which would refer to slave-boats. But in view of the fact that Israel is pictured as actually retracing the steps of the exodus, this cannot be correct and the N.E.B. has instead translated it by a very similar-looking Hebrew word meaning 'sighing', 'groaning'. ✶

THE INTRODUCTION TO MOSES' THIRD ADDRESS

These are the words of the covenant which the LORD **29** 1*a* commanded Moses to make with the Israelites in Moab, in addition to the covenant which he made with them on Horeb.

✶ This verse is better taken as the introduction to 29–30, rather than the conclusion to the earlier laws. Unusually, the covenant in Moab is regarded as quite distinct from that

[a] *28: 69 in H*

of Sinai, whereas elsewhere in Deuteronomy the law revealed by Moses in his farewell address is seen as deduced from the earlier law revealed at Sinai. Once more Moses acts as covenant mediator. ✶

HOPE FOR THE FUTURE

2[a] Moses summoned all the Israelites and said to them: 'You have seen with your own eyes all that the LORD did in Egypt to Pharaoh, to all his servants, and to the whole 3 land, the great challenge which you yourselves witnessed, 4 those great signs and portents, but to this day the LORD has not given you a mind to learn, or eyes to see, or ears 5 to hear. I led you for forty years in the wilderness; your clothes did not wear out on you, nor did your sandals 6 wear out and fall off your feet; you ate no bread and drank no wine or strong drink, in order that you might 7 learn that I am the LORD your God. You came to this place where Sihon king of Heshbon and Og king of 8 Bashan came to attack us, and we defeated them. We took their land and gave it as patrimony to the Reuben- 9 ites, the Gadites, and half the tribe of Manasseh. You shall observe the provisions of this covenant and keep them so that you may be successful in all you do.

10   'You all stand here today before the LORD your God, tribal chiefs,[b] elders, and officers, all the men of Israel, 11 with your dependants, your wives, the aliens who live in your camp – all of them, from those who chop wood 12 to those who draw water – and you are ready to accept the oath and enter into the covenant which the LORD

[a] 29: 1 *in Heb.*
[b] *So Pesh.; Heb.* your chiefs, your tribes.

your God is making with you today. The covenant is to 13
constitute you his people this day, and he will be your
God, as he promised you and as he swore to your forefathers, Abraham, Isaac and Jacob. It is not with you 14
alone that I am making this covenant and this oath, but 15
with all those who stand here with us today before the
LORD our God and also with those who are not here
with us today. For you know how we lived in Egypt and 16
how we and you, as we passed through the nations, saw 17
their loathsome idols and the false gods they had, the
gods of wood and stone, of silver and gold. If there 18
should be among you a man or woman, family or tribe,
who is moved today to turn from the LORD our God and
to go worshipping the gods of those nations – if there is
among you such a root from which springs gall and
wormwood, then when he hears the terms of this oath, 19
he may inwardly flatter himself and think, "All will
be well with me even if I follow the promptings of my
stubborn heart"; but this will bring everything to ruin.[a]
The LORD will not be willing to forgive him; for then 20
his anger and resentment will overwhelm this man, and
the denunciations prescribed in this book will fall
heavily on him, and the LORD will blot out his name
from under heaven. The LORD will single him out from 21
all the tribes of Israel for disaster to fall upon him,
according to the oath required by the covenant and
prescribed in this book of the law.

'The next generation, your sons who follow you and 22
the foreigners who come from distant countries, will
see the plagues of this land and the ulcers which the

[a] but this...ruin: *lit.* to the sweeping away of moist and dry.

23 LORD has brought upon its people, the whole land burnt up with brimstone and salt, so that it cannot be sown, or yield herb or green plant. It will be as desolate as were Sodom and Gomorrah, Admah and Zeboyim, when the
24 LORD overthrew them in his anger and rage. Then they, and all the nations with them, will ask, "Why has the LORD so afflicted this land? Why has there been this
25 great outburst of wrath?" The answer will be: "Because they forsook the covenant of the LORD the God of their fathers which he made with them when he brought them
26 out of Egypt. They began to worship other gods and to bow down to them, gods whom they had not known and
27 whom the LORD had not assigned to them. The anger of the LORD was roused against that land, so that he brought upon it all the maledictions written in this book.
28 The LORD uprooted them from their soil in anger, in wrath and great fury, and banished them to another land, where they are to this day."

29   'There are things hidden, and they belong to the LORD our God, but what is revealed belongs to us and our children for ever; it is for us to observe all that is prescribed in this law.

30   'When these things have befallen you, the blessing and the curse of which I have offered you the choice, if you and your sons take them to heart there in all the countries to which the LORD your God has banished you,
2 if you turn back to him and obey him heart and soul in
3 all that I command you this day, then the LORD your God will show you compassion and restore your fortunes. He will gather you again from all the countries to which
4 he has scattered you. Even though he were to banish you

to the four corners of the world,[a] the LORD your God will gather you from there, from there he will fetch you home. The LORD your God will bring you into the land 5 which your forefathers occupied, and you will occupy it again; then he will bring you prosperity and make you more numerous than your forefathers were. The LORD 6 your God will circumcise[b] your hearts and the hearts of your descendants, so that you will love him with all your heart and soul and you will live. Then the LORD 7 your God will turn all these denunciations against your enemies and the foes who persecute you. You will then 8 again obey the LORD and keep all his commandments which I give you this day. The LORD your God will 9-10 make you more than prosperous in all that you do, in the fruit of your body and of your cattle and in the fruits of the earth; for, when you obey the LORD your God by keeping his commandments and statutes, as they are written in this book of the law, and when you turn back to the LORD your God with all your heart and soul, he will again rejoice over you and be good to you, as he rejoiced over your forefathers.

'The commandment that I lay on you this day is not 11 too difficult for you, it is not too remote. It is not in 12 heaven, that you should say, "Who will go up to heaven for us to fetch it and tell it to us, so that we can keep it?" Nor is it beyond the sea, that you should say, "Who will 13 cross the sea for us to fetch it and tell it to us, so that we can keep it?" It is a thing very near to you, upon your 14 lips[c] and in your heart ready to be kept.

[a] *Lit.* to the end of the heavens.
[b] *Or* incline.   [c] *Lit.* in your mouth.

15 'Today I offer you the choice of life and good, or
16 death and evil. If you obey the commandments of the
LORD your God*ᵃ* which I give you this day, by loving the
LORD your God, by conforming to his ways and by
keeping his commandments, statutes, and laws, then you
will live and increase, and the LORD your God will bless
17 you in the land which you are entering to occupy. But
if your heart turns away and you do not listen and you
are led on to bow down to other gods and worship
18 them, I tell you this day that you will perish; you will not
live long in the land which you will enter to occupy
19 after crossing the Jordan. I summon heaven and earth to
witness against you this day: I offer you the choice of life
or death, blessing or curse. Choose life and then you
20 and your descendants will live; love the LORD your God,
obey him and hold fast to him: that is life for you and
length of days in the land which the LORD swore to give
to your forefathers, Abraham, Isaac and Jacob.'

* This section presupposes that the covenant relationship
has been terminated, and that the curses laid down for its
breach have fallen on disobedient Israel. Her land now
lies desolate, and her leading citizens have been led into exile.
In its present form it must then be attributed to the deuteronomic historian whose intention is to assure scattered Israel
that even now through her repentance she can yet know
God's grace. For by once again submitting to his law, Israel
will find that God has not finally let her go, that she can still
be his chosen people, and can indeed know a future far more
glorious than anything hitherto envisaged. All this would be
worked out in God's own time, once Israel had turned back
to him. The section is again based on the suzerainty-treaty

[a] If you...your God: *so Sept.; Heb. om.*

form (cp. pp. 4f.) as can be seen from the historical prologue (29: 2–8), statement of general principles (29: 9), blessings and curses (30: 16–18), and the call to witnesses (30: 19). The detailed laws are presupposed in what has gone before. As 29: 1 indicates, the deuteronomic historians see the covenant at Moab, whose terms are set out in chs. 12–26, as replacing the earlier covenant at Horeb (Sinai) annulled by the Babylonian conquest. Once more Israel stands at the edge of the promised land: if she will obey the conditions of this new covenant, God will indeed bring about a second exodus and conquest, and Israel will again enjoy the fulness of his blessing. The deuteronomic historians thus seek to dissuade from apostasy a totally bewildered people whose whole theological basis had suddenly collapsed. Despite appearances to the contrary, by holding fast to their God, they can yet have a future.

4. *but to this day the LORD has not given you a mind to learn*: for the deuteronomic historians faced with widespread apostasy, it was clear that the exilic generation did not understand the significance of Israel's salvation history. From the first, Israel was intended to be the people of Yahweh, and the miraculous events of the exodus and desert period should have been understood as self-authenticating evidence of his love and concern for her. Instead even in the deuteronomic historians' own times, Israelites were going after other gods.

5f. *your clothes did not wear out*: cp. on 8: 4.

7f. *Sihon king of Heshbon and Og king of Bashan*: for the conquest of the kings and the division of their land, cp. on 2: 26 – 3: 22.

9. *You shall observe the provisions of this covenant*: the laws hitherto set out in Deut. 12–26 constitute the detailed terms of the Moabite covenant. It is on obedience to them, rather than the Horeb (Sinai) law, that Israel's future depends.

10f. *You all stand here today*: the whole adult population is here drawn into the covenant relationship, male, female and even resident aliens (cp. on 1: 16). As the N.E.B. footnote indicates, the Hebrew 'your chiefs, your tribes, your elders' cannot be right, and the Syriac version is to be accepted. *your dependants* does not indicate all children, but those old enough to be members of the covenant community. The same word occurs in 1:39 where children old enough to become spoils of war are contrasted with those who do not know good from evil. The expression *from those who chop wood to those who draw water* confirms that no adult is excluded from the covenant community no matter how menial his place in society. It was to these lowly tasks that the Gibeonites were assigned after they had tricked the Israelites into making them members of the covenant community Josh.)9).

13. *your forefathers, Abraham, Isaac and Jacob*: cp. on 1:8.

14. *It is not with you alone*: the covenant is not made with one generation, but with Israel, and therefore governs every Israelite in every age. The intention is to drive home to the deuteronomic historians' contemporaries that they are as bound by the covenant law in Deut. 12–26 as any generation who may once have gathered in Moab before entry into the promised land. Cp. on 5:3.

17. *their loathsome idols and the false gods*: for the exilic generation Israel's God appeared to have been defeated by the stronger Babylonian gods, and therefore the temptation to apostasize was very great. Indeed for the deuteronomists the covenant relationship had in effect been reduced to acceptance or rejection of the first commandment which demanded exclusive allegiance to Yahweh.

18ff. *If there should be among you a man or woman*: any individual, family or tribe who, in spite of an outward appearance of conformity with Israelite practice and belief, secretly apostasizes will none the less be singled out by God and punished. Even though the apostate can remain undetected to the rest of Israel, God will find him, and the curses prescribed in Deuteronomy, now thought of as a written book (cp. 28:58), will fall on him. Cp. on 27:14–26.

22. *The next generation...and the foreigners*: perhaps the deuteronomic historians' contemporaries to whom both the devastation of the land and the exile have to be explained.

23. *the whole land burnt up with brimstone and salt*: the land of Israel, the land flowing with milk and honey, now looks like the utterly desolate country near the Dead Sea where once great cities flourished (cp. Gen. 10: 19).

25ff. *Because they forsook the covenant*: by worshipping other gods. Israel's present misfortune is thus entirely attributed to her apostasy, which led God to implement the curses implicit in the covenant relationship. *where they are to this day* indicates that this section was written in the latter part of the exilic period. The Deuteronomic Work is in fact to be dated between 561 B.C., the release of Jehoiachin from prison, and 538 B.C., the return from exile (cp. pp. 3, 10).

29. *There are things hidden*: a note apparently inserted before the hopeful passage of Deut. 30, probably in answer to those faithful people who asked why God's promises were being delayed. This apparent lack of activity on God's part caused considerable concern in the late exilic period as can be seen from Deutero-Isaiah's prophecies (cp. Isa. 40: 27). The note indicates that while God has not revealed all his plans to man, he has revealed his law. It is for man to keep that law, and leave the rest to God. This questioning of God's activity is typical of the post-exilic wisdom literature (cp. Job, Proverbs and Ecclesiastes).

30: 2ff. *if you turn back to him*: through repentance Israel can still know God's grace, and once again experience the covenant relationship. In spite of the destruction of the temple, and the exile of the king and leading citizens, God has not renounced Israel for all time. But it is for Israel to take the initiative: only then can she be restored to what promises to be a far greater glory than anything previously enjoyed (cp. 4: 29–31).

6. *The LORD your God will circumcise your hearts*: cp. on

10: 16. But here the rite is carried out by God himself. As in Jer. 31: 31–4; 32: 39–41; Ezek. 36: 24–8, it is God who will make it impossible for the Israel of the future to renounce him, and so suffer the total collapse of the covenant relationship. It was the Priestly theologians who worked out how such an unbreakable relationship could come about. It was achieved through the abolition of Israel's corporate responsibility for obedience to the covenant law in favour of individual obedience, which determined membership of the elect community of Israel, whose future was guaranteed by her cult. This new understanding of the covenant relationship thus led to a renunciation of the Mosaic covenant principles based on the suzerainty-treaty form upon which the deuteronomists had built their theology (cp. pp. 10f.).

11ff. *it is not too remote*: Israel has no excuse for failing to keep the law. God has openly revealed it to her, and in taking part in the covenant renewal festival every Israelite would hear it recited, and assent to it. It was a feature of the covenant relationship that God could not suddenly place on Israel additional demands. He had specified what were the conditions of the covenant, and he, like Israel, was bound by them.

15ff. *the choice of life . . . or death*: the basic choice for Israel was allegiance to her God or idolatry. The way of the former led to blessing: the latter could only result in curse.

19. *I summon heaven and earth to witness*: cp. on 4: 26.   *✶*

MOSES' IMMINENT DEATH

31 ₁,₂ Moses finished speaking[a] these words to all Israel, and then he said, 'I am now a hundred and twenty years old, and I can no longer move about as I please; and the ₃ LORD has told me that I may not cross the Jordan. The LORD your God will cross over at your head and destroy these nations before your advance, and you shall occupy

[a] *So Scroll; Heb.* Moses went and spoke . . .

their lands; and, as he directed, Joshua will lead you
across. The LORD will do to these nations as he did to 4
Sihon and Og, kings of the Amorites, and to their lands;
he will destroy them. The LORD will deliver them into 5
your power, and you shall do to them as*a* I commanded
you. Be strong, be resolute; you must not dread them 6
or be afraid, for the LORD your God himself goes with
you; he will not fail you or forsake you.'

Moses summoned Joshua and said to him in the pre- 7
sence of all Israel, 'Be strong, be resolute; for it is you
who are to lead this people into the land which the LORD
swore to give their forefathers, and you are to bring
them into possession of it. The LORD himself goes at 8
your head; he will be with you; he will not fail you or
forsake you. Do not be discouraged or afraid.'

Moses wrote down this law and gave it to the priests, 9
the sons of Levi, who carried the Ark of the Covenant
of the LORD, and to all the elders of Israel. Moses gave 10
them this command: 'At the end of every seven years, at
the appointed time for the year of remission, at the
pilgrim-feast of Tabernacles, when all Israel comes to 11
enter the presence of*b* the LORD your God in the place
which he will choose, you shall read this law publicly
in the hearing of all Israel. Assemble the people, men, 12
women, and dependants, together with the aliens who
live in your settlements, so that they may listen, and learn
to fear the LORD your God and observe all these laws
with care. Their children, too, who do not know them, 13
shall hear them, and learn to fear the LORD your God all

[a] *So Sept.; Heb.* according to all the commandment which...
[b] *Lit.* see the face of.

their[a] lives in the land which you will occupy after crossing the Jordan.'

✵ Having completed the recitation of the law revealed to him in Moab, and aware of his imminent death, Moses provides for the future. A successor must be appointed both to lead Israel into the promised land, and to act as covenant mediator. But in order that there should be no doubt as to the content of the covenant law which Israel must henceforth obey, it is straightway written down and provision made for its regular public recitation.

1. *Moses finished speaking these words*: this section continues on from 3: 23–9. As in the Hittite suzerainty treaties, the covenant stipulations are called *words* (cp. on 4: 13).

2. *a hundred and twenty years old* is a round figure indicating that Moses' life spanned three generations. *I may not cross the Jordan*: cp. on 1: 37. It is not merely old age which prevents Moses from entering the promised land, but Israel's disobedience for which he is made to suffer.

3. *The LORD your God will cross over at your head*: probably a reference to the Ark (cp. on 10: 1).

4. *Sihon and Og, kings of the Amorites*: cp. on 2: 26 – 3: 11.

7f. *Moses summoned Joshua*: Joshua is to act both as a military and cultic leader.

9. *Moses wrote down this law*: the political suzerainty treaties provided for the writing down of the treaty stipulations and their deposit in the shrines of both parties. In Israel's case both copies of the law were placed in the Ark (cp. on 4: 13). Both clerical and lay leaders are entrusted with the care of the written law.

10ff. *At the end of every seven years*: the political suzerainty treaties also provided for their regular recitation. Such a ceremony of covenant renewal had regularly taken place in Israel (Pss. 50; 81). Indeed it would seem that here reference

[a] So Sam.; Heb. your.

is being made to ancient practice at Shechem, once the centre
of the confederacy of tribes in pre-monarchical Israel.
What is new is that the recitation every seven years at
Tabernacles is now not merely to include the Ten Commandments, but the whole deuteronomic law. It is by means of
such a ceremony that children will come to know the law,
and be brought within the covenant community. The
singular form of address *you shall read* probably refers to the
covenant mediator, whose task it was to recite the covenant
stipulations. ✻

Joshua appointed successor to Moses

✻ This short section is very confused. The appointment of
Joshua (31: 14–15, 23), which had in fact already taken place
(31: 7–8), is a late insertion by the pentateuchal editor; the
injunction to Moses to write his Song (31: 16–22) is the work
of the person who inserted the Song itself (ch. 32); and the
command to deposit the book of the laws in the Ark (31:
24–9) appears to be a duplicate of the ancient traditions
already referred to in 31: 9–13. ✻

WITNESSES AGAINST ISRAEL'S FUTURE
DISOBEDIENCE

THE LORD SAID to Moses, 'The time of your death 14
is drawing near; call Joshua, and then come and stand
in the Tent of the Presence so that I may give him
his commission.' So Moses and Joshua went and took
their stand in the Tent of the Presence; and the LORD 15

appeared in the tent in a pillar of cloud, and the pillar of cloud stood at the entrance of the tent.

16 The LORD said to Moses, 'You are about to die like your forefathers, and this people, when they come into the land and live among foreigners, will go wantonly after their gods; they will abandon me and break the 17 covenant which I have made with them. Then my anger will be roused against them, and I will abandon them and hide my face from them. They will be an easy prey, and many terrible disasters will come upon them. They will say on that day, "These disasters have come because 18 our God is not among us." On that day I will hide my face because of all the evil they have done in turning to other gods.

19 'Now write down this rule of life*a* and teach it to the Israelites; make them repeat it, so that it may be on record 20 against them. When I have brought them into the land which I swore to give to their forefathers, a land flowing with milk and honey, and they have plenty to eat and grow fat, they will turn to other gods and worship 21 them, they will spurn me and break my covenant; and many calamities and disasters will follow. Then this rule of life will confront them as a record, for it will not be forgotten by their descendants. For even before I bring them into the land which I swore to give them, I know which way their thoughts incline already.'

22 That day Moses wrote down this rule of life and 23 taught it to the Israelites. The LORD*b* gave Joshua son of Nun his commission in these words: 'Be strong, be

[a] rule of life: *or* song.
[b] *Prob. rdg.; Heb.* He.

resolute; for you shall bring the Israelites into the land
which I swore to give them, and I will be with you.'

When Moses had finished writing down these laws 24
in a book, from beginning to end, he gave this command 25
to the Levites who carried the Ark of the Covenant of
the LORD: 'Take this book of the law and put it beside 26
the Ark of the Covenant of the LORD your God to be
a witness against you. For I know how defiant and 27
stubborn you are; even during my lifetime you have
defied the LORD; how much more, then, will you do so
when I am dead? Assemble all the elders of your tribes 28
and your officers; I will say all these things in their
hearing and will summon heaven and earth to witness
against them. For I know that after my death you will 29
take to degrading practices and turn aside from the way
which I told you to follow, and in days to come disaster
will come upon you, because you are doing what is
wrong in the eyes of the LORD and so provoking him to
anger.'

* After God has commissioned Joshua as Moses' successor,
he induces Moses to write down a Song which will anticipate
the Israelites' attempt to avoid responsibility for the disasters
which are to fall on them. Both this Song and the copy of
the law itself will give the true explanation of Israel's misfortune. God is punishing her for disobedience to the covenant law.

14f. *in the Tent of the Presence*: in contrast to verses 1–8, God,
not Moses, commissions Joshua. He does this by meeting
him *in the Tent of the Presence*, where he had hitherto spoken
face to face with Moses (Exod. 33: 11). Since *the Tent of the
Presence* is nowhere else referred to in Deuteronomy, but is
instead found in the Tetrateuch, these verses are best under-

stood as the work of the pentateuchal editor who attached Deuteronomy to the Tetrateuch (cp. p. 2). Traditions concerning *the Tent of the Presence* go back to Israel's earliest sources (Exod. 33: 7–11), though these were later elaborated by the Priestly theologians (Exod. 26–7). Unlike the Ark on which God permanently manifested himself, *the Tent of the Presence* was the place tu which God would specifically descend in order to communicate with man. Its chief function appears to have been connected with oracles, and it lost its importance once Israel entered Canaan and acquired sanctuaries of her own. The *pillar of cloud* protected the Israelites from seeing God, which would have resulted in their immediate death.

17. *our God is not among us*: rather than admit that the disasters facing Israel are due to her own disobedience of the covenant law, she will instead blame God for deserting her. Undoubtedly such an assessment of the cause of the Babylonian conquest and exile was widespread, and accounted for many Israelites giving allegiance to the mightier Babylonian gods whom they considered had vanquished Israel. Ironically it is Israel's desertion of her God which has caused her defeat.

19ff. *Now write down this rule of life*: the Hebrew here refers to Moses' Song which follows in Deut. 32. This is to act as a witness against the Israelites when they falsely accuse God of deserting them. But the language of this passage (verses 19–21) is not applicable to a song, but to a legal document, which shows that the idea of the Song as a witness is secondary. Originally it was the covenant law alone which fulfilled this function (verse 26). But this legal terminology has been borrowed by the person who inserted Moses' Song in order to establish the Song as an integral part of Deuteronomy. There is thus no need to emend the Hebrew, as is done in the N.E.B. translation, by reading *torah* (*rule of life*) for *shirah* ('song'). But the explanation provided by these verses for the origin of the Song is not really satisfactory, for it ignores the fact that the Song itself concludes with God's vindication of Israel in the defeat of her enemies (32: 34–43). *on record*: the same phrase occurs in verse 26, and is best translated as there by 'a witness'.

23. *The LORD gave Joshua son of Nun*: following verses 14–15, God gives Joshua his commission in a truncated form of 31: 7–8.

24ff. *When Moses had finished writing down these laws in a book*: these verses virtually repeat 31: 9–13. The written copy of the law will proclaim clearly enough why disaster will fall on Israel.

28. *summon heaven and earth to witness against them*: cp. on 4: 26. ✵

Two historical poems

✵ Both the Song and the Blessing of Moses are quite independent of Deuteronomy into which they have been inserted. Their origin and date are uncertain, and both have been subject to considerable debate, a great variety of conclusions being offered.

There undoubtedly lies behind the Song the well-known form of the covenant lawsuit (cp. Isa. 1: 2ff.; Mic. 6: 1ff.), in which Israel is charged with breach of the covenant. God, who appears as both plaintiff and judge, first summons witnesses to hear his complaint that in spite of all he has done for Israel, she has none the less broken the covenant relationship: then he pronounces judgement upon her. But the Song goes on to develop into an oracle of salvation. In spite of Israel's disobedience, God promises to vindicate her by punishing the very people whom he had used to execute his judgement upon her. In spite of the fact that there is no mention of the exile, the freedom with which the covenant lawsuit form has been used and the many theological similarities with Ezekiel and Deutero-Isaiah point to an exilic date.

On the other hand, the Blessing clearly reflects a period when the tribes were still conscious of their individual identities. Since tribal identity survived the establishment of the monarchy, this still leaves a considerable period in which to date the Blessing. But literary evidence and comparison with Canaanite material would seem to indicate a date late in the period of the judges. ✳

THE SONG OF MOSES

30 MOSES RECITED this song from beginning to end in the hearing of the whole assembly of Israel:

32   Give ear to what I say, O heavens,
        earth, listen to my words;
2   my teaching shall fall like drops of rain,
        my words shall distil like dew,
        like fine rain upon the grass
        and like the showers on young plants.

3   When I call aloud the name of the LORD,[a]
        you shall respond, 'Great is our God,
4   the creator[b] whose work is perfect,
        and all his ways are just,
        a faithful god, who does no wrong,
        righteous and true is He!'

5   Perverse and crooked generation
        whose faults have proved you no children of his,
6   is this how you repay the LORD,
        you brutish and stupid people?

[a] *Or* the name JEHOVAH.   [b] *Or* rock.

Is he not your father who formed you?
Did he not make you and establish you?
Remember the days of old,   7
think of the generations long ago;
ask your father to recount it
and your elders to tell you the tale.

When the Most High parcelled out the nations,   8
when he dispersed all mankind,
he laid down the boundaries of every people
according to the number of the sons of God;*a*
but the LORD's share was his own people,   9
Jacob was his allotted portion.
He found him in a desert land,   10
in a waste and howling void.
He protected and trained him,
he guarded him as the apple of his eye,
as an eagle watches over its nest,   11
hovers above its young,
spreads its pinions and takes them up,
and carries them upon its wings.
The LORD alone led him,   12
no alien god at his side.
He made him ride on the heights of the earth   13
and fed him on the harvest of the fields;
he satisfied him with honey from the crags
and oil from the flinty rock,
curds from the cattle, milk from the ewes,   14
the fat of lambs' kidneys,*b*

[a] *So Scroll; Heb.* sons of Israel.
[b] kidneys: *transposed from fourth line.*

of rams, the breed of Bashan, and of goats,
with the finest flour of wheat;
and he[a] drank wine from the blood of the grape.

15   Jacob ate and was well fed,[b]
Jeshurun grew fat and unruly,[c]
he[a] grew fat, he[a] grew bloated and sleek.
He forsook God who made him
and dishonoured the Rock of his salvation.

16   They roused his jealousy with foreign gods
and provoked him with abominable practices.

17   They sacrificed to foreign demons that are no gods,
gods who were strangers to them;
they took up with new gods from their neighbours,
gods whom your fathers did not acknowledge.

18   You forsook the creator[d] who begot you
and cared nothing for God who brought you to birth.

19   The LORD saw and spurned them;
his own sons and daughters provoked him.

20   'I will hide my face from them,' he said;
'let me see what their end will be,
for they are a mutinous generation,
sons who are not to be trusted.

21   They roused my jealousy with a god of no account,
with their false gods they provoked me;
so I will rouse their jealousy with a people of no account,
with a brutish nation I will provoke them.

22   For fire is kindled by my anger,
it burns to the depths of Sheol;
it devours earth and its harvest

[a] *So Sept.; Heb.* you.   [b] Jacob...fed: *so Sam.; Heb. om.*
[c] *Or* and kicked.   [d] *Or* rock.

and sets fire to the very roots of the mountains.
I will heap on them one disaster after another,   23
I will use up all my arrows on them:
pangs of hunger, ravages of plague,   24
and bitter pestilence.
I will harry them with the fangs of wild beasts
and the poison of creatures that crawl in the dust.
The sword will make orphans in the streets   25
and widows in their own homes;
it will take toll of young man and maid,
of babes in arms and old men.
I had resolved to strike them down   26
and to destroy all memory of them,
but I feared that I should be provoked by their foes,   27
that their enemies would take the credit
and say, "It was not the LORD,
it was we who raised the hand that did this."'

They are a nation that lacks good counsel,   28
devoid of understanding.
If only they had the wisdom to understand this   29
and give thought to their end!
How could one man pursue a thousand of them,   30
how could two put ten thousand to flight,
if their Rock had not sold them to their enemies,
if the LORD had not handed them over?
For the enemy have no Rock like ours,   31
in themselves they are mere fools.
Their vines are vines of Sodom,   32
grown on the terraces of Gomorrah;
their grapes are poisonous,

the clusters bitter to the taste.

33   Their wine is the venom of serpents,
     the cruel poison of asps;

34   all this I have in reserve,
     sealed up in my storehouses

35   till the day of[a] punishment and vengeance,
     till the moment when they slip and fall;
     for the day of their downfall is near,
     their doom is fast approaching.

36   The LORD will give his people justice
     and have compassion on his servants;
     for he will see that their strength is gone:
     alone, or defended by his clan, no one is left.

37   He will say, 'Where are your gods,
     the rock in which you sought shelter,

38   the gods who ate the fat of your sacrifices
     and drank the wine of your drink-offerings?
     Let them rise to help you!
     Let them give you shelter!

39   See now that I, I am He,
     and there is no god beside me:
     I put to death and I keep alive,
     I wound and I heal;
     there is no rescue from my grasp.

40   I lift my hand to heaven
     and swear: As I live for ever,

41   when I have whetted my flashing sword,
     when I have set my hand to judgement,
     then I will punish my adversaries

[a] till the day of: *so Sam.; Heb.* for me.

and take vengeance on my enemies.
I will make my arrows drunk with blood,   42
my sword shall devour flesh,
blood of slain and captives,
the heads of the enemy princes.'
Rejoice with him, you heavens,   43
bow down, all you gods, before him;*a*
for he will avenge the blood of his sons*b*
and take vengeance on his adversaries;
he will punish those who hate him
and make expiation for his people's land.*c*

This is the song that Moses came and recited in the 44
hearing of the people, he and Joshua*d* son of Nun.

Moses finished speaking to all Israel, and then he said, 45, 46
'Take to heart all these warnings which I solemnly give
you this day: command your children to be careful to
observe all the words of this law. For you they are no 47
empty words; they are your very life, and by them you
shall live long in the land which you are to occupy after
crossing the Jordan.'

* The Song has been inserted into Deuteronomy in order to
contrast the disobedience of Israel with the faithfulness of
her God, a faithfulness which extends even beyond what
could have been expected under the covenant relationship.
Having summoned witnesses, God recites Israel's salvation
history through which she had become his chosen people.
But once she enjoyed the affluence of life in Canaan, Israel

[a] Rejoice...before him: *so Scroll, cp. Sept.; Heb.* Cause his people
to rejoice, O nations.   [b] *So Scroll; Heb.* servants.
[c] he will punish...land: *so Scroll; Heb.* and make expiation for his
land, his people.   [d] *Heb.* Hoshea (*cp. Num. 13: 16*).

abandoned her God in favour of other gods, and for her apostasy must suffer the curse implicit in the covenant relationship. So judgement is heralded. But in discussion with himself, God recognizes that he cannot let Israel go. Even though she deserves utter annihilation, he will yet vindicate her. The Song is thus very close in thought to the deuteronomic historian's own theological position, if not dependent on it (cp. 32: 15ff.), which would account for its later insertion at this point (cp. 4: 31).

32: 1. *Give ear to what I say, O heavens*: since natural phenomena witness the covenant itself (cp. on 4: 26), when a breach is alleged, they are forthwith summoned to attend the court (cp. Mic. 6: 1ff.).

3. *the name of the LORD*: on the pronunciation JEHOVAH (N.E.B. footnote), see on 5: 6.

4. *the creator*: as the N.E.B. footnote indicates, the Hebrew word used here is uncertain. Both in this verse and verse 18 the N.E.B. translates by *the creator* instead of 'the rock'. There is some textual support for this rendering here, but not in verse 18. None the less it is possible that since 'the Rock' occurs elsewhere in the Song, two distinct descriptions of God using words which look very much alike have become confused, and in all cases 'the Rock' has come to be read. This ascription clearly designates the stability and faithfulness of Yahweh in the face of Israel's fecklessness.

5ff. *whose faults have proved you no children of his*: it is because Israel has renounced her true parentage that she finds herself in the dock. This leads God to recount Israel's salvation history through which he gave her birth and brought her to the promised land. But since he loves Israel as a son (1: 31), in spite of her disobedience, he will be unable to let her go (cp. Hos. 11: 1ff.).

8f. *When the Most High parcelled out the nations*: cp. on 2: 5. *according to the number of the sons of God*: this Septuagint reading has been confirmed from the Dead Sea Scrolls over against the Hebrew 'sons of Israel'. The poet, drawing on

Canaanite mythology, identifies Yahweh with the pre-Davidic Canaanite god Elyon, who has not only laid out the boundaries of the nations, but allocated them to their gods, subordinate members of the pantheon, called sons of God (cp. Ps. 82: 6). But Israel he reserved for himself, who should in consequence be supreme among the nations. The reading 'sons of Israel' identifies the number of the nations (Gen. 10) with the number of Jacob's (Israel's) children (Gen. 46: 27).

10. *He found him in a desert land*: as in Hos. 9: 10, Israel's salvation history is only traced back to the desert period, and not to the exodus. This has sometimes been explained as pointing to a special tradition belonging to those tribes who had only joined the covenant community after the exodus. But elsewhere Hosea sees Egypt as the place of Israel's origin (Hos. 2: 15; 11: 1). The Song is simply seeking to stress Israel's ingratitude by contrasting the poverty of life in the desert with its richness in Canaan.

11. *as an eagle watches over its nest*: cp. Exod. 19: 4. The picture is of an eagle stirring up its young to fly from the nest, but being ready to catch them on its wings should they become tired. In the same way God supports immature Israel, until she is able to fend for herself (cp. Hos. 11: 3).

12. *The LORD alone led him*: God had guided Israel to the promised land utterly unaided. Thus Israel's apostasy could only be interpreted as crass ingratitude.

13. *He made him ride on the heights of the earth*: the picture is of an irresistible power going forward with extreme speed. As master of creation, God can provide food from the most unlikely places.

14. *the breed of Bashan*: cp. on 3: 1.

15ff. *Jacob ate and was well fed*: once Israel found security in the fertile promised land, she forgot her God on whom she had hitherto been dependent, and apostasized with the formerly unknown gods of Canaan. This reduction of the covenant obligations to the first and fundamental commandment of exclusive allegiance to Yahweh is typical of deuteronomic theology (cp. 6: 4ff.), and perhaps indicates that the Song is not as early as has sometimes been supposed. (Cp. on verse 39.) *Jeshurun* is a rare name for Israel (cp. Deut. 33: 5, 26; Isa. 44: 2). It comes from a word meaning 'upright', and its application to Israel in this passage is, therefore, peculiarly ironic.

19ff. *The LORD saw and spurned them*: Israel's repudiation of God could only result in the complete breakdown of the covenant relationship.

21. *They roused my jealousy*: cp. on 4: 24. *a people of no account*: usually explained as the Babylonians. But the fact that there is no hint of exile has led to other suggestions. None the less the utter destruction envisaged, and the complete obliteration of Israel's memory would seem to point to the events of 587 B.C.

22. *it burns to the depths of Sheol*: God's wrath is going to be exercised on such a scale that it will extend even to the place where the dead rest (cp. Amos 9: 2).

26. *to destroy all memory of them*: God has resolved to terminate the covenant relationship irrevocably by the complete annihilation of Israel. It would be as if she had never existed.

27. *but I feared that I should be provoked by their foes*: God realized that the heathen nation whom he had used as his agent of destruction would fail to recognize that they owed their victory to Israel's God and not to their own military prowess. Indeed they would interpret their victory as a defeat of Yahweh himself. Consequently there would be no one left on earth to acknowledge him. God was thus in a considerable dilemma. To carry out the terms of the covenant relationship would harm him as much as it would harm Israel. In the aftermath of the Babylonian conquest, God's predicament was clearly recognized (Ezek. 20; Isa. 48: 9–11).

28ff. *They are a nation that lacks good counsel*: refers to the alien enemy who is totally without any understanding of how he has gained the victory. The wise man is the man who can see the order in things, how one thing relates to another. This wisdom is denied to the conquering power who cannot see that Israel's God is Lord of history.

32. *Their vines are vines of Sodom*: Israel's enemies are like the poisonous and bitter fruit of that region of the Dead Sea where once the great cities of Sodom and Gomorrah flourished, but which is now barren under sulphurous and saline deposits.

36. *The LORD will give his people justice*: once again God will intervene and rescue Israel from her enemies. The Song thus ends in expectant hope. In spite of the fact that Israel is guilty, yet God is going to acquit her by an act of sheer grace.

37ff. *Where are your gods*: at the moment of judgement, God reminds Israel that she owes her future not to her false gods who have proved utterly useless to her in her moment of need, but to the God whom she had forsaken, and yet who alone and unaided determines the fate of all mankind.

39. *See now that I, I am He*: cp. Isa. 43: 11. In contrast to the non-existent heathen gods, Yahweh undoubtedly exists. *and there is no god beside me*: this phrase does not have to be interpreted as meaning that there is no other god at all, that Yahweh is the only God (monotheism). It can mean that what Yahweh does, he does on his own unaided by any other divine being (cp. 4: 35). But in view of the very great similarity with Deutero-Isaiah's theology where monotheism is clearly enunciated (Isa. 44: 6; 45: 5–7; 46: 9), it is probable that similar ideas are being expressed here. This would certainly imply a post-exilic date for the Song (cp. verses 15ff.).

40. *I lift my hand to heaven and swear*: God raises his hand to take an oath that he will execute vengeance on Israel's enemies. Normally in oath-taking, the raised hand indicated an appeal to the god that if the oath proved false, then he should inflict immediate punishment. It was thus a sign of the self-imprecation implicit in every oath. In God's case, he swears by himself since there is no one greater to whom he can appeal.

43. *Rejoice with him, you heavens*: as the N.E.B. footnote indicates, the text of this concluding verse is extremely confused, but it appears to be a general summons to all creation to praise Yahweh for effecting Israel's salvation. *and make expiation*: a sacrificial term used metaphorically, indicating that God's activity on Israel's behalf in securing her salvation is always costly in that it demands the exercise of his love for a people who do not deserve it, and who have consistently rejected it.

44. *Joshua son of Nun*: the Hebrew Hoshea (N.E.B. footnote) seems to be a mistake (cp. Num. 13: 16).

46. *to observe all the words of this law*: after the insertion of the Song, there is a further reminder to keep the covenant law. This literary arrangement echoes 31: 14–29, where the law and then the Song are to act as witnesses to the covenant.

47. *no empty words*: points to the creative power of Yahweh's word. Once Yahweh has spoken ('Thus says the Lord'), then his words take immediate effect (cp. Isa. 55: 11). 'The words' of the law, if heeded, will bring abundant life. ✲

MOSES ORDERED TO CLIMB MOUNT NEBO

48, 49 That same day the LORD spoke to Moses and said, 'Go up this mount Abarim, Mount Nebo in Moab, to the east of Jericho, and look out over the land of Canaan
50 that I am giving to the Israelites for their possession. On this mountain you shall die and be gathered to your father's kin, just as Aaron your brother died on Mount
51 Hor and was gathered to his father's kin. This is because both of you were unfaithful to me at the waters of Meribah-by-Kadesh in the wilderness of Zin, when you
52 did not uphold my holiness among the Israelites. You shall see the land from a distance but you may not enter the land I am giving to the Israelites.'

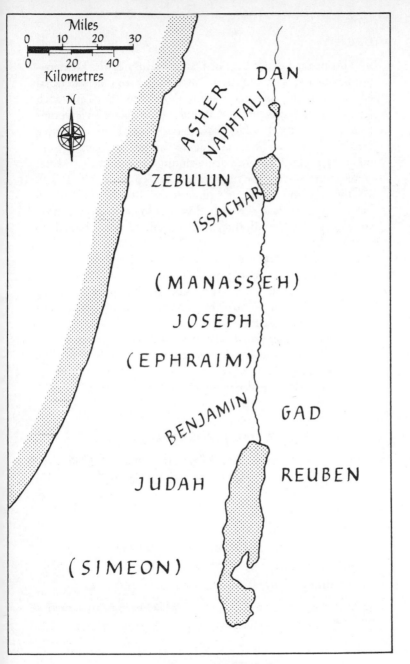

2. The tribes of Israel.

✼ This passage is not part of Deuteronomy or the Deuteronomic Work, but has been inserted by the pentateuchal editor when he attached Deuteronomy to the Tetrateuch (cp. p. 2). It represents the Priestly theologians' viewpoint (Num. 27: 12–14) which saw Moses' death before entry into the promised land as due to sin on his part (Num. 20: 1–13), rather than the deuteronomic tradition that Moses suffered vicariously for his people's sin (cp. on Deut. 1: 37). By the time the Pentateuch came to be formed, the Priestly version had become the orthodox theological interpretation of Moses' death, and therefore the editor felt obliged to make this insertion.

48. *That same day*: that is the day referred to in 1: 3.

49. *Abarim*: means 'regions beyond', and was applied to the mountains on the eastern side of the Jordan among which was Mount Nebo. This indicates that the writer was situated in Israel itself.

50. *just as Aaron your brother died on Mount Hor*: cp. 10: 6. For the Priestly theologians' account of Aaron's death, cp. Num. 20: 22–9.

51. *at the waters of Meribah-by-Kadesh*: cp. Num. 20: 1–13. ✼

THE BLESSING OF MOSES

33 This is the blessing that Moses the man of God pronounced upon the Israelites before his death:

2 The LORD came from Sinai
   and shone forth from Seir.
   He showed himself from Mount Paran,
   and with him were myriads of holy ones[a]
   streaming along at his right hand.

[a] and with...holy ones: *prob. rdg.; Heb.* and he came from myriads of holiness.

Truly he loves his people[a]   3
and blesses[b] his saints.[c]
They sit at his[d] feet
and receive his[d] instruction,
    the law which Moses laid upon us,   4
as a possession for the assembly of Jacob.
Then a king arose[e] in Jeshurun,   5
    when the chiefs of the people were assembled
together with all the tribes of Israel.

Of Reuben he said:[f]   6

May Reuben live and not die out,
but may he be few in number.

And of Judah he said this: 7

Hear, O LORD, the cry of Judah
and join him to his people,
thou whose hands fight for him,
who art his helper against his foes.

Of Levi he said: 8

Thou didst give thy Thummim to Levi,
thy Urim to thy loyal servant[g]
whom thou didst prove at Massah,
for whom thou didst plead at the waters of Meribah,
who said of his parents, I do not know them,   9

[a] his people: *so Sept.; Heb.* peoples.   [b] *So Pesh.; Heb.* in thy hand.
[c] *Or* holy ones.   [d] *So Vulg.; Heb.* thy.
[e] *Or* Then there was a king...
[f] Of Reuben he said: *prob. rdg.; Heb. om.*
[g] Thou didst...servant: *so Sept.; Heb.* Thy Thummim and Urim
belong to thy loyal servant.

who did not acknowledge his brothers,
nor recognize his children.
They observe thy word
and keep thy covenant;
10   they teach thy precepts to Jacob,
thy law to Israel.
They offer thee the smoke of sacrifice
and offerings on thy altar.
11   Bless all his powers,*a* O LORD,
and accept the work of his hands.
Strike his adversaries hip and thigh,
and may his enemies rise no more.

12   Of Benjamin he said:

The LORD's beloved dwells in security,
the High God*b* shields him all the day long,
and he dwells under his protection.*c*

13   Of Joseph he said:

The LORD's blessing is on his land
with precious fruit watered from heaven above*d*
and from the deep that lurks below,
14   with precious fruit ripened by the sun,
precious fruit, the produce of the months,
15   with all good things from the ancient mountains,
the precious fruit of the everlasting hills,
16   the precious fruits of earth and all its store,
by the favour of him who dwells in the burning bush.

[a] Or skill.   [b] the High God: *prob. rdg.; Heb.* upon him.
[c] under his protection: *lit.* between his shoulders.
[d] above: *so some MSS.; others* with dew.

This shall rest[a] upon the head of Joseph,
on the brow of him who was prince among[b] his brothers.
In majesty he shall be like a first-born ox,   17
his horns those of a wild ox
with which he will gore nations
and drive[c] them to the ends of earth.
Such will be the myriads of Ephraim,
and such the thousands of Manasseh.

Of Zebulun he said: 18

Rejoice, Zebulun, when you sally forth,
rejoice in your tents, Issachar.
They shall summon nations to the mountain,   19
there they will offer true sacrifices,
for they shall suck the abundance of the seas
and draw out[d] the hidden wealth of the sand.

Of Gad he said: 20

Blessed be Gad, in his wide domain;
he couches like a lion[e]
tearing an arm or a scalp.
He chose the best for himself,   21
for to him was allotted a ruler's portion,
when the chiefs of the people were assembled together.[f]
He did what the LORD deemed right,
observing his ordinances for Israel.

[a] *Prob. rdg., cp. Gen. 49: 26; Heb. has an unintelligible form.*
[b] him...among: *or* the one cursed by.
[c] and drive: *prob. rdg.; Heb.* together.
[d] draw out: *prob. rdg.; Heb.* obscure.
[e] *Lit.* lioness.
[f] were assembled together: *so Sept.; Heb.* obscure.

22 Of Dan he said:

> Dan is a lion's cub
> springing out from Bashan.

23 Of Naphtali he said:

> Naphtali is richly favoured
> and full of the blessings of the LORD;
> his patrimony stretches to the sea and southward.

24 Of Asher he said:

> Asher is most blest of sons,
> may he be the favourite among*a* his brothers
> and bathe his feet in oil.

25 May your bolts be of iron and bronze,
> and your strength last as long as you live.

26 There is none like the God of Jeshurun
> who rides the heavens to your help,
> riding the clouds in his glory,

27 who humbled the gods of old
> and subdued*b* the ancient powers;
> who drove out the enemy before you
> and gave the word to destroy.

28 Israel lives in security,
> the tribes of Jacob by themselves,
> in a land of corn and wine*c*
> where the skies drip with dew.

29 Happy are you, people of Israel, peerless, set free;
> the LORD is the shield that guards you,

[*a*] *Or* of.
[*b*] *Prob. rdg.; Heb.* under.
[*c*] *Or* new wine.

the Blessed One*[a]* is your glorious sword.
Your enemies come cringing to you,
and you shall trample their bodies under foot.

* Facing death, Moses gives his Blessing to the tribes. Such
a blessing acted as a kind of will, for the words uttered were
understood to have a creative power which would influence
future events. This is clearlys een in Isaac's Blessing of Esau
and Jacob (Gen. 27), and Jacob's Blessing of his twelve sons
(Gen. 49), with which Moses' Blessing should be compared.
This is now surrounded by a psalm (verses 2–5, 26–9).

2ff. *The LORD came from Sinai*: these verses are very
obscure, but are probably best seen as indicating a festival
procession to the sanctuary at which the law was recited
(cp. on 31: 10ff.). Under the monarchy, the king (verse 5)
would have played a central part in such a festival, and it is
possible that this psalm refers to his enthronement as the
representative of Yahweh. Such a festival of enthronement is
known from Babylon, and is held by some scholars to be
reflected in such psalms as 47, 93 and 96–9. It is argued that the
festival celebrated Yahweh's original triumph over the primeval forces of chaos, and looked forward to his eventual
victory over all gods and nations opposed to his rule. Only
here in Deuteronomy is *Sinai* used in place of Horeb. For
Jeshurun cp. on 32: 15.

6. *Reuben*: as the first-born is to be protected from extinc-
tion, but because he challenged his father's authority by
laying claim to his harem (Gen. 49: 4), he is not to thrive.
Evidently the tribe was in a very precarious state. Simeon,
who as Leah's second son should follow at this point, is not
even mentioned, which must indicate that that tribe had
already become absorbed into Judah. In Gen. 49: 5–7 Simeon
and Levi are in conflict.

7. *Judah*: apparently faces enemy attack which makes it

[a] the Blessed One: *Heb.* Asher.

impossible for that tribe to have contact with the other tribes. There is no need to interpret this prayer for Judah as referring to the situation after the division of the united kingdom of David and Solomon. It may, however, reflect Judah's inability to attend the central sanctuary of the pre-monarchical tribal confederacy.

8–11. *Levi*: is presented as a priestly tribe in charge of oracles, teaching of the law, and sacrifices. But it is probable that only verse 11 originally formed part of the Blessing, verses 8–10 being a later elaboration. The *Thummim* and *Urim* were lots used in giving oracles (cp. 1 Sam. 14: 41). The meaning of the names and the nature of the objects are quite unknown. Neither of the narratives concerning *Massah* and *Meribah* (Exod. 17: 1–7; Num. 20: 2–13) refers to Levi, whereas that tribe does figure prominently in the incident of the golden calf recorded in Exod. 32: 26–9. There the Levites alone proclaim their loyalty to Yahweh illustrated by their willingness to renounce family ties in order to serve him. For the deuteronomists, the Levites constituted Israel's only legitimate priesthood (cp. on 10: 8).

12. *Benjamin*: is especially loved and enjoys God's protection. The meaning of the last line is uncertain. Literally the Hebrew reads 'and he dwells between his shoulders'. If the subject is Yahweh, then this must refer to his presence at a sanctuary: but if, as the N.E.B. translates, the subject is Benjamin, then the phrase must be an expression indicating protection.

13ff. *Joseph*: the Blessing stresses the tribe's agricultural wealth and its military prowess. *who dwells in the burning bush*: the only Old Testament reference to the incident in Exod. 3 leading to Yahweh's revelation of his identity to Moses.

18f. *Zebulun*: together with *Issachar* is responsible for a mountain sanctuary, usually identified as Tabor, where the foreigners whom they meet in their trade will come and worship.

20f. *Gad*: is the largest tribe in Transjordan. The meaning of verse 21*b* is obscure. Perhaps it belongs with the psalm which surrounds the Blessing, and should be transferred to verse 5, or it may indicate that although Gad had already acquired her territory, she none the less took part in the conquest of Canaan (cp. 3: 12ff.).

22. *Dan*: has now migrated to the north (Josh. 19: 40–8; Judg. 18).

23. *Naphtali*: *the sea* refers to the Lake of Galilee. Naphtali's land is very rich.

24f. *Asher*: has the richest territory of all the tribes. Verse 25 may refer to her precarious position in the north of Israel. Her fertile country would naturally be envied by aggressive neighbours.

26–9. *There is none like the God of Jeshurun*: the psalm of verses 2–5 continues in praise of Israel's God who has subdued the primeval forces and driven out the inhabitants of Canaan, in whose fertile land Israel now dwells secure under his protection. Yahweh is both lord of nature and lord of history, and all is in his ultimate control. *who rides the heavens to your help*: such imagery was frequently applied to Baal, and the psalm reflects how the attributes of Baal were taken over by Yahweh who ousted him as God of Canaan and lord of creation. ✻

The death of Moses

✻ As a result of the formation of the Pentateuch by attaching Deuteronomy to the Tetrateuch (cp. p. 2), the deuteronomic historian's conclusion has now been supplemented by the Priestly theologians' record of the death of Moses (34: 1, 7–9). An account of his death must once have appeared at the end of Numbers, but this has now been dovetailed into the conclusion of Deuteronomy. The final verses 10–12 lead straight into the book of Joshua, and the deuteronomic historian's description of the conquest of the promised land. ✻

MOSES COMPLETES HIS MINISTRY

34 THEN MOSES WENT UP from the lowlands of
Moab to Mount Nebo, to the top of Pisgah, east-
wards from Jericho, and the LORD showed him the whole
2 land: Gilead as far as Dan; the whole of Naphtali;
the territory of Ephraim and Manasseh, and all Judah as
3 far as the western sea; the Negeb and the Plain; the
valley of Jericho, the Vale of Palm Trees, as far as Zoar.
4 The LORD said to him, 'This is the land which I swore
to Abraham, Isaac and Jacob that I would give to their
descendants. I have let you see it with your own eyes,
but you shall not cross over into it.'

5   There in the land of Moab Moses the servant of the
6 LORD died, as the LORD had said. He was buried in a
valley in Moab opposite Beth-peor, but to this day no
7 one knows his burial-place. Moses was a hundred and
twenty years old when he died; his sight was not dimmed
8 nor had his vigour failed.[a] The Israelites wept for Moses
in the lowlands of Moab for thirty days; then the time
9 of mourning for Moses was ended. And Joshua son of
Nun was filled with the spirit of wisdom, for Moses had
laid his hands on him, and the Israelites listened to him
and did what the LORD had commanded Moses.

10   There has never yet risen in Israel a prophet like Moses,
11 whom the LORD knew face to face: remember all the
signs and portents which the LORD sent him to show in
Egypt to Pharaoh and all his servants and the whole
12 land; remember the strong hand of Moses and the
terrible deeds which he did in the sight of all Israel.

[a] nor...failed: *or, with Pesh.*, and his cheeks were not sunken.

✵ Moses climbs Mount Nebo, and looking out over the promised land, takes legal possession of it for Israel. His death and burial follow, and Joshua, who inherits Moses' authority, is left to lead Israel across the Jordan to her promised inheritance.

1ff. *and the LORD showed him the whole land*: the legal transfer of land was secured by the purchaser's formal inspection. Here God invites Moses to take possession of Canaan on Israel's behalf (cp. on 3: 27). This was the climax of his ministry. He had brought the tribes to the edge of Jordan and had secured their legal right to Canaan. The conquest was thus assured of success, provided Israel obeyed the covenant law which Moses had given them. The geographical boundaries indicate the whole of the land which was to become Israel, though in fact the full extent of the territory could not be seen from Mount Nebo.

4. *I swore to Abraham, Isaac and Jacob*: the promised inheritance has now been secured (cp. on 1: 8). *but you shall not cross over into it*: for the deuteronomists, Moses died vicariously for Israel's sin (cp. on 1: 37): but for the Priestly theologians his death was God's punishment for his own sin (cp. on 32: 48–52).

6. *He was buried in a valley in Moab*: though once known, the site of Moses' grave has now long since been lost.

7. *his sight was not dimmed*: in spite of his great age, Moses was in full possession of all his faculties at his death. This Priestly viewpoint does not really accord with 31: 2, where the deuteronomic historian pictures him as enfeebled by old age and ready to die.

9. *And Joshua son of Nun was filled with the spirit of wisdom*: Joshua inherits Moses' authority, and with it divine inspiration to continue his work as covenant mediator (cp. Num. 27: 18–23).

10ff. *a prophet like Moses*: cp. on 18: 15. In the deuteronomists' eyes, no one in Israel's history ever matched Moses as God's spokesman. It was he who had given Israel her covenant law, the very means of life, through which she had come into being as the elect people of God. Despite all kinds of vicissitudes he had led the Israelites to the edge of the promised land, and then as the culmination of his ministry given his life for their sin, in order that they might enjoy unimaginable prosperity in Canaan. No wonder he alone was thought of as the man with whom God had spoken *face to face* (cp. Exod. 33: 11; Num. 12: 1–8). ✳

✳ ✳ ✳ ✳ ✳ ✳ ✳ ✳ ✳ ✳ ✳ ✳ ✳

THE IMPORTANCE OF THE BOOK

In spite of the logic of the covenant relationship which demanded Israel's utter annihilation for breach of the covenant law, the deuteronomists recognized that God could not let Israel go. To do so was foreign to his nature. While it was left to the Priestly theologians to work out a new understanding of God's relationship with Israel (cp. pp. 10f.), the deuteronomists none the less categorically affirmed God's irrepressible love for man.

Although many of the presuppositions behind Deuteronomy no longer apply, making much of the law redundant, no one could fail to be moved by its overriding concern for the defenceless in society. Those in need have an inalienable right to the charity of those who enjoy prosperity. For the affluent West confronting an impoverished 'third world', Deuteronomy's humanitarianism is uncomfortably relevant.

But Deuteronomy's greatest importance lies in the persistent warning to Israel that when she enjoys the affluence of Canaan she should not forget her God. Far from any demand for puritanical renunciation of the good things of life, God has willed Israel's prosperity, and brought her to the land flowing with milk and honey in which she is to luxuriate. But Deuteronomy expresses the fear that once Israel has become self-sufficient, she might be tempted to abandon her

God as no longer necessary for her survival. To do so would inevitably lead to diabolical chaos as man exploited man for his own self-gratification. Of such a society, the prophets bear eloquent witness. Deuteronomy thus affirms that while there can be no doubt that the eradication of poverty and the securing of a prosperous world free of hunger and disease is God's will, that prosperity cannot be maintained unless man continues to acknowledge and co-operate with him who wills it. God is the supreme humanist: but without him, man made in his image can only become less than human. Thus the deuteronomists rightly recognize that man is not called to make a choice between God and the world. Rather he is to affirm both, and, in fellowship with his Creator, enjoy his creation.

A NOTE ON FURTHER READING

A fuller commentary on Deuteronomy is provided by G. von Rad in the *Old Testament Library* series (S.C.M., 1966). Readers will also find a simple but valuable assessment of Deuteronomy's theology in Ronald Clements, *God's Chosen People* (S.C.M., 1968). In order to compare the deuteronomic laws with those in Exodus, they should consult Clements' commentary on Exodus (C.U.P., 1972) in this present series. Readers interested in the Ten Commandments and their place in Israel's law may like to refer to my *Ancient Israel's Criminal Law* (Basil Blackwell, 1971). For those who want to learn more about ancient Israel's institutions in general, R. de Vaux, *Ancient Israel* (Darton, Longman and Todd, 1961) will be of considerable help, in addition to articles in the Bible dictionaries and one-volume commentaries.

INDEX

237